Be More Confident

Teach Yourself®

Be More Confident
Paul Jenner

For UK order enquiries: please contact Bookpoint Ltd, 130 Milton Park, Abingdon, Oxon OX14 4SB. Telephone: +44 (0) 1235 827720. Fax: +44 (0) 1235 400454. Lines are open 09.00–17.00, Monday to Saturday, with a 24-hour message answering service. Details about our titles and how to order are available at www.teachyourself.com

For USA order enquiries: please contact McGraw-Hill Customer Services, PO Box 545, Blacklick, OH 43004-0545, USA. Telephone: 1-800-722-4726. Fax: 1-614-755-5645.

For Canada order enquiries: please contact McGraw-Hill Ryerson Ltd, 300 Water St, Whitby, Ontario L1N 9B6, Canada. Telephone: 905 430 5000. Fax: 905 430 5020.

Long renowned as the authoritative source for self-guided learning – with more than 50 million copies sold worldwide – the **Teach Yourself** series includes over 500 titles in the fields of languages, crafts, hobbies, business, computing and education.

British Library Cataloguing in Publication Data: a catalogue record for this title is available from the British Library.

Library of Congress Catalog Card Number: on file.

First published in UK 2009 by Hodder Education, part of Hachette UK, 338 Euston Road, London NW1 3BH.

First published in US 2009 by The McGraw-Hill Companies, Inc.

This edition published 2010.

Previously published as *Teach Yourself Confidence and Social Skills*

The **Teach Yourself** name is a registered trade mark of Hodder Headline.

Copyright © 2009, 2010 Paul Jenner

Typeset by MPS Limited, a Macmillan Company.

Printed in Great Britain for Hodder Education, an Hachette UK Company, 338 Euston Road, London NW1 3BH, by CPI Cox & Wyman, Reading, Berkshire RG1 8EX.

The publisher has used its best endeavours to ensure that the URLs for external websites referred to in this book are correct and active at the time of going to press. However, the publisher and the author have no responsibility for the websites and can make no guarantee that a site will remain live or that the content will remain relevant, decent or appropriate.

Hachette UK's policy is to use papers that are natural, renewable and recyclable products and made from wood grown in sustainable forests. The logging and manufacturing processes are expected to conform to the environmental regulations of the country of origin.

Impression number 10 9 8 7 6 5 4 3 2 1

Year 2014 2013 2012 2011 2010

Acknowledgements

A very special thank you to Victoria Roddam, my publisher at Hodder Education, and to Laura Davis, my Desk Editor.

For CMS

Contents

Image Credits

Front cover: © Digital Zoo/Digital Vision/Getty Images

Back cover: © Jakub Semeniuk/iStockphoto.com, © Royalty-Free/
Corbis, © agencyby/iStockphoto.com, © Andy Cook/iStockphoto.
com, © Christopher Ewing/iStockphoto.com, © zebicho – Fotolia.
com, © Geoffrey Holman/iStockphoto.com, © Photodisc/Getty
Images, © James C. Pruitt/iStockphoto.com, © Mohamed Saber –
Fotolia.com

Meet the author

Welcome to *Be More Confident*!

A few years ago I had the job of interviewing eight new electronics millionaires for a series in a magazine. One I remember in particular because his self-confidence was so fragile. He'd bought a boat, hoping to impress everyone, and then become depressed when, in the marina, he saw there were even wealthier people with even bigger boats. Our conversation turned to travel and as he listed the places he'd been to and the luxury hotels he'd stayed in, I was able to tick them off on my fingers and say: 'Yes, I've stayed there, too'. In my case I'd not paid a thing because I'd been invited by the hotel in a professional capacity. And he was absolutely furious. His sense of self-worth came from externals such as staying at exclusive hotels and now I'd taken that away from him.

Many people think confidence has to be based on achievements. But it isn't true. And thank goodness. It would make my job a lot harder. Because I can't make you rich. And I can't make you more handsome or more beautiful, either. But I can make you more confident. Confidence comes from inside. And in this book I'll be showing you how to achieve that.

But, surely, you say, externals must count too. And, of course, you're right. But maybe not the externals you're thinking of. If it was essential to drive a Ferrari in order to have self-confidence, there wouldn't be many self-confident people. I'll be telling you about the externals that really count.

Paul Jenner
Spain, 2010

Only got a minute?

- Cognitive therapy (CT) can help you feel more confident by changing such thoughts as 'I'm a loser'.

- Suggestion, role-playing, visualization and self-hypnosis are all good techniques for building a confident mindset.

- Show you like other people and they'll like you.

- By revealing yourself you become more intimate with others.

- Attune your body language to the people you're with.

- Find out who you really are and be that person.

- You'll win more arguments by reason and reasonableness than by being aggressive.

- Overcome nerves by using positive visualizations and by exposing yourself gradually to the challenges that intimidate you.

- Exercise generates 'confidence chemicals'.
- Reward is more effective than punishment – people try to live up to praise.
- Think of members of the opposite sex first of all as people.
- Don't project your fantasies onto dates.
- Deal with relationship problems amicably – use 'cooling off' and never make personal attacks.
- It's not criticism that makes you feel upset, angry or devalued, it's you who 'chooses' to feel that way.
- Disarm your critic by finding something to agree with.
- You'll be more confident if you follow the recommendations in this book.

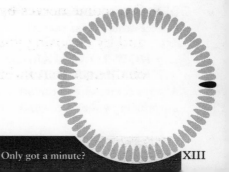

5 Only got five minutes?

1 YOUR SECRET WEAPONS
Cognitive therapy (CT) can help you feel more confident by
eliminating negative thoughts.

2 MORE SECRET WEAPONS
You can program confidence into your unconscious mind by using
suggestion, cinematic visualization and self-hypnosis; rehearse the
way you'd like to be in front of a video camera or with a friend.

3 HOW TO MAKE PEOPLE LIKE YOU – AND
LOVE YOU
Project warmth towards people, accept them as they are, show you
like them, and they will like you; keep a record so you don't forget
important information.

4 THE EASY ART OF CONVERSATION
Research the people you're going to meet, introduce yourself with
a 'hook' (so they immediately know something about you) and
'trade' personal information.

5 DOES YOUR BODY SAY HELLO?
Make full use of your voice and your body language; 'prime'
people by choosing your locations and accessories with care.

6 I'LL BE ME, YOU BE YOU
Discover who you are (take time to experiment), be who you are,
and let others be as they are.

7 HOW TO WIN ARGUMENTS BY BEING ASSERTIVE,
NOT AGGRESSIVE
Always acknowledge the other person's point of view before
introducing your own – and then plant a suggestion.

8 IF YOU'RE AFRAID OF IT, DO IT

Stop imagining a terrible outcome and visualize a positive one instead – then gradually expose yourself to the thing you're afraid of.

9 THE CONFIDENCE CHEMICALS

Exercise generates 'confidence' chemicals as well as improving body image.

10 THE CONFIDENCE TO LEAD

Reward success, give people reputations to live up to and back them with good training.

11 DEVELOPING CONFIDENCE WITH THE OPPOSITE SEX

▶ Think of members of the opposite sex as people first.
▶ Try dating different kinds of people – don't project fantasies onto them.
▶ When relationship problems arise, keep the emotional temperature down.

12 PEOPLE WHO PUT YOU DOWN

When you're criticized, 'disarm' your critic by finding something to agree with; the person whose approval counts the most is you, so, afterwards, laugh about it.

13 YOUR ONE-MONTH CONFIDENCE PLAN

If you follow all the recommendations in this book you will be a far more confident person within one month.

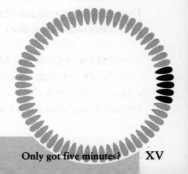

10 Only got ten minutes?

1 YOUR SECRET WEAPONS

▶ Cognitive therapy (CT) is an important 'secret weapon' for becoming more confident – and it can be used to help you in other ways as well.

▶ The belief behind CT is that the way you feel is entirely due to the way you think.

▶ By changing your thoughts you can therefore increase your confidence.

▶ Examples of negative thoughts that need to be changed are, 'They're better than me', 'I'm not first so therefore I'm a loser' and 'I know they're not going to like me'.

2 MORE SECRET WEAPONS

▶ To become more confident it's important to enlist the help of your unconscious mind.

▶ One way of influencing your unconscious is to plant suggestions repeatedly at a receptive time – in bed just before going to sleep is ideal.

▶ Practise the way you'd like to be in front of a video camera, and by role-playing with a friend.

▶ In Neuro-Linguistic Programming (NLP) the qualities of visualizations are known as 'submodalities'. By changing the submodalities you can change the impact of the visualizations.

▶ The *Circle of Confidence* is an NLP visualization technique in which you recall a previous occasion on which you've felt confident and then transfer that confidence to a situation about which you're feeling apprehensive.

▶ Self-hypnosis is a way of using deep trance to make visualizations more effective.

3 HOW TO MAKE PEOPLE LIKE YOU – AND LOVE YOU

▶ If you want other people to like you it's important to project warmth towards them, to accept them as they are (the right attitude is encapsulated by the phrase, 'I'm okay and you're okay'), to be curious about them and never to indulge in *Schadenfreude* when things go wrong in their lives.
▶ Like other people and they'll like you.
▶ Prepare a calendar of the birthdays of people important to you, so you don't forget them – annotate it with key information about likes and dislikes, children's names, and so on.

4 THE EASY ART OF CONVERSATION

▶ Don't make yourself tongue-tied by trying to think of something incredibly witty or intelligent to start a conversation – a perfectly normal question or remark will do fine.
▶ When you introduce yourself add a 'hook' so the other person immediately knows something about you.
▶ Use 'open' questions as much as possible – they're questions that can't be answered by a simple 'yes' or 'no'.
▶ When you know you're going to be meeting certain people for the first time, try to do a little research about them.
▶ Use mnemonics to remember people's names – for example, the gorgeous one is George, the rich-looking one is Richard, and so on.
▶ Be a good listener.
▶ *Small* talk can make a *big* difference – don't just make factual statements, ask people how they've been affected by things.
▶ If you want to hear about intimate things you'll have to be willing to 'trade secrets'.
▶ If you want to be entertaining, now and then flick through a book of jokes or quotations.

5 DOES YOUR BODY SAY HELLO?

▶ Experts say that about 85 per cent of communication is by body language, so it's important to pay attention to it.
▶ Handshake strength in men really is a sign of testosterone level.
▶ You can accelerate the process of bonding by deliberately matching and mirroring someone else's body language – but do it subtly, otherwise people will think you're weird.
▶ The impression someone forms about you is partly determined by the surroundings in which you meet and the accessories you use – deliberately manipulating these things is known as 'priming'.
▶ Your voice is one of the hardest things to control – joining a debating society or an amateur theatrical company are good ways of learning how.

6 I'LL BE ME, YOU BE YOU

▶ The way to find out who you really are is to keep trying different things.
▶ It's important to let chance enter your life so you'll have experiences you've never thought of.
▶ Don't be afraid to be different, if you feel that you are – the world would be a poorer place without difference.
▶ Meditation can help you understand yourself 'from the inside'.
▶ Spend less time doing things you 'should' and more time doing things you feel are right for you.
▶ Spend some time alone, experimenting with your personality.

7 HOW TO WIN ARGUMENTS BY BEING ASSERTIVE, NOT AGGRESSIVE

▶ The three steps to assertiveness are firstly, acknowledging the other person's point of view, secondly, introducing your own and thirdly, suggesting a reasonable way the conflict might be resolved.

- Planting the seed of an idea in someone else's mind can prove more effective than either ordering or arguing.
- You'll be more persuasive if you employ the techniques of the 'Milton Model' – they include using questions rather than instructions, relating anecdotes that make your point for you, speaking at a 'hypnotic' pace and 'presupposing' agreement thus making it harder for the other person to oppose you.

8 IF YOU'RE AFRAID OF IT, DO IT

- Using euphemisms can reduce the power of things you fear.
- Imagining terrible outcomes increases fear; visualize successful outcomes instead.
- You can reduce your fear of things by a step-by-step process of gradual exposure.
- Keep on challenging yourself and you'll develop confidence in yourself.

9 THE CONFIDENCE CHEMICALS

- Exercise generates chemicals (such as PEA, noradrenaline/ norepinephrine and endorphins) that will make you feel more confident – and happier, too.
- Exercise will also tone you up, make you fitter and improve your body image.
- Activities helpful to confidence include self-defence, tai chi, jogging, swimming, cycling, dancing and working out at the gym.

10 THE CONFIDENCE TO LEAD

- It's more effective to reward people for the things they do well than punish them for the things they do badly (and it's easier for a leader, too).
- People try to live up to their reputations – so give them reputations that are a little bit higher than where they are now.
- Good training is vital – when people don't perform well it's often a sign that the training was inadequate.

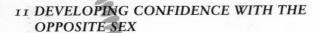

11 DEVELOPING CONFIDENCE WITH THE OPPOSITE SEX

- Men and women are different, but not *that* different – think of members of the opposite sex as people first.
- When you meet someone you're attracted to, don't project exalted qualities onto them or you'll make yourself nervous.
- Don't only date people who fit the template you've drawn up.
- Cognitive therapy can help you overcome self-doubt in dating.
- When discussing relationship problems it's important to keep the emotional temperature down – once heart rates go above 100, arguments tend to become irrational.

12 PEOPLE WHO PUT YOU DOWN

- If you become upset or angry when criticized that's because *you choose* to feel that way – you can equally choose to laugh, to take no notice or to make changes while remaining cheerful.
- When you're attacked, it's usually better to 'disarm' a critic rather than to either 'run away' or 'fight back'; first defuse the situation by inviting your critic to detail the criticism, then find something to agree with before making your own suggestions for dealing with the situation.
- It's nice to have people express their approval of you, but being too affected by approval and criticism will make you emotionally vulnerable; approve of yourself and you can always be confident and happy.

13 YOUR ONE-MONTH CONFIDENCE PLAN

- If you follow all the recommendations in this book you will be a far more confident person within one month.

1

Your secret weapons

In this chapter you will learn:
- *how to use this book*
- *how your brain is 'plastic'*
- *the power of cognitive therapy.*

> *Attitudes are more important than facts.*
>
> Dr Karl Menninger (1893–1990), American psychiatrist

On what does a strong sense of self-worth – confidence – depend? Money? Good looks? High intelligence? Nice clothes? An important job? An expensive car? Love? Helping other people?

What if I were to tell you you can be confident without any of that? Don't believe me? Well, in fact, it's true. Just as you can smile for no particular reason (simply raise the corners of your mouth) and laugh for no particular reason (try it) so you can also be confident 'without any particular reason'.

You don't need permission from anybody to be confident. There's no law that says you have to conduct yourself as an 'inferior' being because you're none of those things. You don't need an external justification to have a strong sense of self-worth. You are entitled to self-worth, right now, just as you are, and I shall prove it to you in this book. You can feel self-confident. I guarantee it.

This book is for you if:

▶ *you lack confidence in general*
▶ *you lack confidence in specific circumstances*
▶ *you find it difficult to be assertive without being aggressive*
▶ *you find it difficult to take charge of other people*
▶ *you feel you can't be yourself when you're with other people*
▶ *you find it hard to make friends*
▶ *you can't cope with criticism*
▶ *you get tongue-tied with people you're attracted to*
▶ *you find it difficult to make conversation*
▶ *you're afraid of things that other people seem to manage quite effortlessly*
▶ *you're embarrassed about your appearance*
▶ *you're easily discouraged by any setbacks in your life*
▶ *you're afraid to apply for a better job even though you could do it.*

If you carefully follow the instructions in this book you'll:

▶ *feel more confident in all circumstances*
▶ *find it easier to get what you want*
▶ *be more relaxed with people you're attracted to*
▶ *have more friends*
▶ *become a better conversationalist*
▶ *cope more easily with disappointments*
▶ *be a popular and successful manager of other people*
▶ *aim for the things you really want in your life.*

Confidence is entirely a matter of mind. It may be a fact that you're not tall, or able to wear designer clothes, or drive a fancy sports car, or anything like that, but you can still be confident. It's attitude that counts. In this chapter and the next I'll be teaching you five secret weapons for building confidence using the power of your own mind. But not just your conscious mind. We'll also be harnessing the power of your unconscious. That's why I call them 'secret weapons'. They are:

▶ *Cognitive therapy (CT)*
▶ *Suggestion*

- ► *Trial runs*
- ► *Visualization*
- ► *Self-hypnosis.*

In this chapter I'll be explaining how you can gain confidence by eliminating negative ways of thinking – the principle of CT. And in the next chapter I'll be explaining how you can reinforce that by actively cultivating positive ways of thinking.

Insight

It may not be good to lack confidence but it can also be harmful to have too much. A team at the University of Georgia, led by Dr Keith Campbell, found that although highly confident people created a positive impression at the first meeting, they later came to be rated as arrogant, conceited, hostile and less able than they themselves thought.

WHERE ARE YOU NOW?

Here's a little test to find out how confident you are right now. When you've finished the book do it again – if you've followed my advice your eventual score will be much higher (but not too high!). I'm 100% confident about that!

1 You enter a room full of strangers. Do you:
   a) Slink into a corner and watch?
   b) Look for a person alone and team up?
   c) Stride expansively around the room, greeting everyone as you go?
2 In a discussion everyone is agreed on a particular course of action except you. Do you:
   a) Go along with them without putting forward your own ideas?
   b) Say you don't agree but that you'll accept the majority view?
   c) Try to persuade them all that they're wrong?
3 As regards fashion, which statement most closely represents your view?
   a) It's important to be fashionable because otherwise people will ridicule you.

b) It's important to be fashionable so you fit in with other people.

c) You shouldn't follow fashion but develop your own personal style.

4 At a dinner party you find yourself sitting next to someone who has little to say. Do you:

    a) Feel anxious and pass most of the time in silence?

    b) See your neighbour's attitude as a challenge to your conversational skills?

    c) Make conversation with the entire table?

5 You have to give a speech. How do you feel?

    a) Petrified.

    b) You'd rather not but you'll try your best.

    c) Euphoric at the opportunity to be the centre of attention.

6 You have the task of showing a group of people around at work but when you enter the room where they're waiting, several of them fail to notice you and carry on talking. Do you:

    a) Go out again and hope they'll pay attention if you return in a few minutes?

    b) Ask the nearest sympathetic-looking person to come with you and hope the rest will follow?

    c) Bang on something to get attention, make a welcoming speech and then lead the party off?

7 You've been put in charge of overseeing a group working on a certain task. One of the group has come up with an unorthodox but clearly better way of doing things. Do you:

    a) Refer to your superior to make a decision?

    b) Insist things are done in the usual way?

    c) Give your approval to the new approach?

8 You're having riding lessons and the horse isn't doing what you want. Do you:

    a) Let the horse make the decisions?

    b) Beat the horse because it's making you look stupid?

    c) Calmly and persistently continue to give the horse the correct signals?

9 You're looking for a job and see various suitable positions advertised. Do you:
   a) Apply for one which pays badly and for which you're rather over-qualified because you think you have a good chance?
   b) Apply for one that exactly matches your qualifications?
   c) Apply for one for which you're under-qualified because you feel you're ready for a step up?
10 You learn that you've been turned down for a job. Do you:
   a) Feel despondent and vow never to apply for a job again?
   b) Curse the company for having been so stupid?
   c) Tell yourself that there will always be failures and get on with some more applications?
11 You buy a business suit but when you get it home you realize part of the lining is coming unstitched. Do you:
   a) Sigh, then put it right yourself (or get your partner to)?
   b) Return to the shop in a rage and shout at the assistant?
   c) Return calmly to the shop and ask for your money back?
12 On a plane you find yourself sitting next to someone you find very attractive. Do you:
   a) Keep quiet and fantasize?
   b) Confine comment to practical matters such as asking to be allowed out for the loo?
   c) Begin a conversation with the aim of starting a relationship?

How did you score?

Mostly a: You won't be surprised to hear that you're severely lacking in self-confidence. Just about every area can be dramatically improved by working methodically through this book.

Mostly b: You've developed various mechanisms for coping with life's challenges and disappointments but you haven't yet achieved real self-confidence. This book will give it to you.

Mostly c: You're already a pretty confident person but, no doubt, there are still areas that could be improved by selectively working through this book.

THE POWER OF YOUR UNCONSCIOUS

Think about this for a moment... As you read this your heart is beating. Your lungs are filling with air. Your digestive system is converting food to energy. Your kidneys are eliminating waste products. And so on. And yet you're making no conscious effort at all. How can this be? It's because all of these things and much more are under the control of your unconscious mind.

Just suppose that, instead of using your unconscious, you had to make a conscious effort to control all these processes. In fact, you wouldn't be able to. Your conscious mind just wouldn't be able to deal with so much data. You'd die.

It's pretty clear, then, that your unconscious mind is incredibly powerful. Far more powerful, in fact, than your conscious mind. But, nevertheless, it's very easily upset by your conscious thoughts. The proof of that is in the way so many people get some sort of stomach upset or headache when they're apprehensive about a challenging situation.

How can that be? How can such an omnipotent force be deflected by a lesser one? Here's a simple analogy. Suppose you were to enter the control room at the Kennedy Space Center during a mission. You probably wouldn't have much of a clue about what was going on there. But that wouldn't stop you being able to disrupt the smooth operation of the mission by pressing a few buttons. Do you see what I'm getting at? The control room represents your unconscious mind and you represent the conscious mind. You don't know how to run the control room but you can, nevertheless, very easily interfere with its proper functioning. You can cause the Kennedy Space Center equivalent of a stomach upset or a headache.

So how are we going to stop ourselves wrecking our own control rooms? The answer is CT – and it's something you can learn to do on your own.

COGNITIVE THERAPY

The brain is a 'plastic' structure. That's to say, it changes *physically* in response to what you've learnt and what you think. In other words you can develop a 'self-doubting brain', a brain that's physically different to a 'confident brain'. Once that sets in, it takes time to change it.

But it can be done.

It's rather like letting a muscle wither through lack of use. Ten press-ups aren't going to alter it. But over weeks and months of programmed exercise you can completely transform that muscle. Of course, it's easiest when you're young. But even if you're well past middle age you can still do it. And it's much the same with the brain.

One of the key people in the development of a technique for profoundly changing thought patterns is Dr Aaron Beck of the University of Pennsylvania School of Medicine. In the 1960s Dr Beck was researching the causes of depression. He began to notice a rather striking pattern. People who were depressed very often had a self-image that really didn't match with their true abilities and achievements. That's to say, they often regarded themselves as failures when the facts said differently.

Dr Beck concluded that their depression stemmed not from the reality of their lives but from their perception of their lives. In other words, there was a sort of malfunction in their way of thinking. That's why Dr Karl Menninger, quoted earlier, concluded that 'attitudes are more important than facts'. The truth is that when you lack self-confidence your opinion of yourself – your attitude – is much lower than it should be.

Dr Beck began to develop a treatment for correcting this condition and gave it the rather scientific-sounding name of 'cognitive therapy'. In essence, it's simply a way of eliminating negative thoughts. It works for depression and it can also work for all kinds of other things, including lack of self-confidence.

There are ten different kinds of negative thoughts, or what psychotherapists call 'cognitive distortions'. Here are ten examples as related to a lack of self-confidence:

▶ *They're better than me*
▶ *I'm not first so therefore I'm a loser*
▶ *The things I do have faults so I'm obviously no good*
▶ *I'm always making an idiot of myself*
▶ *I know they're not going to like me*
▶ *I feel like a failure so I must be a failure*
▶ *I'm a label (stupid/boring/unattractive or whatever)*
▶ *I feel guilty that I'm not doing the things I should*
▶ *It's obviously my fault (again)*
▶ *They're only saying that to be nice.*

Now let's look at these in detail and see how you can tackle them.

They're better than me

You look at other people and convince yourself they're superior to you. At the same time you focus on what you see as your inferior qualities. This is what psychotherapists call the 'mental filter'. You see others as more capable, more successful and less troubled by self-doubts and problems. But are they really better than you? It was the famous lexicographer Dr Samuel Johnson who observed that by examining your own mind you could also know what passed in the minds of others. In other words, other people are just like you. They do have self-doubts, do have moments when they lose confidence in themselves, and do have times when they look around and think everyone else is more successful than they are. It's part of being human. But they overcome those feelings and move ahead – possibly with less justification than you have. Those people are not better than you. They're just different. Better at some things, maybe. And certainly a lot worse at others.

PRACTICAL EXERCISE
In our celebrity-worshipping society we're all encouraged to compare ourselves with the richest and most attractive-seeming

people on the planet. But when you think about it, that's ludicrous, because those people are literally one in a million. Let's get real:

1 *The first thing I want you to do is the opposite. That is, compare yourself with the most unfortunate people on the planet. When you do that your situation isn't so bad, eh?*

2 *Next, compare yourself with other people in the UK. Take a good look around you. Don't focus on that one person at the top of the heap. What about the neighbour who's unemployed? What about the friend who does two jobs to make ends meet? What about the colleague who lives alone and hates it? You're probably doing much better than you think.*

3 *And here's another thing I want you to do. I'm going to prove to you that you're just as good as anybody else. I want you to write down ten of the fine qualities you possess. Don't believe you've got any? Let me start you off with some suggestions. Well, to begin with you're obviously not arrogant. So that's a good thing. You're obviously not domineering. That's another good thing. And you're sensitive. So that's three excellent qualities for a start. Now you continue and don't stop until you have ten.*

4 *Take a convenient piece of card and head it up: 'Good things about me'. Underneath, list your ten fine qualities. Keep the card handy and look at it every day.*

I'm not first so therefore I'm a loser
This is the old 'black and white' issue. The 'all-or-nothing' mentality. If you have this way of looking at the world you tend to take up extreme positions. 'As I'm not the most successful salesman in my company I'm obviously a failure', 'I didn't get that job – I just can't do anything right'. Black-and-whiters ignore the 'grey' of which most of the world is composed. Only one person can be the top salesman. That certainly doesn't make everyone else a failure. Only one person can fill one job vacancy. Not being that person doesn't mean you can't do anything right.

1 *Write down the names of people you know or have heard of who are not number one.*

2 *Ask yourself: Are those people really failures? What about politics, for example? Are all those politicians failures because they're not a prime minister or president? Are all those actors and actresses in a film failures because they're not the star? Are all the world's tennis players failures, except for the one who is at the very top of the rankings? Of course not. And nor are you a failure.*

The things I do have faults so I'm obviously no good
I've got news for you. Everything everybody does has faults. Nothing is perfect. By focusing on the faults in what you do you're committing the error that's known as 'magnification'. You let that one little slip devalue everything else you've achieved.

If you think perfection exists you're mistaken. And I'll prove it to you. The test is this. If something is perfect it's incapable of improvement. So now you tell me what things you consider to be perfect. A speech you've just heard? But couldn't it have been clearer? Wasn't there some dull material that needed to be cut? Or maybe a party you just went to? But couldn't the music have been better? The food less rich? Or maybe there's an item of clothing you covet? But couldn't the finishing be better? Or the price be lower?

I could go on. When you think about it, I'm sure you'll agree that nothing is perfect. In which case, striving for perfection is a fool's quest. Don't do it. And don't be dissatisfied because you haven't achieved perfection. Nobody does.

It's true that some mystics teach that everything is perfect. But that really only confirms what I'm saying. It's their attitude that makes something 'perfect'. In other words, their acceptance of things as they are. You, too, need to accept that there's a level beyond which it isn't sensible to try to go. So try to see the whole and don't go looking for little faults and then magnifying them out of all proportion.

In whatever it is you're doing – at work, around the house, at play – aim for a good and competent standard but certainly not for perfection. You'll find you'll accomplish a lot more. And be more satisfied.

I'm always making an idiot of myself

No you're not. This is yet another example of attitudes and facts being out of sync. You're destroying your own self-confidence by a style of exaggeration known as 'generalization'.

This is how it happens. You walk into a room full of people, slip over and say to yourself: 'I'm always making an idiot of myself'. You get up to make a speech, spill a drink over your clothes and think the same thing. You go for a job interview, give a bad answer and, again, think the same thing. But it's actually the rarity of these misfortunes that makes them memorable, not the frequency. You probably give a bad answer once in 100 times, spill something on your clothes once a month and slip over once a year.

Insight

Research shows that we all overestimate how much other people notice our gaffes – by a factor of at least two.

PRACTICAL EXERCISE

Have a little notebook handy tomorrow and, as the day goes on, record:

▶ *all the things you do well*
▶ *all the things you do badly*
▶ *all the occasions you don't make an idiot of yourself.*

I'll bet that all the things you do well, plus all the occasions you didn't make an idiot of yourself, will far outweigh the small number of things you do badly (if any). Keep the notebook and refer to it whenever you feel like moaning about 'making an idiot' of yourself. And then stop thinking it ever again.

I know they're not going to like me

This is what cognitive therapists term 'jumping to negative conclusions'. The problem is that this kind of thinking can become a self-fulfilling prophecy. Either you work so hard to make people like you that, instead, they become frightened of getting involved with someone so desperate. Or, at the other extreme, you retire into your shell, having already decided there's no point in making any effort at all. In which case, people can't like you because they can't know you.

PRACTICAL EXERCISE

We all make negative predictions and sometimes, of course, they turn out to be right. Then, in a mixture of bitterness and triumph, we call out: 'There, I told you so'. But how often are they right? Let's find out.

1 *Every time you make a negative prediction such as 'They're not going to like me', I want you to make a note of it.*
2 *Later, record whether or not the prediction turned out to be true. I bet you'll find that on most occasions you were wrong.*

I feel like a failure so I must be a failure

This is something that psychologists call 'emotional reasoning'. Because you feel a certain way you assume you are that way. It may seem logical but it's not. In fact, it's a trick. It's your circular way of thinking that's the problem. You think you're a failure because you feel like a failure which means you think you're a failure ... And on and on and on. You've got to cut right through that circle and head off in a new direction.

PRACTICAL EXERCISE

1 *Make a list of all the things you believe you're bad at.*
2 *For each of them give yourself a score from one to ten.*
3 *List everything you can think of that contradicts your low score. For example, suppose you had listed: 'I'm a poor conversationalist', well, let's see. Can you deal with life's day-to-day communication challenges, like buying something in a shop? Can you explain to someone else how to work a piece*

of equipment? Can you offer words of reassurance to others? Can you pass on gossip? Can you recount what you've done today? Have you ever made anyone laugh? In all probability you've scored yourself, say, a two when in reality you're more like a seven.

4   Now start thinking of yourself as someone with the higher score you really deserve. Tell yourself: 'I feel like a good conversationalist and I am a good conversationalist'. Keep feeling it and thinking it and break out of the circle.

I'm a label

We all fall into this trap to a certain extent. It simplifies things so much if we can put other people into pigeonholes. He's a bore. She's popular. He's a winner. She's a loser. And so on. It saves us having to delve any deeper. But it can be a terrible mistake. And so it is, too, when we apply labels to ourselves. I'm dull. I'm a poor conversationalist. I'm unattractive.

PRACTICAL EXERCISE
The first thing is stop applying labels.

If you find it difficult to break the habit then try putting those labels to the test to see how valid they really are. Have you, for example, ever done anything to overcome your 'problem labels'? I'll bet you haven't. You see, that's how we human beings are. Unless we can do something straightaway, we get discouraged. Then we give up. But nobody achieves anything without effort. Nobody learns to become a good conversationalist, or to dress well, or to perform under pressure in interviews, without quite a bit of practice. If the labels we give ourselves stop us ever really trying, then they become a self-fulfilling prophecy.

Here's what you have to do now:

1   Write down the labels you have for yourself: No good at languages. Two left feet. Hopeless in romantic situations. And so on. Whatever they may be.

2 *Next write down the things you've tried in order to overcome those problems. I'll bet you won't be writing down very much. Now ask yourself this: 'Can I really be expected to excel in this category given how little training and experience I've had?'*

3 *Select one of the items on your list, organize some lessons and get practising. Aim to be able to cross out that label within a year. And proudly proclaim: 'Good at ...'*

I feel guilty that I'm not doing the things I should
Ah, the 'should' word. It causes such a lot of guilt, anxiety and self-recrimination. What a pity it was ever invented!

Let's just think about this for a moment. Who says what you should and shouldn't do? The government? Other people? That little voice inside your head?

Rather than talk in terms of 'should' let's talk in terms of 'want'. What do you want to do? And what don't you want to do? Forget what other people say. You're not them. You're different. In fact, you're unique and you have to follow your own path.

As to that little voice inside, well, you have to be able to know when it's your own authentic voice and when, on the other hand, it's something implanted in your unconscious by others – a kind of brainwashing, in fact.

Let's say you've been invited to a party. You feel you should go. It's only polite. You don't want to let people down. And, anyway, you're trying to improve your social life. On the other hand, you don't enjoy dancing, don't drink much and don't like the other people who've been invited. So what do you do? Perhaps you'll go. Or perhaps you'll conclude your social life will improve more if you meet people in the sort of setting that appeals to you. Take a look at the practical exercises below and see if they help you make up your mind.

PRACTICAL EXERCISE

Next time you're berating yourself over something you should do
or should have done, stop and ask yourself the following questions:

▶ *Who says I should?*
▶ *Is it realistic that I should?*
▶ *What do I truly want?*

Another thing you can do is make a note every time a 'should
statement' comes into your head. Just make a tick in a notebook
or use one of those wrist counters you can buy in sports shops.
For the first few days you'll probably find the number of 'shoulds'
increases as you get better at spotting them. But, then, you'll
probably notice a steady decline as you begin to recognize your
faulty thinking.

Finally, try replacing any 'shoulds' with a softer phrase. Such as: 'It
would be nice if ...'

It's obviously my fault (again)
It's noble to take responsibility for your mistakes. But, on the
other hand, it's damaging to blame yourself for things that
just aren't your fault at all. It's what psychotherapists call
'personalization'.

See if you recognize this sort of self-reproach: 'If only I hadn't
taken a long time getting ready, this never would have happened.'
Or how about this: 'If only I'd spent more time ironing Gerry's

clothes, I'm sure he would have done better at the interview.' Well, I've got two pieces of news for you. One, you're not responsible for everything that goes wrong. And two, other people have to take responsibility for themselves. Gerry is perfectly capable of ironing his own clothes.

Well, ironing may not be the issue in your case. But you take the point. If you have this kind of mindset it may be that your parents were always putting the blame on you. And maybe that set a pattern that's hard to break. The mindset can carry on into adult relationships and eventually destroy every bit of self-confidence.

PRACTICAL EXERCISE
Next time there's a problem and you think it's your fault or someone else says it's your fault, just analyse the situation and ask yourself these kinds of questions:

1 *Was this really my responsibility?*
2 *Or is there somebody else who really had responsibility?*
3 *Was I given proper training to take on this responsibility?*
4 *Would another person have done any better?*

Never lose sight of the fact that everybody makes mistakes every day. That's life. It just isn't possible to do everything perfectly. If you don't believe me, just make a list of all the things you think your least favourite politician has got wrong. You'll probably need quite a lot of paper for that.

Accept responsibility when it's appropriate. Everyone will admire you for it. But never make yourself a scapegoat. And don't let anybody else turn you into one.

They're only saying that to be nice
If someone pays you a compliment do you dismiss it as undeserved? Maybe you think like this: 'He wants something' or 'She's only being nice'. If that sounds like you then you're suffering from a mindset called 'disqualifying the positive'.

Another manifestation is never being satisfied with your own achievements. You set goals but even when you reach them you tell yourself the goals were too easy and move the goalposts to make things harder.

There's nothing at all wrong with setting goals. And there's nothing wrong with setting more difficult challenges as you progress. On the contrary. What's wrong with this particular mindset is that, instead of each achievement creating a sense of self-worth and boosting confidence, it instead becomes a source of dissatisfaction. That's ridiculous.

PRACTICAL EXERCISE

1 *Think of something you enjoy, in which the source of pleasure comes from the thing itself, not the achievement of a particular goal. It could be listening to music, or dancing around the room, or looking at a beautiful view or just lying in bed, all warm and cosy. In fact, when you start to think about it, there are so many things where goals would be meaningless. After all, how can you lie in a bath better than anyone else or better than you did the last time?*

2 *Now hold on to that concept of enjoying something for itself and try to carry it over into those areas where you're always competing with yourself or other people. Giving a speech at a wedding? Then just revel in the happiness of the couple and the company of your friends. Playing a game? Then just enjoy taking part. Going swimming? Then just enjoy the feeling of the water flowing over your body.*

3 *Learn to accept compliments. Don't analyse them. Don't weigh them up to decide to what extent they're deserved. Take them at face value and be happy.*

USING NLP

Neuro-Linguistic Programming (NLP), which began with the collaboration of Richard Bandler and John Grinder in the 1970s, has certain things in common with CT. Here are three NLP 'presuppositions' that can be useful in combating negative thinking.

IF ONE PERSON CAN DO SOMETHING, ANYONE CAN LEARN TO DO IT
This isn't strictly true, of course, but it encapsulates a truth which stands good in most circumstances. It might be better to say 'If most people can do it, I must be able to do it too.' And you will be able to.

IF WHAT YOU ARE DOING ISN'T WORKING, DO SOMETHING ELSE
We often keep doing something because we believe it should work, and when it doesn't we get demoralized. This presupposition cuts to the heart of the matter. As they say, 'If you always do what you've always done, you'll always get what you've always got.' Rather than feel demoralized and lose confidence in yourself, simply switch tactics.

THERE'S NO SUCH THING AS FAILURE, ONLY FEEDBACK
This presupposition is particularly appropriate when it comes to confidence. Think of infants learning to walk. No matter how many times they fall they keep on trying and eventually they succeed. It's only as adults that we develop a fear of what we call 'failure'. But you haven't failed until you've given up trying. Be like an infant and treat each fall as a lesson in what doesn't work and what does.

NLP has quite a lot to teach about confidence and I'll be returning to it from time to time throughout the book.

DEALING WITH BAD DAYS

We all have them. There we are, going along quite nicely, then suddenly … wham! Something bad happens. Just as it did to the psychologist at the cocktail party …

The psychologist was talking to some friends when a man suddenly came up to him, punched him in the face, knocked him to the ground, then kicked him as he lay there. Eventually the assailant walked off and the psychologist staggered to his feet, brushed down his clothes, straightened his tie and smoothed back his hair. Looking at his fellow guests he shrugged his shoulders and said, 'That's his problem'.

Just a little joke to introduce a phrase with which you're no doubt familiar. I'll be using it quite often in this book. In fact, it's a very important concept and the psychologist was, indeed, a master. In their lives, other people have their different ways of looking at things, their misconceptions and their traumas. They may, unfortunately, bring their problems into your life. But that doesn't mean you've done anything wrong. The psychologist didn't allow the assault to damage his self-confidence. When things happen to you, as they do to all of us, try to remember the psychologist and those three little words.

Insight

Here's another tip for making sure those days don't set you back.

Keep a calendar in a prominent place. It needs to be the type that shows just one day at a time on printed paper. At the end of every 'working day' go to the calendar, tear the page off, screw it up and throw it into the waste paper basket while reciting something like this:

▶ *I did my best today. Some things went well. Some things didn't go so well. But now it's over. I'm going to relax and enjoy myself. Tomorrow, when I wake up, it will be a brand new day.*

10 THINGS TO REMEMBER

1 *You can be confident 'without any particular reason'.*

2 *You are entitled to self-worth, right now, just as you are.*

3 *You can literally change the physical make-up of a 'self-doubting brain' into that of a 'confident brain'.*

4 *It's important to tackle the unconscious as well as the conscious mind.*

5 *Cognitive therapy is a way of eliminating negative thoughts.*

6 *Dr Aaron Beck is the 'father of cognitive therapy'.*

7 *If you lack confidence it's because your thoughts are unrealistic.*

8 *There are ten different kinds of negative thoughts you must learn to eliminate.*

9 *Making a list of your good qualities is a simple way of boosting your self-worth.*

10 *Put bad days behind you and forget about them.*

HOW CONFIDENT ARE YOU NOW?

- ▶ *Have you realized that other people are not 'better' than you?*
- ▶ *Have you accepted that coming second or third or fifteenth doesn't make you a 'loser'?*
- ▶ *Have you understood that nothing is ever perfect?*
- ▶ *Have you stopped imagining that other people are paying attention to your occasional mistakes?*
- ▶ *Have you stopped anticipating that other people won't like you?*
- ▶ *Have you stopped feeling like a failure?*
- ▶ *Have you stopped giving yourself negative labels?*
- ▶ *Have you stopped feeling guilty about things you 'should' do?*
- ▶ *Have you stopped blaming yourself when other people are actually responsible?*
- ▶ *Have you stopped dismissing compliments?*

Score:

If you answered 'yes' to most questions, then you're obviously already a pretty confident, happy and resilient person. Go straight on to the next chapter.

If you answered 'yes' to between five and seven questions, then you can also go on to the next chapter but revisit this one from time to time and think about the issues it raises.

If you could answer 'yes' to only four questions or fewer, then you're obviously being far, far too hard on yourself. Keep working on the practical exercises in this chapter until you raise your score to five or higher.

2

More secret weapons

In this chapter you will learn:
- *how to harness the power of suggestion*
- *how trial runs can eliminate fear*
- *how to succeed with visualization and self-hypnosis.*

Nobody can make you feel inferior without your consent.

Eleanor Roosevelt (1884–1962)

You now know about eliminating negative thoughts. Next let's take a look at the opposite side of the coin and learn ways of actively promoting positive thoughts.

SUGGESTION

The unconscious will always be associated with the Austrian physician Sigmund Freud (1856–1939), but in fact others wrote about it before him, notably the French psychiatrist and philosopher Pierre Janet (1859–1947). Freud's vital contribution was to devise systems for both uncovering and altering its contents.

We now understand how, simply by using suggestion, we can reprogram our unconscious minds. There's an easy but very powerful technique which anybody can master. All you have to do is devise a 'suggestion' and keep repeating it to yourself. But make sure the suggestion is couched in positive terms.

Here's a common experience. I was at a seminar with some important people – well, important to me – and on the first morning I got two of them mixed up and called them by the wrong names. (In fact, they looked very similar.) Next morning I saw Vincent heading towards me and told myself: 'This is Vincent. Do not call him Hubert. Do not call him Hubert. Do not call him Hubert.' Yet as soon as I opened my mouth I heard myself say, 'Hello Hubert'. And he was pretty upset.

How could it have happened? The answer is simple. I'd been concentrating on the wrong thing. On the negative. I'd been focusing on the avoidance of failure, not on the achievement of success. It's a very important distinction. I shouldn't have said to myself, 'Do not call him Hubert'. I should simply have visualized myself saying, 'Hello Vincent'.

Do you see the difference? The two methods seem similar and have the same goal. But one is doomed to failure because your mind is mesmerized by the negative possibilities. The other is zeroed in on success.

And, therefore, it will succeed.

PRACTICAL EXERCISE

1 *Select a time when you can completely relax. I suggest you do this in bed at night, just before going to sleep. That's when the 'pathway' between the conscious and unconscious minds is most accessible.*

2 *Now simply repeat your suggestion in your mind, over and over. For example, suppose you feel that people don't warm to you. You feel inadequate and anxious in social situations. Then you might say something like this: 'I'm a kind and loving human being with a lot to give. I take an interest in people and like to help. When I show that side of myself people find me attractive and enjoy my company.' Remember you mustn't frame your suggestions in negative terms. For example, never say anything like this: 'There's no reason people shouldn't like*

me'. That would be to implant negative expectations into your unconscious which would have the opposite effect to the one you want. Always be positive.

3   It doesn't matter if you vary the words a little every night because you can't quite remember them. In fact, long suggestions seem to work better than short ones. Possibly they permeate more of the unconscious. So don't worry about being word perfect. The important thing is that the sentiment – the positive sentiment – remains the same.

Insight

Choose or invent a confidence-boosting motto for yourself. Repeat it every night just before you go to sleep and whenever you start to have doubts about your ability to succeed.

Here are a few standard mottos to give you some ideas:

▶ *Beaten paths are for beaten people.*
▶ *Boldness be my friend.*
▶ *Boldness has genius, power, and magic in it (Goethe).*
▶ *Every day in every way I'm getting better and better.*
▶ *If at first you don't succeed, try, try, try again.*
▶ *I can.*
▶ *Imagination is more important than knowledge (Einstein).*
▶ *Never give in (Winston Churchill).*
▶ *Serve to lead (Royal Military Academy Sandhurst).*
▶ *The only ones who fail are those who do not try.*
▶ *Train hard, fight easy.*
▶ *Whatever it takes.*
▶ *Who dares wins (UK Special Air Service).*
▶ *You're as good as you think you are.*
▶ *You've got to be in it to win it.*

And here are some in Latin:

▶ Acta non verba – *Actions not words.*
▶ Alis grave nil – *Nothing is heavy to those who have wings.*

- ▶ Audeamus – *Let us dare.*
- ▶ Audentes fortuna iuvat – *Fortune favours the bold.*
- ▶ Audere est facere – *To dare is to do (the motto of Tottenham Hotspur Football Club).*
- ▶ Aut viam inveniam aut faciam – *Either I shall find a way or I shall make one (Hannibal).*
- ▶ Carpe diem – *Seize the day.*
- ▶ Fortes fortuna adiuvat – *Fortune favours the brave (3rd Regiment of the US Marine Corps).*
- ▶ In somnis veritas – *In dreams there is truth.*
- ▶ Non progredi est regredi – *Not to progress is to go backwards.*
- ▶ Semper excelsius – *Always higher.*

And, finally, a few funny ones:

- ▶ *For every action there is an equal and opposite criticism.*
- ▶ *Hard work pays off in the future; laziness pays off now.*
- ▶ *No one is listening until you make a mistake.*
- ▶ *Repeat after me: We are all individuals.*
- ▶ *The sooner you fall behind the more time you'll have to catch up.*

TRIAL RUNS

Rehearsing or making a 'trial run' is something you can do for all sorts of situations to combat nerves. Lack of confidence is, after all, often just a fear of the unknown. If you've never done something before you're bound to feel apprehensive. You have no way of knowing how you'll cope or if you'll succeed. That makes you apprehensive.

The idea of the trial run is very simple but also very effective. Let's say you're job hunting. There's one particular position you'd desperately like and you're feeling anxious. How can you prepare yourself? The answer is really very simple. Apply for other similar jobs and use those interviews as trial runs. Here are the advantages:

- ▶ *You'll be able to practise your interview technique in a real situation.*

▶ *You might get offered one of those other jobs – which will make you feel more confident and relaxed at the interview for the job you really want.*

You can use the technique of trial runs in all sorts of situations. And if you can't organize a real-life test then, at the very least, try to practise with the help of friends. If the goal is a job interview, for example, ask someone to act the role of the prospective employer and to throw questions at you. Similarly, if you know there's going to be some kind of psychometric test then get hold of some previous test papers and go through them.

Here are some of the situations where a trial run is always a good idea:

▶ *job interview*
▶ *television, radio or press interview*
▶ *court appearance*
▶ *making a speech*
▶ *giving a presentation*
▶ *making important phone calls*
▶ *selling*
▶ *negotiating*
▶ *telling jokes*
▶ *giving an important dinner party*
▶ *going out with a new boyfriend or girlfriend*
▶ *dealing with a difficult person*
▶ *any kind of physical challenge.*

PRACTICAL EXERCISE
The following exercise is a trial run to help you get through a job interview. But you can adapt the concept for just about anything.

1 *Enlist the help of a friend. You're going to be role-playing.*
2 *Ask your friend to take the part of a prospective employer (or whatever it may be).*
3 *Get your friend to spend a little time preparing questions.*
4 *Your friend fires the questions at you and you do your best to answer.*

5 *When it's over, analyse your responses together and see how they could be improved (if you can actually record your voice, so much the better).*

Insight

Of course, you can't always know what questions people are going to throw at you in an interview. Nor can you know what life's going to throw at you in general. So how can you prepare yourself with a trial run?

The answer is to regularly challenge yourself in as many different ways as possible. There's no direct connection between, say, climbing a mountain and giving a speech to a roomful of people. But there's an indirect connection. As you step up to that podium you can say to yourself: 'I've done harder things than this before'.

VISUALIZATION

Some people find visualization very easy while others find it quite difficult. It's all a question of how your mind works. But one thing's for sure. The more you practise the better you'll get at it.

Let's say you've been asked to talk about your company's products. On the face of it, a straightforward task. But in your mind you change it into something quite different. You build it up into a test of the way you look, the way you dress, your skill as an entertainer and your ability to make people laugh. In reality, no one is going to be judging you that way. In fact, they're not going to be judging you at all. They want to hear about your company's products and if you give them the information they need they'll be perfectly satisfied. Job done.

What you need to do is harness the power of your imagination to 'see' yourself providing that information and the audience appreciating it.

Without doubt you're already using visualization but you're probably using it in a negative way. Maybe you're visualizing people being bored by you, taking a dislike to you, laughing at you. You need to turn that round and use visualization in a positive way, just as top sports stars do. They visualize themselves making the correct movements. They visualize themselves winning. You can do the same. In the following exercise I'll stick with the idea of giving a speech, but you can substitute any other situation you find challenging.

PRACTICAL EXERCISE

1 *Sit or lie down and relax. If you like, have on some music – but make sure it's something you find inspiring and energizing.*

2 *Now just close your eyes, let your mouth crease up into a smile and breathe slowly and regularly. You're going to visualize yourself being very relaxed, so it will help if you feel relaxed while doing it.*

3 *See yourself being very relaxed. Hear yourself talking in a calm, easy voice. Imagine yourself making eye contact from time to time with the people around you. (Some people can conjure up scenes quite clearly in their imaginations and other people only manage hazy fragments. It doesn't matter if your visualization isn't very detailed. The important thing is to concentrate on the key elements.)*

4 *Now let's take a look at those people. See your audience concentrating on what you have to say. See their appreciative expressions. See them, now and then, exchanging glances with those sitting next to them and nodding in agreement.*

5 *Hear the applause at the end.*

Of course, visualization isn't something you can only do in a quiet room. You can do it on a train or bus, during any free moment, and even while walking or running. The key is to repeat the visualization over and over. And be sure to reinforce it one more time just before the event you'd previously been worried about.

Insight

Some people find that visualization makes them feel worse. So they prefer not to think about the situation at all. Their mistake is that they allow their imagination to entertain negative thoughts. Don't ever make the same error. Never allow any negatives to enter your visualization. If you do, you'll end up making the situation worse, not better. Close your mind to negatives. They don't exist.

Watch yourself

If you have a video camera, or can borrow one, you can get a very good impression of how you look to other people. You can also practise different ways of using your voice, different ways of holding yourself and so on. Don't ask someone else to film you. That will only make you inhibited and less willing to experiment. Instead, set your camera up on a tripod and use your TV as a monitor with the leads provided. That way, you'll be able to check you're in frame.

Try talking both directly to the camera and talking to an imaginary person a little to one side of the camera. If you do that, you'll be able to see how you come across to someone you're speaking to and you'll also be able to see how you look to a third party.

You'll be surprised. You'll look much better than you imagined. What's more, you'll very quickly see what expressions, gestures and postures work and which ones don't.

Keep on making adjustments and re-filming until you think you've got it right. Once you've done that, then ask someone you can trust to watch you in action and suggest improvements. But here's a warning. Don't be artificial because it will be too much of a strain to keep up. In other words, try to develop a style that reflects the real you.

If you can't lay your hands on a video camera at least use some kind of voice recorder.

BUT DON'T MAKE UNFAIR COMPARISONS

We all watch the professionals at work every day and once you get to grips with a video camera you'll inevitably be comparing yourself with Fiona Bruce or Bruce Forsyth, Johnny Ball or Zoë Ball. But don't forget they've had professional training and years of practice. You just can't compare yourself with those people. In fact, when you think about it, very few people can match their skills. It's great to have their example as an ideal but don't go thinking you're a failure because you're not on their level. That's asking the impossible. Just be yourself, which requires no effort, and focus on getting the job done.

It's also worth reflecting that none of those people developed their presentational abilities by accident. They've all done what you're practising – that is, rehearsing in private before ever being allowed on air.

Advanced visualization

Now that you're using visualization in a positive rather than a negative way, let's take the whole thing to a new level. We easily can, thanks to the work of John Grinder and Richard Bandler on Neuro-Linguistic Programming (NLP), which we met briefly in the previous chapter. One of their innovations was the manipulation of what they called 'submodalities'. It's a rather clumsy word, simply meaning the qualities possessed by internal images, sounds and feelings – that's to say, the angle and distance from which a scene is viewed, the brightness of the colours, the pitch of the sounds and so on.

By changing the submodalities you can alter the emotional impact of the scene. When we're afraid of things, for example, we tend to imagine them big. If you lack confidence with dogs, then when you think about them you probably have a dog's face completely filling your 'screen', its huge fangs bared and seeming to be the size of ice picks. When you're nervous about asking someone for a date, you probably see that person in vivid colour and see yourself, by contrast, as blurry and drab. When you're anxious about an interview you probably hear questioning voices that are distinguished and superior while your own voice sounds timid and unworthy.

The concept behind NLP is that you can turn all this back to front. That is, instead of the way you feel creating the submodalities, you deliberately create the submodalities that will make you feel the way you would prefer to be. In other words, instead of seeing the dog full screen you reduce the size. Instead of the possible date being more vividly coloured than you, the two of you become more equal. Instead of the interviewers sounding intimidating they sound comical.

Most people have probably never given a thought to the submodalities of their internal cinema. So, if that includes you, here's a little exercise.

PRACTICAL EXERCISE
Lie down somewhere comfortable and have a notebook and pen handy.

Call up an image of a person you really love. Write down in your notebook the submodalities. For example, is the image in colour or in black and white? Is it vivid or faint? Is it large or small? Is it central or to one side? Can you hear music?

Next think of someone you really dislike and once again write down the submodalities.

Here are some possibilities that may help you:

Visual qualities (visual submodalities)

- ▶ *colour or black and white*
- ▶ *large or small*
- ▶ *near or far*
- ▶ *bright or dull*
- ▶ *moving or still*
- ▶ *clear or blurred*

Audio qualities (audio submodalities)

- *loud or soft*
- *high pitched or low pitched*
- *clear or muffled*
- *near or far*
- *pleasant or unpleasant*

Qualities of feelings (kinaesthetic submodalities)

- *heavy or light*
- *rough or smooth*
- *hot or cold*
- *constant or intermittent*
- *strong or weak*
- *moving or still*
- *intense or faint*
- *sharp or dull*
- *increasing or decreasing heart rate*
- *faster or slower breathing rate*

Once you've got the hang of identifying submodalities the next step is to begin manipulating them deliberately.

PRACTICAL EXERCISE
Call up one of your favourite daydreams but this time, instead of just watching it, start manipulating it in various ways.

Here are some ideas:

- *See the scene through your own eyes.*
- *Now 'switch cameras' to see the scene from another person's viewpoint.*
- *Pull back to see everyone in the scene simultaneously.*
- *Make a split screen and show different images side by side.*
- *Run a section in slow motion.*
- *Show a series of stills.*

- ▶ *Change 'camera angles'.*
- ▶ *Play some music.*
- ▶ *Play some completely different music.*
- ▶ *Use soft focus.*
- ▶ *Introduce a voiceover.*
- ▶ *Zoom in for a close-up.*
- ▶ *Move in closer still.*
- ▶ *Pull right back so you can now see for miles.*
- ▶ *Turn down the lights.*
- ▶ *Switch from colour to black and white.*
- ▶ *Have a pianist, as in the silent movie days.*
- ▶ *Have the image fill the entire 'screen'.*
- ▶ *Shrink the image to half the screen then a quarter then an eighth.*

The more you practise the more effective you'll be. Don't worry if you can't actually see an image very clearly or for very long. That's how it is for most people.

Each time you manipulate the image ask yourself what effect it has on you. How does it impact your emotions?

For example, you might feel:

- ▶ *more/less excited*
- ▶ *more/less involved*
- ▶ *more/less positive*
- ▶ *more/less happy*
- ▶ *more/less afraid*
- ▶ *more/less confident.*

Insight
Make time to carry out these experiments in submodalities every day. See if you can improve your ability to visualize. If you have to commute by train regularly this is a good way of creatively passing the journey.

THE CIRCLE OF CONFIDENCE

The *Circle of Confidence* is an NLP visualization technique for transferring confidence from a situation in which you feel mastery to a situation in which you feel inadequate. Some people climb mountains or sail round the world single-handed to try to convince themselves that they can have the self-confidence to tackle just about any situation. They theorize that if they take on the world's hardest challenges then nothing else will ever seem difficult again. But life isn't quite like that.

This technique does things differently. It lets you take the self-confidence you felt in any previous situation, including one that was *easy*. And then it transfers that feeling to the more difficult situation.

Step 1 Something important is coming up and you're going to need plenty of self-confidence to deal with it. Search your memory for a past situation in which you felt that necessary confidence. It doesn't have to have been an especially difficult situation. Relive that confident time, seeing and hearing everything in as much detail as possible. Particularly notice how you looked and how the confidence was oozing out of you.

Step 2 Imagine a circle on the floor. Take the confidence you feel and pour it into the circle. Immediately the circle takes on a colour – the colour that, to you, is the colour of confidence. It also makes a noise. Maybe it's a buzzing sound or even music – again, it's whatever expresses confidence to you.

Step 3 Are there any other qualities you'll need? Maybe patience? Maybe judgement? If so, repeat the procedure, also pouring those qualities into your circle.

Step 4 Turn your thoughts to the future occasion when you'll be wanting to feel those qualities. Select a cue to that moment. For example, if you're going to give a speech, the cue could be someone introducing you. Or, if you're going to an interview, it could be a secretary calling your name. (But don't make

*it too specific otherwise you might never get the cue you
envisaged.)*

*Step 5 Holding that cue in your mind, step into the circle and
visualize all those qualities rising up from the floor, permeating
and enveloping you. As you move around so that cocoon of
confidence will move with you.*

*Step 6 Visualize the future unfolding from that cue moment. See
yourself behaving with confidence and all the other qualities
you've selected.*

*Step 7 When the cue moment arrives for real, visualize the circle on
the floor, step into it and go and do what you have to do.*

Insight

NLP makes the presupposition that people already have
all the resources they need. You should try hard to find
the necessary qualities within you. However, if you can't,
then visualize another person who embodies the necessary
qualities, perhaps a character in a film.

SELF-HYPNOSIS

Visualizing something in detail, as in the *Circle of Confidence*, both
induces a mild trance and creates a 'program'. So the very act of
visualization *automatically* channels the new program into your
unconscious, which is where it needs to be if it's to be effective. But
there is a special way of deepening the trance and increasing the
power of the program. That's self-hypnosis.

Because self-hypnosis can be so powerful, it's important to
carry out what's known as an 'ecology check' before attempting
to make any changes to your behaviour. That simply means
investigating all the ramifications before going ahead. The key
questions are:

▶ *What will happen if I succeed in making this change?*
▶ *What won't happen if I succeed in making this change?*
▶ *What will happen if I don't succeed in making this change?*
▶ *What won't happen if I don't succeed in making this change?*

PRACTICAL EXERCISE

Step 1 Get yourself comfortable in a place you won't be disturbed.
It's not a good idea to lie on the bed because you might fall
asleep. But you could sit up on the bed supported by pillows,
or arrange yourself in a nice, comfy chair.

Step 2 Decide the length of time you wish to spend in
self-hypnosis. Initially I'd suggest ten minutes. That should
give you enough time to achieve a deep state of trance
without feeling anxiety about 'wasting' time or needing to
get on with something else. As you get used to self-hypnosis
you can vary the time. For example, if the aim is to relax
after a strenuous or demanding day then you might like
to enjoy that state for half an hour or more. On the other
hand, just before a difficult meeting you might only have five
minutes available. So, having got comfortable, you should
say something like this: 'I am now going to hypnotize myself
for ten minutes'. You might like to append the actual time
by adding '... which means I will come out of self-hypnosis
at 19.30 (or whatever)'.

Step 3 This is a key step because it's where you state the purpose of
your hypnosis. Here we're concerned with confidence but you
can use the technique for all kinds of things. During your initial
experiments I'd suggest starting with one of your more minor
problems, leaving your biggest problems to be dealt with once
you've become proficient in the technique. The exact words
aren't important. Something along these lines will do fine.
'I am entering into a state of self-hypnosis so that I can hand
over to my unconscious mind the task of ....' Or: 'I am entering
into a trance for the purpose of allowing my unconscious mind
to make the adjustments that will help me ...' Whatever you
say, make sure it includes the message that you are inviting your
unconscious to deal with the matter.

Step 4 State how you want to feel when you come out of your trance. It may be you will simply want to experience your 'normal waking state'. It might be you will immediately want to make use of the change your unconscious has made. In that case you might say, for example, '… and as I come out of my trance I will feel full of confidence and ready to take the next step'. Or it may be that you simply want to continue feeling relaxed or even go to sleep.

Step 5 This is the actual process of self-hypnosis. Basically you're going to engage your three main representational systems (seeing, hearing, feeling) in turn to bring the trance about. In the first part of the process you will be noting things you can actually see, hear and feel *in the room where you are*. In the second part you will be noting things you can see, hear and feel *in an imaginary scene*.

Insight

The things you *feel* should be *physical* sensations at the interface of your body and the environment. In other words, saying 'I can feel a breeze on my face' will be more effective than saying 'I feel happy'.

Below is a diagram that represents the whole process. In the diagram, V = Visual System, A = Auditory System, and K = Kinaesthetic System.

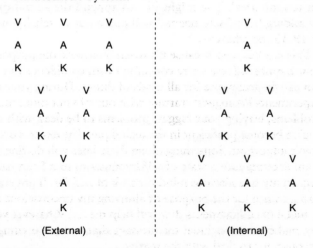

Figure 2.1 Diagrammatic representation of self-hypnosis.

In this process, some people talk to themselves internally but I recommend that you say everything out loud. For that reason you'll want to be in a private place. You might imagine that you'd 'wake' yourself up but, in fact, the sound of your own voice, done the right way, will intensify the effect. (If, however, speaking out loud doesn't work for you, then by all means speak internally.)

5.1 From your comfortable position look at some small thing in the room in front of you and say out loud what you are looking at. Choose things you can see without moving your head. For example, 'I am looking at the door handle.' Then, without rushing, focus on another small item. For example, 'I am now looking at a glass of water on the table.' Then move on to a third item. For example, 'I am looking at the light switch.' When you have your three visual references, move on to 5.2.

5.2 Switch attention to sounds and, in the same way, note one after another until you have three, each time saying out loud what you're hearing. Then move on to 5.3.

5.3 Note things that you can feel with your body. For example, you might say, 'I can feel the seat pressing against my buttocks.' When you have your three, move on.

5.4 Now repeat steps 5.1 to 5.3 but with only two items for each sense, that's to say, two images, two sounds and two feelings. They must be different from the ones you used before. Speak a little more slowly.

5.5 Again repeat steps 5.1 to 5.3 but with only one item per sense, that's to say, one image, one sound and one feeling. Again, they must be different from any that have gone before. Speak even more slowly.

5.6 Close your eyes, if they're not already closed, and think of the particular scene in which you would like to be more confident. Let's say, for example, you want to be more confident when asking someone for a date. In that case you would see yourself talking to that other person in a confident way, and the other person smiling, laughing and happily accepting.

5.7 Using this imagined scene, go through the same process you already used for the real scene, but beginning with just one instance of each of the three senses, that is, one image, one sound and one feeling. For example, you might say: 'I see my eyes twinkling, I hear myself confidently suggesting that we meet in a restaurant, I feel my potential date touch my hand.' When you've done that, increase to two instances and then three. (Three is usually enough, but if you've stipulated a lengthy session you may need to continue with your fantasy scene by going on to name four images, sounds and feelings, or five or even more.) Remember, each instance must be different. You'll probably find you're automatically speaking very slowly now but, if not, make a point of slowing your voice down more and more.

Step 6 After the allotted time you should begin to come out of trance automatically. But it may help to announce, 'I'll count to three and when I reach three I'll be (whatever you said in step 5.4).' Don't worry about getting 'stuck' in a trance. That won't happen. You may feel a little woozy for a while. If so, don't drive a car or do anything demanding until you're sure you're okay to do so.

10 THINGS TO REMEMBER

1 *Simply repeating a suggestion over and over again can have an important impact on your behaviour – but make sure the suggestion is couched in positive, not negative, terms.*

2 *Mottos work in exactly that way – through the repetition of positive suggestions.*

3 *Lack of confidence is often just a fear of the unknown – so use trial runs to convert the unknown into the known.*

4 *It's useful to develop the skill of visualization.*

5 *If you visualize yourself succeeding then you'll increase your chance of success.*

6 *Never allow anything negative into your visualization or you'll do more harm than good.*

7 *You can learn a lot by acting out scenarios in front of a video recorder and then playing them back – you'll be surprised how good you become.*

8 *Changing the submodalities of a visualization can change the whole way you feel.*

9 *The* Circle of Confidence *lets you 'borrow' confidence so that you can use it in a situation about which you feel nervous.*

10 *Self-hypnosis is an extremely powerful technique for reprogramming your mind.*

HOW CONFIDENT ARE YOU NOW?

▶ *Have you unleashed the power of positive suggestion?*
▶ *Have you adopted a positive motto?*
▶ *Have you had at least one trial run?*
▶ *Have you practised in front of a video recorder?*
▶ *Have you been practising your visualization skills?*
▶ *Have you been able to change submodalities?*
▶ *Have you been able to change your emotional response by changing submodalities?*
▶ *Have you successfully used the* Circle of Confidence?
▶ *Have you been able to put yourself into a trance?*
▶ *Have you been able to use the trance state to reprogram your unconscious mind?*

Score:

If you answered 'yes' to eight or more questions, move on to the next chapter.

If you answered 'yes' to between five and seven questions, you can move on to the next chapter if you wish but be sure to return to this one to practise the various techniques.

If you answered 'yes' to four questions or fewer, then you need to work on the practical exercises in this chapter before moving on to new topics.

3

How to make people like
you – and love you

In this chapter you will learn:
- *the special quality you have that everybody values*
- *how to project your warmth towards other people*
- *what to do if somebody doesn't respond positively to you.*

The only way to have a friend is to be one.

Ralph Waldo Emerson (1803–82), American poet

Some people lack confidence because they erroneously believe they
have nothing to give to others. They devalue themselves because
they're not rich, or highly educated, or expert in anything, or don't
see themselves as attractive. Does that sound like you in any way?
Then let me prove to you that you do have something very special
to give if only you'd use it. It's something other people value above
all else. You don't have to have money, you don't have to have
position, you don't have to have looks, you don't have to have a
fine education or a high IQ. All you have to have is the willingness
to project the warmth that's inside you.

Just think about it for a moment. What is it that draws you to
other human beings? Undoubtedly, you need to feel that you have
things in common. But then what? Is it their money, their house,
their car, their expertise in accountancy or electrical engineering,
their university degree? Very unlikely. Isn't it the warmth they
project towards you? Well, you have just as much warmth as
anybody else.

WARMTH

Energy is Eternal Delight.

William Blake, English poet

Every actor wants it by the tonne. Those that have it command fees in the millions. No one can define it but everyone recognizes it when they see it. What is it? Some people call it 'charisma' but it's really a special kind of warmth. And it's just about the most elusive of human qualities.

We can certainly pin down one of the ingredients. It's energy. Not the running up and down the stairs kind of energy, but a more subtle kind that emanates from a person. When someone has that special warmth we talk about them being 'electric'. And that's literally true.

Human beings actually run on electricity. We're not normally aware of it because the charge is very small – about 0.1 volts. Nevertheless, in the context of the human membranes across which the current flows, it's more significant than it seems. In terms of volts per metre it's actually 20 times more powerful than a bolt of lightning. So, yes, you may not be aware of it but, you have a lot of power at your disposal if you know how to use it. We'll be looking at ways of projecting that power in a moment.

On the other hand, there are people who, far from being 'electric', actually seem to suck energy out of anyone who comes near them. Everyone instinctively keeps away. It may not be very kind but it's a normal reaction. What is it that creates this 'energy sink'? It's all due to being negative. 'Energy sinks' are people who are constantly:

▶ *self-pitying*
▶ *pessimistic*
▶ *gloomy*
▶ *apathetic*

- *critical*
- *defeatist*
- *overly introverted.*

So how do you create energy? That list should give you a clue. And in fact, it's quite easy. All you have to do is put a stop to the 'negativity' that's diverting and blocking your natural electricity. That means developing the qualities of:

- *acceptance*
- *supportive friendship*
- *inclusivity*
- *optimism*
- *curiosity.*

ACCEPTANCE

One quality, above all, is important if people are going to like you and love you. And it's just as important if you're going to like and love yourself. The word for it is 'acceptance'.

It isn't, on the face of it, a very exciting word. It certainly doesn't seem to be a very noble word. On the contrary, it almost sounds contemptible. And yet it's the key to so much.

Think about it for a moment. What do you want most from other people? Criticisms of the way you do things? Suggestions for how you can improve yourself? Reasons why your beliefs are invalid?

Of course not. You want people to value you for yourself exactly as you are. In other words, you want to be accepted.

In the same way, you have to accept other people as they are. You have to accept yourself as you are. And while you're at it, you might as well accept the world the way it is, too. You'll be a lot happier and have a lot more self-confidence if you do. In fact, let's take things even further. Because accepting is really only the minimum requirement. Better still, find as much as possible to celebrate.

Let me elaborate. I'm not saying you should meekly and passively put up with unpleasant things other people and life in general dish out to you. I'm not saying you, other people and the world shouldn't ever change. (In fact, change is inevitable and that's another thing you're going to have to accept.) But I am saying acceptance is the prerequisite for everything else. Because if you don't accept other people they're certainly not going to accept you. They're not going to like you. They're not going to be friends.

In fact, when it comes to other people, psychologists say there are just four basic outlooks on life. Here they are:

- *I'm okay and you're okay.*
- *I'm okay but you're not okay.*
- *I'm not okay but you're okay.*
- *I'm not okay and you're not okay.*

Just spend a moment taking that in. You'll fairly quickly see that the first position is the ideal way to be. When you genuinely feel that, other people sense it and are drawn to you. The other three positions will all cause you problems in your social life (and your happiness, too).

Insight

Unfortunately, these positions are set very early in life – between the ages of four and five according to many psychologists. After that it becomes difficult to change them. But not impossible.

If you want to be more at ease on social occasions, here's another thought to slip into your unconscious at bedtime:

- *I'm a nice person and everyone I meet will be a nice person, too.*

PRACTICAL EXERCISE

The failure to signal acceptance is often part of a downward spiral that begins like this. When you're apprehensive about meeting people you're bound to give out negative vibes which other people will pick up. They may not necessarily guess the reason for your negativity. All they'll know is that you are negative. That will make them wary. In turn you'll probably start thinking something like this:

▶ *I knew I shouldn't have come. They don't like me and I don't like them. I'm completely out of place here.*

Once you start feeling defensive you're more likely to be critical of everyone else. Maybe you'll respond by thinking like this:

▶ *I don't like the look of him; he looks like a drunk. I'm not going to get on with her; she's far too full of herself.*

And so on.

You need to avoid that kind of judgmental thinking at all costs. Try retraining your unconscious by saying this to yourself every night just before you go to sleep:

▶ *It's a pleasure to meet new people. Everyone I meet is a potential new friend. Every way they're like me makes me feel exhilarated. Every way they're different to me is fascinating and stimulating. I love everybody and I look forward to every encounter.*

Is that going too far for you? Loving everybody? Then that may be the basis of your problem with socializing. When you're about to meet somebody new do you, in fact, ever say this to yourself, 'I hope I'm going to like them'? Well, the answer to that lies with you, not with the other person. Hope doesn't come into it. If you don't like them that's because you decide not to like them. You can just as easily decide to like them. I suggest you do. Your social encounters will go much better like that.

SUPPORTIVE FRIENDSHIP

A little while ago I accidentally set light to some bushes on my land. A neighbour rushed to help me put out the blaze and as the two of us were beating side by side, he grinned and said: 'Don't worry. I did the same thing myself last year'. The neighbour could have behaved very differently, especially as his own land was threatened. He could have been angry. He could have laughed at my utter stupidity. He could have revelled in his superiority. He did none of that. Instead he basically said to me: 'I'm all right and you're all right'. In other words, he was supportive, not critical. I appreciated that even more than his help. The two of us are now great friends.

PRACTICAL EXERCISE
The Germans have long had a word for it and the English language has imported it. You are now going to ban it from your life. It's *Schadenfreude* and it means taking a delight in other people's misfortunes. Whenever someone in your life does something stupid, like setting fire to their own garden, don't indulge in Schadenfreude. Instead, offer the words of support the other person needs. Show them that, as far as you're concerned, they're 'all right'.

INCLUSIVITY

When you're driving your car on a crowded road do you ever find yourself thinking something like this: 'I'm in a hurry and I can't get along because all these stupid people are blocking the road up'? Or if you go to the beach and find it so packed you can hardly spread your towel out, do you ever think like this: 'Why aren't these people at work? They shouldn't be here!'?

Do you? If so, do you see what you're doing? You're setting yourself apart from other people. You've got an attitude of 'them and me'. In fact, you probably have no better reason for being on the road or at the beach than anybody else. What you have to understand is that everyone is in the jam together. In other words, you need to be inclusive, not exclusive. When you're exclusive other people sense it, even if you don't say anything.

Next time you're caught up in a traffic jam or something similar say this to yourself:

▶ *I'm contributing to this jam just as much as anybody else. We're all in this together. I'm all right but they're all right, too.*

OPTIMISM

People who are optimistic and positive are fun to be around. And you can make a policy decision to become one of them. In everyone's life there are good and bad things. Why mope over the bad ones when that only makes you unhappy? Instead, choose to focus on the good ones. (This is a whole subject in itself – you might care to read *Teach Yourself How To Be Happier* for more information.)

PRACTICAL EXERCISE
Next time someone asks you how things are, don't say:

▶ *not so bad*
▶ *okay*
▶ *could be better.*

In fact, don't say anything like that. Instead say:

▶ *wonderful*
▶ *marvellous*
▶ *incredible.*

And then elaborate a little in universal terms: Because it's such a beautiful day. Because life is full of such exciting possibilities. Because it's just great to be alive.

See what effect that has. You'll like it so much you'll want to keep on doing it. Everyone can share in those feelings because they're not specific to you. People will react by thinking:

'That's right! And he's all right', and feel energized by contact with you.

CURIOSITY

Everything and everybody is fascinating when you delve under the surface. So cultivate a spirit of curiosity and tease out the secrets that lie hidden from view. When you do, you're showing that whatever it is, is 'all right'. You'll never be bored and you'll never be boring.

PRACTICAL EXERCISE
Next time someone is boring you, see if you can't discover a more interesting dimension. Suppose a friend is showing you a new electric kettle. Boring? That all depends on your point of view. How, for example, does the plastic withstand steam? How does the kettle know the water is boiling? Why does calcium deposit itself as limescale inside a kettle? Why does water behave so violently at around 100 degrees centigrade? Why doesn't the handle get hot? And so on. When you start to think this way you become a more stimulating companion.

PUSHING YOUR WARMTH AHEAD OF YOU

So, you've now unblocked some of that warmth. The next stage is to project it onto other people. Unfortunately, most of us hide the warmth that's inside us. Which is a great pity. We're conditioned to be that way because it's part of our culture. But it's also because we're afraid of rejection. Our attitude is: You show warmth first and I'll return it. Which usually means that nobody shows any warmth.

Imagine that wherever you went you found the people friendly and eager to help rather than cold and distant. Well, it could be that way. You can change the human landscape around you not by changing the people (which would be very difficult) but by changing yourself (which is relatively easy). Just project your warmth onto other people and plenty of them will reflect it back. They'll change from cold to warm because of the way you are.

Notice I say 'plenty' not 'all'. Some people will be so unused to it they'll be taken by surprise. They'll be confused and suspicious. Never mind. You can work on them over time.

Insight

This business of 'projection' explains how two people can go on holiday to the same destination and come back with totally different experiences. One says the people were very friendly. The other says the opposite. How is it possible? Because one projected warmth and the other concealed it. It's that simple.

PRACTICAL EXERCISE

All this week project warmth wherever you go.

1 *Project it with your body. Think of being on a crowded train. What do you do? Probably sit or stand with your arms close to your body, your knees pressed together and your head down or buried in a newspaper. Effectively you're trying to shut everyone else out. Well, projecting warmth with your body is the opposite. Your body is relaxed. Your arms are spread out, your legs are slightly apart or crossed, and you look around at everything with interest. Increase the effect by imagining that every time you breathe in you absorb energy which you then project from every pore. As you walk, visualize the warmth flowing out in front of you.*

2 *Project it with your eyes. Make eye contact with people when you talk to them. Put a little twinkle into your eyes and smile. If you're not sure how to make your eyes sparkle, practise in front of a mirror. Or, better still, use a video camera linked to a monitor (your TV).*

3 *Project it with focus. It's much better to spend a quarter of an hour giving someone your full attention than to spend an hour constantly distracted by other preoccupations.*

Insight

Keep a contacts book or electronic file with details about everyone you're acquainted with – children's names, pets' names, food fancies and so on. When you know you're going to be meeting up, consult your records so you can ask after family members by name, provide food they like and generally show that you care. I also make a note of everyone's birthdays and keep the list in a prominent place – everyone appreciates getting a birthday card (electronic or paper) on time.

USING COGNITIVE THERAPY

In Chapter 1 I described ten 'cognitive distortions' connected with self-confidence. All of them can have a negative impact on friendship, intimate relations and the projection of warmth, but here I want to focus on two of them in particular:

▶ *I know they're not going to like me.*
▶ *They're only saying that to be nice.*

Deciding in advance that people aren't going to like you is an example of a style of thinking psychotherapists call 'jumping to conclusions'. In fact, you have no reason at all to think that and I'm going to prove it to you. I want you to take a sheet of paper and draw a line down the middle. On the left-hand side I want you to head it up 'Reasons I think they won't like me' and on the right-hand side 'Why I'm mistaken'. Then I want you to fill it in. Try to step back from your negative feelings and analyse them as logically as you can. Below I've given some ideas to get you started. But I want you to add to them according to your own thoughts and feelings. When you've finished I think you'll see how unjustified your negative feelings were.

Reasons I think they won't like me	*Why I'm mistaken*
Nobody likes me.	That's not actually true. I have family and friends who enjoy getting together with me.
	(Contd)

We're too different.	I know people who are different to me and I still like them. I enjoy being with them precisely because of their unusual ideas and ways of doing things.
They're far more successful than I am.	Successful in what? Okay, they earn more money. But money isn't everything and I'm sure they know that. I have other qualities to contribute.

Now let's turn to the second statement. It's an example of what psychotherapists call 'disqualifying the positive'. People with this mindset readily accept anything negative they hear but subject the positive to immediate critical scrutiny. If someone calls them a 'loser' they accept the description, but if someone describes them as a 'winner' they reject the tag. Do you see the inconsistency? It's a bias towards the negative.

Insight

Apart from causing depression, this mindset makes it difficult to generate warmth. It's also rather tedious for everyone around. It means you're contradicting people and no one likes that. Just as bad, you're giving off negative vibes and they drive people away.

Let's just think about this for a moment. If people say things to you 'to be nice', that's already good. Well, isn't it? It means they care enough about you to want to please you and make you happy. You're special to them. That should already be very good for your self-confidence. But why assume that the compliment isn't justified? Once again, I want you to divide a sheet of paper vertically into two columns. On the left-hand side head it up 'Reasons the compliment is unjustified'. And on the right head it up 'Reasons the compliment is justified'. Let's suppose, for example, that your boss has said he's impressed by a report you've just written. Then your sheet of paper might start off like this:

Reasons the compliment is unjustified	Reasons the compliment is justified
I was rushed and had to miss out some of the data.	Of course, any piece of work can always be improved on but considering the time I was given I covered the subject in great detail.
Maybe my forecasts will turn out to be wrong.	Nobody can guarantee their predictions will turn out to be right but mine are consistent with everything that's known.
My boss would have done it better.	Being the boss certainly doesn't mean you can do everything better than anyone else. My boss's job is to manage and I was chosen for this task because of my skill in this area.

Insight

This technique of subjecting your negative feelings to logical, balanced analysis is extremely useful. Use it whenever you recognize any of those ten 'cognitive distortions' (see Chapter 1) in your way of thinking.

USING VISUALIZATION AND SELF-HYPNOSIS

Here's an application for the techniques of visualization and self-hypnosis you learned in Chapter 2. What you're going to do is program yourself to radiate charisma and warmth. I'm going to describe how to do that under self-hypnosis which, as you now know, is simply a technique for deepening trance and thereby installing a 'program' more effectively. But if time is short or you're somewhere it wouldn't be appropriate to go into a deep trance, then you can just use the visualization without self-hypnosis.

PRACTICAL EXERCISE

1 *Select a DVD featuring a character who exudes charisma and warmth.*

2 *Choose a scene in which the character displays those qualities to the maximum and play it several times, taking careful note of the way the actor/actress speaks, looks and moves.*

3 *Complete the 'external' phase of the process of self-hypnosis described in Chapter 2, stating the purpose of the self-hypnosis as follows: 'I am entering into a trance for the purpose of allowing my unconscious mind to make the adjustments that will help me radiate charisma and warmth, just like the character in the DVD.'*

4 *Having completed the 'external' phase, close your eyes and, for the 'internal' phase, visualize the scene from the DVD, but substituting yourself for the character you wish to emulate. Deepen the trance by selecting things you can 'see', 'hear' and 'feel', as described in Chapter 2.*

5 *Come out of the trance, as described.*

6 *Repeat the process from time to time until the behaviour is automatic.*

WARNING: NOBODY IS LOVED BY EVERYBODY

Once you've mastered these techniques you'll find people respond to you in a very positive way. Most of them. The vast majority. But not everybody. That's something you're just going to have to be prepared for. You see, you can't be liked by everybody. Nobody is liked, let alone loved, by everybody. That's impossible.

The sooner you get used to that idea the happier and more resilient you'll become.

Instead, content yourself with a more reasonable score. And what would that be? Well, suppose you were to be introduced to 20 people at a party. How many do you think should like you? How many should want to become friends? How many should invite you home for dinner?

Consider this. In the first place, some people are simply suspicious of newcomers. They're very liable to take an 'instant dislike' to someone for no very good reason. If you remind them of someone they don't like, or if you wear the wrong kind of clothes or support the wrong political party, they immediately decide they don't like you.

Charlotte says she can't stand her mother-in-law. Why not? 'Because she's always happy and pretending everything is fine even if it's not.' Well, to me that seems a good personality trait. I like that kind of person. Charlotte doesn't. Two people. Two different ideas. That's just something you have to accept.

Generally speaking, we only make friends with people like ourselves. Some people take that to an extreme. You'll see a group of people all dressed the same way, with the same hairstyle, the same accessories, eating the same food, drinking the same drink and thinking the same thoughts. Other people are more flexible. But the principle is there. Everyone wants to be with people who make them feel comfortable.

Insight

Even when people do like you – like you a lot – bear in mind that only a small number are looking to add new friends to their 'lists'. Yes, it's wonderful to have friends, but friends take time and time is something most people are short of.

So, whenever you don't succeed in making friends there's a useful phrase to keep in mind. Here it is ...

That's their problem
By now you should be pretty familiar with this phrase. Think it whenever:

- ▶ *you're warm to people and they don't respond*
- ▶ *people act as if they don't like you*

- ▶ *people exclude you*
- ▶ *people turn down your perfectly reasonable requests.*

The fact is, they're the ones who are behaving badly, not you. So just say to yourself: That's their problem.

And move on. With optimism.

10 THINGS TO REMEMBER

1 *To make people like you or love you all you have to do is project your warmth onto them.*

2 *Your warmth can be blocked by negative attitudes.*

3 *The most important quality for unblocking warmth is acceptance.*

4 *The correct attitude is: 'I'm okay and you're okay.'*

5 *Demonstrate supportive friendship in difficult situations – never indulge in* Schadenfreude.

6 *Don't think of yourself as apart from everyone else – think of everyone being in the same boat together.*

7 *Develop the habits of optimism and curiosity.*

8 *Imagine your warmth flowing from every pore and push it ahead of you.*

9 *When you have negative feelings subject them to careful analysis – you'll usually find they're unjustified.*

10 *Nobody can be loved by everybody – when your warmth is rejected say to yourself: 'That's their problem'.*

HOW CONFIDENT ARE YOU NOW?

▶ *Have you accepted yourself as you are?*
▶ *Have you accepted other people as they are?*
▶ *Do you believe 'I'm okay and you're okay'?*
▶ *Have you banished* Schadenfreude?
▶ *When people ask how you are do you say, 'Wonderful ... marvellous ... incredible ...'?*
▶ *Are you curious?*
▶ *Are you pushing your warmth ahead of you?*
▶ *Have you made a list of birthdays?*
▶ *Have you stopped anticipating that people won't like you?*
▶ *Are you happily accepting compliments?*

Score:

If you answered 'yes' to most questions, then you obviously like other people and other people like you. Go straight on to the next chapter.

If you answered 'yes' to between five and seven questions, then you can also go on to the next chapter but revisit this one from time to time and think about the issues it raises.

If you could answer 'yes' to only four questions or fewer, then you're obviously finding it hard to believe that other people could like you and, in self-defence, you've decided not to like them. Keep working on the practical exercises in this chapter until you raise your score to five or higher before reading on.

4

The easy art of conversation

In this chapter you will learn:
- *why breaking the silence is more important than being brilliant*
- *how you can always have something to say*
- *the way to establish a meaningful connection*
- *what it means to be a good host or hostess.*

Each person's life is lived as a series of conversations.

Deborah Tannen, Professor of Linguistics

Let me see if I can guess what happened last time you were at a dinner party. You were sitting next to people you didn't know. You were racking your brains for something to say. And every time an idea came into your head you rejected it on various grounds. 'She'll be bored by that ... he'll think I'm weird if I say that ... she'll think I'm being too familiar if I say that ...' And so on and so on.

Am I right? You see, it's trying to think of clever things that makes it impossible for you to speak. But you probably can't give a worse impression than by saying nothing at all. So open your mouth and say anything. Well, just about anything.

You really don't have to say something brilliant. As we saw in Chapter 1, you should never aim for perfection in anything you do. Don't sit there racking your brains for a stunning thing to say. The longer the silence goes on the harder it will be. So break it straightaway and you'll soon find some common ground.

Here's a simple silence breaker:

▶ *Hello. I'm (your name).*

You, then, immediately add something for the other person to latch onto:

▶ *I'm a friend of Susan's from schooldays.*
▶ *I'm a neighbour of Jack's.*
▶ *Gary and I are in the same cricket team.*
▶ *Jill and I work for the same company.*

And, then, for good measure throw in a quick follow-up observation or question:

▶ *This is a really nice party.*
▶ *What a beautiful house/apartment/garden/day/night.*
▶ *What do you think of the wine/music/performance?*
▶ *I just love that painting/chair/view. What about you?*
▶ *How long have you known (the host/hostess)?*
▶ *Where did you meet (the host/hostess)?*
▶ *Doesn't (name) look beautiful/handsome/happy?*
▶ *Great/awful news about (whatever).*

That should be plenty to get a conversation started.

In fact, there are literally hundreds of things you could say. The problem isn't really what to say. As with so many other things, it's much more to do with an attitude of mind.

Insight

Some of the above follow-ups are statements, some can be answered with a 'yes' or 'no' and some demand a more lengthy response. A question that can be answered with a brusque 'yes' or 'no' is known as a 'closed' question. An example would be: 'Do you like the wine?'

A better way of approaching the subject would be to ask: 'What do you think of the wine?' The other person is then

prompted to give a longer answer which will, in turn, present opportunities for further developing the conversation.
Sentences that begin with a W – When, Where, Who, Why, Which, What – are generally 'open'. Use them frequently.

PRACTICAL EXERCISE
Your first exercise is to break the silence in a variety of different situations all this week (and no getting out of it).

1 *In a train, bus, coach, plane or restaurant say the following to someone:*
    ▷ *Excuse me, I'm just reading on the back of your newspaper about (whatever). Do you mind if I just take a look at that?*
2 *In a pub or bar identify someone alone and engage them in conversation. (Top tip: Maybe they're watching sport on television so you can say 'Good shot'.)*
3 *At work wait by the coffee machine or photocopier and speak to someone you've never spoken to before. (Top tip: Maybe you can say 'I wouldn't touch the tea'.)*
4 *In a shop engage the assistant in conversation. (Top tip: Maybe you can begin by saying 'Do you think this suits me?')*

PREPARING YOUR MIND FOR CONVERSATION

So you've been invited to some sort of social gathering. A dinner, a party, a wedding or whatever. And you're feeling nervous because you can never think of witty things to say.

Well, I've got news for you. You don't need to. Most people would much rather settle for words of interest, concern and support than froth, however witty it might be.

So let's prime your unconscious accordingly, using the techniques described in Chapter 2.

Before you go to sleep each night say something like this to yourself. I am going to a party. I will be happy to meet everyone. I will enjoy myself. I will be relaxed. I will find it easy to speak. I will open my mouth and words will flow out.

Employ visualization. See yourself at the party looking relaxed and happy. See yourself chatting in an easy-going manner. See yourself moving from one group to another and being accepted. See other people talking back to you.

Use self-hypnosis – put yourself into a trance before starting the visualization.

DO SOME HOMEWORK BEFORE YOU GO

I know someone who met David Niven, the late actor and writer, twice. On successive nights. She'd been invited to a dinner party and to her great excitement she found herself at the table with the man who had entertained the world with *The Moon's A Balloon*. All evening his anecdotes had everyone in stitches. She was delighted and thoroughly impressed. Next night it was another dinner party. And who should be there but David Niven! And guess what? Yes, he told exactly the same stories in exactly the same way. He'd done his homework and perfected his act.

▶ *When something looks effortless it's usually the result of constant practice.*

Now David Niven was a professional. You're not and I've already counselled you against setting your sights too high. But there's no reason you can't prepare yourself just as he did. (Just make sure you have a few stories in reserve!)

Let's say, for example, you've been invited to a dinner party. Don't just turn up without doing a little preparation:

▶ *Find out from your host or hostess who else is coming, their names, and a little bit about them.*
▶ *Write all the details down and do your best to memorize them.*
▶ *Do some background research. For example, if you're told that someone is a keen golfer you might check to see who won the big tournaments recently.*

- *Work out some things you might say. The biggest mistake 'poor conversationalists' make is not to have planned in advance.*
- *Keep your crib sheet in your pocket or handbag so you can discreetly refer to it.*
- *As you meet people at the party you can say things like: 'Well, Hannah, I hear you're a keen golfer'.*
- *Afterwards, if there are people you expect to be meeting again, write down the extra information you've gathered as soon as you get the opportunity (names of children and partner, job, hobbies and so on).*

Insight

When you're meeting a group of new people it's not easy to take in their names. And if you've already convinced yourself you're one of those people who 'can never remember a name' you're just making it harder for yourself. So the first step is to start thinking of yourself as someone who can remember. When you shake hands, use the person's name. Don't just say 'Nice to meet you'. Say 'Nice to meet you, Name'. At the same time try to relate the name to the person in some way. It could be something quite stupid. George is gorgeous. Anita has nice knees. Richard looks rich. Use the name again as quickly as possible: 'You know, George, I think ...' Or something like that.

Write names down as soon as you get the opportunity and add the names of partners and children, too, if you've been told them.

If you do forget a name at a gathering, discreetly ask the host or hostess to remind you. Otherwise, just be straightforward about it. Rather than failing to use a person's name, say something like:

- *I'm terribly sorry, I didn't catch your name when we were introduced.*
- *I'm awfully sorry, I've forgotten your name.*

And be sure to use it from then onwards.

THE SKILL OF LISTENING

I have one friend – call him John – who always shows a keen interest in new acquaintances, asking them all kinds of questions about themselves. At first, people are flattered. But soon they become irritated by the relentless barrage. They eventually realize that John isn't interested in them as people, but is simply filing the information away in case it might be useful to him. What's more, John only makes disclosures about himself when he wants to achieve a particular effect.

At the other end of the spectrum is a woman – I'll call her Cathy – who talks very openly about herself in quite intimate detail. Within a few minutes of meeting Cathy you'll be thinking she's one of the friendliest and most interesting people in the world. But after an evening you'll know better. Because she won't have asked a single thing about you.

Neither John nor Cathy is genuinely empathetic. They seem so at first. But although their conversational approaches are almost opposites, they're very similar people. They're really only interested in themselves.

Insight
In a genuine friendship there should be a rough balance between talking and listening.

Improving your listening skills
An actor once remarked that the skill in his profession consisted of learning to look as if you're listening. As an actor, you already know what the other person is going to say but you have to pretend you don't.

In real life, some people behave like bad actors. They don't pay attention to what anyone else is saying, only to what they themselves are going to say next. That isn't conversation.

Listening doesn't sound a very difficult thing to do. But it's harder than you think. It consists of:

▶ *paying full attention to what the other person is saying*
▶ *understanding what's been said*
▶ *working out the significance of things left unsaid.*

Once you comprehend both the 'said' and the 'unsaid' you'll be a much better conversationalist.

PRACTICAL EXERCISE
1 *Listen to someone speaking on the TV or radio and, when they've finished, make a note of all the things you can recall.*
2 *You can always ask a friend to help you with this one. Both of you listen to someone speaking on TV or radio and, when they've finished, both of you make notes on what was said. Then compare your notes. Quite likely you'll have opposite recollections of some things. Which just goes to prove how hard listening really is.*
3 *Next, discuss the things that weren't said.*

Giving feedback
When someone tells you something, it's a good idea to give them some positive feedback. One way of doing that is to confirm what they've said in different words. Of course, you don't want to carry the principle to the point of tedium. Let's say someone tells you: 'I've just finished reading a biography of Diana'.

Don't say: 'Uhu!'

Say something more like: 'Yes, I've always wondered what it's like to be a member of the royal family'. That way, you confirm you've taken in what was said and you also move the conversation forward. Now the other person has an opening and can respond with something like: 'It was really hard for her'.

Of course, it might be you have no interest whatsoever in Diana. In which case you could have said: 'I really find the subject very

boring'. But that would have been a mistake for two reasons.
Firstly, it would have been a metaphorical slap round the face
to the person talking to you. Secondly, you can find something
interesting in everything if you:

▶ *Develop the skill of curiosity (remember Chapter 3!).*

Insight

Learn to be fascinated. It's not so hard because, in fact, most
things are fascinating when you start looking into them.

LISTENING MAKES PEOPLE FEEL GOOD

A young woman dined with Gladstone one evening and Disraeli
the next. When asked her opinion of the two great statesmen of the
Victorian age she said this: 'When I left the table after sitting next
to Mr Gladstone I thought he was the cleverest man in England.
But after sitting next to Mr Disraeli I thought I was the cleverest
woman in England.'

BREAKING INTO A CONVERSATION

It's one of the most intimidating moments at any social gathering.
There you are totally alone. And what do you see? Half a dozen
tight circles of people talking and laughing together, their collective
backs forming little defensive walls, effectively shutting you out.
What do you do?

Here is something to bear in mind. Most people go to parties to
enjoy the company and that includes your company. So let them
have it. Don't drop your shoulders and slink around. By doing that
you're announcing: 'I'm boring'. Instead, get a grip on your body,
hold your head up, smile and do the following:

1 *If you already know just one person in one group, then walk
   up to that group, listen for a clue to what they're talking
   about, catch the person's eye and slide yourself in alongside.*
2 *If you don't know anybody, listen out for a conversation
   that sounds interesting then charge in. If you can't physically*

penetrate that tight wall then in a loud voice say something like: 'Hi everyone'. They'll have to turn to look at you which will give you the physical space to join the group.

3 *Introduce yourself to the group: 'Hello, I'm Charlotte'.*

4 *Hold out your hand and shake with everyone. Or kiss cheeks. Or whatever is the appropriate style of greeting in that culture. Repeat your own name each time. That way, everyone in the group will hear your name several times over which will make it easier for them to remember it. At the same time, do your best to remember all their names (see earlier).*

5 *Follow up with something along the lines of: 'I'm really interested in what you were saying'.*

There's nothing physically difficult about any of that. Psychologically, though, it can call for a certain amount of courage. You need to develop a positive attitude. If you don't think you can manage it, take a look again at Chapter 2. And ask yourself this question: What are they going to do to me that might be so awful? Kill me?

Insight

People who are nervous about social gatherings often arrive late to minimize the 'agony'. But that makes it more likely the other guests will have formed little cliques before you arrive. By getting there early you can become an automatic part of a clique and not have to break in. Another good tactic is to volunteer for a task such as carrying around a tray of drinks or nibbles. That automatically gives you an introduction to everyone in the room.

That's their problem

Since it's a social event there's no reason at all to imagine you might be frozen out. But if the others should react with a show of resentment then ... altogether now ... that's their problem. You have done nothing wrong. On the contrary, you've behaved exactly as someone at a party should behave. They're the ones who have behaved badly. If it happens, don't let it bother you. Just move on to another group. But it almost certainly won't happen.

IMPROVING YOUR CONVERSATIONAL SKILLS

Anthropologists identify several different kinds of conversation.
At social gatherings the most common is 'grooming talking'. That
is, talking that substitutes for the mutual grooming behaviour
exhibited by many other species. If we were as hairy and unwashed
as our nearest animal relatives we'd pick parasites off one another.
But we're not. Instead we have grooming talking whose function
is to signal friendly co-operation and to create some low-level
bonding. Examples of grooming talking are phrases such as 'Lovely
weather' and 'Nice party'. In other words, this is 'small talk'.

Some people loathe small talk. If you're one of them then let me
tell you why you shouldn't. Yes, the words are insignificant. Yes,
the superficial meaning is insignificant. But the subtext is: 'I'm
friendly; let's feel one another out and see how we get on'. And
that's pretty important.

So always be willing to indulge in some small talk. The problem
is if all of the subsequent conversations continue to be small talk.
That really means one of you (or both) is signalling: 'This is
as intimate as I want to get with you'. If it's the other person
who's appearing aloof, have a shot at something a little more
self-revealing and if that doesn't elicit a response, move on.

When grooming talking is successful, men tend to progress to a
different category of conversation known as 'information talking'.
This is the realm in which they excel. How to repair a boiler.

The best way to train for a marathon. What equity might go up in value next week. And so on. Sometimes the information is genuinely useful but at other times it may only be another form of grooming talking. You listen with apparent interest even though you don't have a boiler, have no intention of running a marathon and will never have enough spare cash to speculate on the stock market.

Yet another male style is 'discussion'. That's to say, giving opinions and debating them. Discussions can certainly be invigorating and they can't fail to reveal something about each of the speakers.

But none of this is very intimate. When grooming talking is completed women behave differently to men. They tend to move on to 'exploratory talking'. That's finding out about other people, discovering what 'makes them tick', sharing confidences, teasing out secrets. That's a lot more interesting. If you're a man I suggest you practise more exploratory talking. Because it's all about connection it's so much more satisfying. (For more on the differences between men and women in conversation see Chapter 11.)

Here are some examples to make the point:

▶ *Information: 'Inflation has reached four per cent.'*
▶ *Discussion: 'I think the central bankers have mishandled the economy.'*
▶ *Conversation: 'The economic situation is making life very difficult for me. How is it affecting you?'*

Do you see the difference? Conversation is all about personal experience, feelings and emotions.

PRACTICAL EXERCISE
▶ *Next time you're talking with someone, work the following phrases into your conversation:*
▶ *How has that affected you personally?*
▶ *How did you feel about that?*
▶ *I understand how you feel.*

- *How has that changed things?*
- *What would you like to happen?*

USING NLP

Neuro-Linguistic Programming (NLP) holds that people favour certain 'representational systems'. That's to say, some people think most of all in pictures, others in sounds, others in feelings and still others in smells and tastes. Consider these sentences and see if you can work out each speaker's primary representational system:

- *You'll see that I'm looking for a clear-cut solution.*
- *I heard you loud and clear and I'm speechless.*
- *I feel this is too much for me to handle unless I have support.*
- *I don't like the smell of this – it's going to leave a bad taste.*

You probably don't need me to tell you that they were, in order, visual, auditory, kinaesthetic and, in the final sentence, olfactory followed by gustatory (VAKOG in NLP shorthand).

NLP considers this to be very important for conversation. Personally, I'm not convinced. But if you *do* identify a consistent representational system in someone's speech then it certainly won't do any harm to copy it and, as NLP holds, it may very well help the conversation along.

Trading intimacies

Some people are immediately very happy to talk about personal things. But, in general, getting onto an intimate footing with someone else involves an element of 'trading'. That's to say, if you want someone to reveal themselves to you, you have to be willing to reveal yourself to them. Put like that it can all sound a little manipulative. But, as long as you're being genuine, then it isn't like that at all. It's much more a question of building confidence in one another.

PRACTICAL EXERCISE
1 *Tell someone close to you something personal they didn't already know about you.*

2 *Next time you're talking to someone you'd like to know better, reveal something intimate about yourself. Don't just stick to facts. Describe feelings as well.*

Don't just say	Add this as well
What a storm last night!	I adore lying in bed and hearing the rain on the roof. Don't you find it romantic?
My dog has disappeared.	I'm really upset about it – I love that dog. Do you have any pets?
The stock market is down 200 points.	I'm desperately worried. Have you got any shares?

'CHAT-UP' LINES

As a generalization, women tend to get involved in relationships despite the chat-up lines, not because of them. In other words, most chat-up lines simply confirm women's fears that men are not serious. Avoid them. For more on 'chatting up' see Chapter 11.

Asking strangers for help
Asking for help from someone you don't know very well or even at all can be one of the hardest things to do.

I have a friend called Luke whose car broke down. He walked to the nearest bar and, being an engaging sort of fellow, was fairly soon in conversation. Within a few minutes that person's friends had become his friends, too. He bought them all a drink. They were having a good time together. Presently, there was a suitable conversational opening for him to mention his car. And before the evening was over his new friends had sorted the problem out for him. Luke says you only have to give people the opportunity to help you and most of them will. The fact is:

▶ *We all feel good about ourselves when we help other people.*

So make someone happy and give them the chance.

PRACTICAL EXERCISE
Your exercise is to get someone you don't know at all, or don't know very well, to help you in some way.

(Top tip: Luke didn't go into the bar and ask for help. That would only have worked if he'd been in such desperate circumstances that people felt obliged to help. He made friends first. Then he gave his friends the opportunity to help him.)

STOP WORRYING WHAT PEOPLE THINK OF YOU

One thing you can be sure of, no matter how rich, how famous or how powerful the other person is, they'll also have worries about meeting you. You see, we all want other people to see us as we like to see ourselves. And the thing we fear most in a new encounter is somebody who doesn't do that. Just as in the fairy story, we're all scared of that little boy. The one who says the Emperor isn't actually wearing any clothes at all. And, in fact, the rich, the famous and the powerful are more scared than most because they have the most to lose. In the old boxing adage, the bigger they are the harder they fall. So you should never be frightened about meeting someone 'important'.

And if you're not worried about meeting somebody 'important' then you don't have to worry about meeting anybody at all. Of course, it's easy to write. But it's also easy to do. How?

▶ *Focus instead on the other person's worries.*

In other words, stop thinking about yourself and concentrate on putting the other person at ease. Once you do that your own concerns will disappear.

Insight
The most important thing is to signal acceptance.

In other words, whatever the other person is like, you're signalling: 'That's okay with me'.

It's not just a question of words. It's also a question of body language.

We're all much better at body language than we realize. We use it all day long. In fact, some scientists say as much as 85 per cent of our communication with other people is non-verbal – by body language. When you go into a room and conclude 'you could cut the atmosphere with a knife', that's largely down to body language. So make sure your mouth and body language agree. It's no use saying, 'Nice to meet you' if at the same time you're leaning back. When you find people attractive you generally lean towards them. (There are two exceptions. One is the open-armed preparation for the bear hug – the sort of 'I'm ready, come and get it' pose. The other is the casual superiority pose, in which you sit leaning back, with your hands clasped behind your head.)

To learn a lot more about body language see Chapter 5.

DEALING WITH PEOPLE WHO DON'T WANT TO TALK TO YOU

No matter how friendly you are there's one thing you're going to have to learn to accept. From time to time you're going to encounter people who make it clear they're not interested in talking to you. And you won't be able to do a thing about it. So remember this:

▶ *That's no reason for your self-confidence to go down.*

You see, there are people who, for various reasons, are just not the warm, open, friendly human beings that most of us are. Probably they've had experiences earlier, perhaps in childhood, that have created quirks in their personalities. Chips on the shoulders. Negative attitudes. Jealousies. Insecurities. Maybe depression. These problems have nothing to do with you. They existed before you came along and they'll continue to exist after you've said goodbye. When people's personalities have been damaged:

▶ *They don't have to have any good reason to dislike someone.*

That means their negative response to you is meaningless. Don't agonize over it.

The fact is, no one can score 100 per cent success with other people, even well-balanced people. Just think about it for a moment. Is there any film star about whom all of your friends are in agreement? It's very, very rare that ten women will agree about a male celebrity or that ten men will agree about a female celebrity. And that's when the celebrity is effectively a fantasy figure. In real life, the 'success rate' is much lower.

So if you're getting nowhere with a conversation at, say, a party, just forget about it and move on.

BEING THE HOST OR HOSTESS

If you're the one who's throwing the party, of whatever kind it might be, it's your job to get everyone mingling happily together. So pay attention to those introductions. They can make all the difference between a great party and a flop.

If it's an occasion where nobody knows anybody else, you can try asking your guests to take turns introducing themselves to the room generally. ('I'm Jill. I'm a make-up artist and I like playing tennis.') If you do that, have the music turned down so everyone can hear.

Alternatively, if only a few people are newcomers, make a point of taking each one by the arm and introducing them to someone you think they'll like. And watch out during the evening for people standing unhappily alone. Either send someone to talk to them, finesse them into a group ('You must meet Gerald') or find them a task to do.

Dinner party topics

When conversation flags over dinner, or guests are only talking to immediate neighbours and you want to get a more convivial atmosphere, you might like to throw out a topic for general conversation.

Here are some suggestions:

- *If you were trapped in a lift for a while, which six famous people would you like to be trapped with?*
- *You know, I was just reading about perfect weekends and I'm wondering what your perfect weekends would be?*
- *Who would you have in a football team if you could have anyone you wanted?*
- *If heaven existed, what would yours be like?*
- *If you were marooned on a desert island, which eight CDs/films/books would you like to have with you?*

DIFFICULT TELEPHONE CALLS

Telephone calls about difficult issues can be a real sweat. In the first place, in order to speak to the person you want you may first have to convince an intermediary (a secretary, for example) to put you through. Once connected you then have nothing other than your voice with which to make your point. No hand gestures, no facial expressions, no props and, what's more, the other person can't see how nice you are.

As a writer and journalist I'm always having to phone people. The most intimidating calls are those to editors when I'm trying to pitch an article. How do I cope? The first thing I say to myself is this:

- *If the person turns me down, in what way am I worse off than I am now?*

The answer, of course, is in no way at all. Before making the phone call I don't have a commission and, if I'm turned down, I still don't have a commission. The situation is no different. I have absolutely nothing to lose.

I look upon the failed phone call as practice for another try in the future. I analyse it. Maybe instead of saying this I should have said that. Maybe I should have tried to sound more friendly or more learned or more enthusiastic. Or whatever.

On the positive side, I reflect that at least I've 'broken the ice' with that particular person. When I phone again they may remember me.

I try to have several possibilities. It just isn't realistic to expect a hit rate of 100 per cent. Or even 50 per cent. Or even ten per cent. In some types of telesales a hit rate of two per cent is considered good. Think about it. That means that out of every 100 phone calls you get turned down 98 times. That can be pretty demoralizing unless you have the right mental attitude. Which is what I call the 'one-armed bandit'. If you've ever put money in one of those machines I'm sure you didn't expect a win first time. Nor even in ten pulls. Well, you need to have the same outlook when making those kinds of telephone calls.

▶ *If your expectations are realistic, your self-confidence won't suffer.*

PRACTICAL EXERCISE
You have to make an important telephone call. Let's say you're seeking a job, but the same principles can apply to any difficult call.

1 *In addition to the job you want, try to find another nine other jobs advertised.*
2 *Before phoning about the job you really want work through the nine you don't really want.*
3 *Before phoning any of the nine say this to yourself: 'I have absolutely nothing to lose by making this phone call because I don't really want the job anyway'.*
4 *After each call reflect on the outcome. If you have some sort of voice recorder, use it to play back what you said and how you said it. In what way could you have handled it better?*

5 *Eventually you come to the phone call you really wanted to make. Review your experience with the other nine calls and incorporate your new knowledge into your approach.*

6 *Ask yourself: 'What's the worst thing that can happen to me if I make a mess of this call?' Will you die? No. Will you be tortured? No.*

7 *Say to yourself: 'I have nothing to lose by making this call.' And then go ahead and make it.*

Insight

Don't assume you'll be able to think fast enough on your feet – you'll be more confident if you have a clear note of all the points you want to raise and tick them off as you go. Write down any significant statements by the person you're talking to – use the loudspeaker facility, if you have one, so your hands are free. Don't get angry – it will only make the other person's position more entrenched.

TELLING JOKES

Telling jokes is, of course, an art. As everyone knows, it isn't so much the joke itself as 'the way you tell 'em'.

Even so, you may as well get the best jokes you can. Maybe someone's already told you a joke that you like. Maybe you heard it on TV. Or buy yourself a couple of books of jokes and comb them for a few gems.

The next thing is to tailor the joke to your own taste and situation. Change it around until you feel comfortable with it. Try it out in your head and then on a few friends.

PRACTICAL EXERCISE

Where jokes are concerned, nervousness is like an old bra. It doesn't matter how good the joke is, if there's a hint of tension in your voice it won't raise a titter. (Ouch!)

The only way to get rid of nerves is to keep practising in front of an 'audience'. So your practical exercise is to tell your joke to as many people as possible this week. At the very least, you must tell it 15 times in 15 slightly different ways. Then try to work out what was special in your most successful 'performance'.

'ADVANCED' CONVERSATION

Although I've counselled against becoming paralyzed by trying to make witty remarks it certainly doesn't do any harm to steal a few. Now and then flick through a dictionary of quotations and memorize any that particularly appeal to you. Some people try to pass quotations off as their own, perhaps after a little tinkering. Others own up. It doesn't really matter. The main thing is to entertain other people with some sharp observations. Here are a few to get you started:

- ▶ *For a discussion on politics: In the country of the blind, the one-eyed man is king. (Erasmus c.1469–1536.)*
- ▶ *For a discussion about life: It's a funny old world – a man's lucky if he gets out of it alive. (From the film* You're Telling Me, *1934.)*
- ▶ *For a discussion about love: Yet each man kills the thing he loves. (Oscar Wilde, 1854–1900.)*
- ▶ *For a discussion about parenthood: The value of marriage is not that adults produce children but that children produce adults. (From* The Tunnel Of Love *by Peter de Vries 1910–93.)*
- ▶ *For a discussion about sport: Nice guys finish last. (Leo Durocher 1906–91.)*
- ▶ *For a discussion about religion: If God did not exist it would be necessary to invent Him. (Voltaire 1694–1778.)*
- ▶ *For a discussion about death: This is no time for making new enemies. (Attributed to Voltaire who, on his deathbed, was asked to renounce the Devil.)*

However, if you insist on coming up with your own witty lines, here are a few pointers:

1 *Don't think too generally. Focus on the event you're going to and the people who are going to be there. That in itself may throw up a few ideas.*

2 *Make a little 'diagram' of these ideas as they come to you. For example, if you're going to a wedding, draw a little box in the centre of the paper and write 'wedding' inside it. Then you might wonder why, in this day and age, anyone would get married. So you draw a line coming out of the box to a new box inside which you write 'Why?' That might provoke thoughts about morality – a third box. Eventually, your chain of thoughts might lead you to your witticism:*
   Morality isn't anything other than married people forming a trade union.

3 *Opposites. One of the easiest ways to get a laugh is to surprise people by setting them up with a familiar phrase or sentiment but then ending it in the opposite way.*
   For example:
   ▷ *If a thing's worth doing, it's worth doing badly.*
   Or as a writer I could say something like this:
   ▷ *I'm dedicating my book to my partner without whose helpful comments it would … have been finished much sooner.*

4 *Contradictions. Contradictions are a subtle variation on Opposites. They're phrases that, at first sight, seem logical but are then seen to contain something that doesn't quite add up.*
   For example:
   ▷ *I can resist everything except temptation.*
   ▷ *She ran the whole gamut of the emotions from A to B.*
   (With thanks to Oscar Wilde and Dorothy Parker.)

5 *Thinking backwards. The idea here is that you start with a well-known phrase and then try to think of an unusual twist – something that might have preceded it which would then make it funny.*
   For example:
   ▷ *They say that money talks – all of mine just said goodbye.*

6   *Exaggeration. Start with a truth and just make it a little more emphatic. For example, if you think having ex-UK Prime Minister Tony Blair as a Middle East envoy is a strange choice you might say:*
      ▷ *He's about as suitable as a comb for a bald man/wheels on a duck/a wolf in a chicken shed ...*
      (See how many more you can come up with!)
7   *Repartee. The most admired form of wit seems to be the sharp reply. After all, if you don't know what line you're going to be fed you surely need rapier-like intelligence to come back instantly with a humorous response. Don't you? Well, actually, no. Because, you see, you do know what lines you're going to be fed. More or less, anyway, because people are always saying the same kinds of things.*

It's simply a case of devising some basic ripostes you can then fashion on the spot. A formula, if you like.

For example, at some point someone is bound to say something like:

▶ *What an interesting family!*

To which you can then reply:

▶ *All families are interesting once you know the truth about them.*

The formula works for just about any subject. Interesting women. Interesting places. Interesting discoveries. It's just a question of adapting it to the circumstances.

Another formula is to use the technique of 'opposites' described above. It works best when you contradict someone in an oblique sort of way. For example, at a job interview a prospective employer might say:

▶ *Money won't be a problem.*

To which you can reply:

> ▶ *I could make it a problem.*

It may not help you get the job but, at least, you'll have been entertaining.

Alternatively, you can confirm what someone else says but in a slightly unexpected way. For example, someone might set you up with:

> ▶ *The best things in life are free.*

To which you reply:

> ▶ *Try telling that to my wife/husband/daughter (or whoever).*

And there are always situations in which you can use 'standards'. For example:

> ▶ *When driving: It's the overtakers who keep the undertakers busy.*
> ▶ *When talking philosophy: Apart from the known and the unknown, what else is there?*
> ▶ *When talking politics/medicine/science (or whatever): It's not necessary to think up jokes. All you have to do is watch the politicians (or whatever) and report the facts.*
> ▶ *When talking gossip: They're so boring they'd never be ashamed to sell the family parrot.*
> ▶ *When talking about anything that's lost: It's easier to replace a dead man/woman than a good (whatever).*

(With thanks and apologies to William Pitt, Harold Pinter, Will Rogers and George Bernard Shaw.)

PRACTICAL EXERCISE
Get hold of a book of quotations and select a dozen fairly universal ones that appeal to you. Memorize them. Then use at least two every day this week, either as written or, better still, as adapted by you.

TELLING STORIES

The best stories usually aren't true.

If you're one of those commendable people who likes to tell the truth and get the facts straight, then you'll very rarely have a good tale to tell. Because truth may be stranger than fiction but it's also very messy. Truth doesn't tend to have a good beginning, middle and end. In particular, truth seldom has a pay-off – a funny line or incident that rounds the whole thing off and brings it to a neat conclusion. Those kinds of things are inevitably thought of long after the event.

So if you want to tell some good 'true' stories be prepared to use some 'artistic licence'. Events that happened on different days can be made to happen on the same day. Dialogue can be improved. And, of course, your own role can be enhanced.

PRACTICAL EXERCISE
Think of something unusual that's happened to you recently. Then set about improving on reality. Give the story shape and, above all, a funny ending. One of the easiest ways is:

'So I said to him …'.

Of course, you never actually did. But no one need ever know that.

Then try your 'true story' out on various people, watch their reactions, and improve it accordingly.

10 THINGS TO REMEMBER

1 *Don't aim for perfection or you'll get 'talker's block' – just start by giving your name together with some information for the other person to latch onto and then pose an 'open' question.*

2 *The biggest mistake 'poor conversationalists' make is not to have prepared in advance – get your unconscious on your side before you go.*

3 *Listening is as important as talking – encourage others by giving feedback.*

4 *If you want to hear intimacies, you'll also have to be prepared to tell some.*

5 *Don't worry what people think of you – they'll be worrying what you think of them.*

6 *Learn to accept that there are bound to be people who don't want to talk to you.*

7 *If you're the host/hostess, it's your job to make useful introductions.*

8 *Make sure you've prepared your case before you make those difficult telephone calls – and don't get angry.*

9 *Stealing witty remarks is easier than thinking of your own, but it's not so difficult, either, to invent your own witticisms if you stick to the simple formulae – Opposites, Contradictions and Exaggerations.*

10 *The best stories aren't true.*

HOW CONFIDENT ARE
YOU NOW?

▶ *Have you begun at least one conversation with a stranger?*
▶ *Did you prepare suitable conversation before attending your last social gathering?*
▶ *Has anyone indicated to you that you're a 'good listener'?*
▶ *Have you been able to break into at least one conversation?*
▶ *Have you discovered anything interesting through exploratory talking?*
▶ *Have you traded intimacies?*
▶ *Have you stopped worrying what other people think?*
▶ *Have you made the difficult phone call you'd been putting off?*
▶ *Have you told a joke or a story and enjoyed the response?*
▶ *Have you 'stolen' and memorized a few witticisms?*

Score:

If you answered 'yes' to most questions, then you're obviously comfortable in social situations, with a good balance between listening and entertaining. Go straight on to the next chapter.

If you answered 'yes' to between five and seven questions, then you can also go on to the next chapter but revisit this one from time to time and think about the issues it raises.

If you could answer 'yes' to only four questions or fewer, then you're obviously struggling in social situations. Keep working on the practical exercises in this chapter until you raise your score to five or higher before reading on.

5

......

Does your body say hello?

In this chapter you will learn:
- *how to use body language to project an aura of confidence*
- *how to power dress*
- *how to control your voice.*

> *Movements of the hands and arms act as a window on the human mind; they make thought visible.*
>
> Professor Geoffrey Beattie, University of Manchester

Have you ever visited a fortune-teller? And if you did, was the seer able to tell you things about yourself that astonished you? Well, be astonished no longer. Because it's not necessary to say a word to convey a huge amount about yourself to other people. Your face, your eyes, your clothes, the way you walk and sit, your gestures, your breathing and many other non-verbal things, all combine to tell your story. In fact, the spoken word accounts for only about 15 per cent of everything we 'say'. And that's the secret of 'fortune-telling'.

In this chapter we're concerned specifically with your physical presence.

Let's start with two basics, the handshake and the greetings kiss.

HANDSHAKES

People can tell quite a lot about you from the way you shake hands. So what's a confident handshake? Nowadays it could be any number of things:

▶ *The high five: Instead of holding your arm out horizontally, you raise your forearm, palm forwards and at roughly head height, and then slap it against the other person's hand. This says: 'We're cool and we're equal'.*

▶ *The half-turned thumb-lock: When the other person holds out a hand to shake in the ordinary way you turn your hand so the fingers are pointing up. You now press the palms together and encircle the other person's thumb with your thumb and forefinger. It sounds complicated but it's a very natural movement which increases skin contact and therefore sends out the message: 'I accept you; I like you'.*

▶ *The never-let-me-go: You do a normal handshake but then you don't let go. At least, not for several seconds. The message is: 'I find you particularly interesting'. (But it can also be a signal of dominance. If someone uses a dominating handshake on you, you may wish to counter it. You can do that by using your free hand to take hold of their arm or shoulder. That just shows that you feel equal. Maintain eye contact. Looking down or away suggests submission.)*

▶ *The two-handed: A variation on the above. You do a normal handshake but then you place your left hand on top of the two clasped hands as if to reinforce the message.*

....

Insight

In men a strong grip is taken as a sign of confidence and it's basically true. Research shows that men with the strongest grips are the healthiest, the most masculine, the most dominant – and the most sexually successful. Your natural grip is largely determined by your genes and your testosterone – but you can always fake it with exercises and resolve.

....

KISSES

Kissing as a greeting is a ritual that British and American people are increasingly borrowing from continental Europe.

If you're not quite clear how to kiss as greeting, here's an explanation. Don't actually put your lips on the other person's cheek. Rather, touch cheeks while making a kissing sound. Some people don't even touch but merely make the head movement, remaining a few centimetres out of range.

The next problem is which cheek to begin with and how many kisses. In fact, customs vary by social group, country and region. For example:

▶ *France. This really is the home of kissing and the Côte d'Azur is the world capital. There anything up to six kisses are given. In Paris the norm is four. In Brittany three. In the rest of France two. Always begin with the left cheek. On leaving, you repeat the ritual all over again – which can be very time-consuming.*
▶ *Netherlands. The Dutch begin with the right cheek and give three kisses.*
▶ *Spain. Two kisses, beginning on the right cheek.*
▶ *Scandinavia and Austria. Two kisses.*
▶ *Belgium. One kiss is the norm.*
▶ *Germany and Italy. Kissing is for family and friends only.*

None of this is set in stone so the best advice is to watch what other people are doing. In the UK and the USA, if there's no one to copy, you can always just ask. Say something like:

▶ *Shall we do this the European way?*

Insight

Men kiss women, for sure, and women kiss men and women. But what about men with men? I've spent many years in both France and Spain and, even though it's commonly done,

(Contd)

seldom kissed a man. And then, only reluctantly. I'm really not very keen on it. And that sums the whole thing up. If a slap on the back or a handshake feel more appropriate to you, then that's fine.

ADVANCED BODY LANGUAGE

I was at a dinner party. The woman sitting on my right was talking to the person on her right and was therefore turned slightly away from me. That was okay. But in addition she had her left hand resting on the side of her face like a horse's blinkers so that she'd completely shut me out of her vision. That wasn't okay. The body language was very clear: 'I don't want to talk to you at all. I'm sorry you even exist.'

I don't know what I'd done to annoy or upset her so much but I decided to take it as a challenge.

Body language is a reflection of how you feel and at that moment I felt pretty crushed. But that's not to say you can't control it to a certain extent. Research shows, for example, that if you smile for no reason you, nevertheless, make yourself feel more cheerful. Similarly, if you hold your body in a confident way, you can make yourself feel more confident.

So I listened for a moment and then I tapped her arm and said: 'That's very interesting'. Of course, she was now obliged to turn towards me and take her hand away and, as she did so, I looked past her to the person on her right, tilted my head a little to one side, and said: 'I absolutely agree with you'. Now the woman in blinkers found herself in the middle and couldn't shut me out. I made increasing eye contact with her, mirrored her body language and by the end of the dinner she didn't seem to hate me at all.

Here are some of the principal guidelines for body language that makes you feel more confident:

Do	Don't
Walk briskly with your head up.	Slouch along, head and shoulders down.
Sit still.	Jiggle about, bite your nails, or fiddle with your ear (indecision) or hair (nervousness). Note that caressing the hair is different and flirtatious.
Sit in an 'open' position, legs comfortably apart, arms stretched out. In other words, not afraid to take up space. In casual situations you might sit with hands clasped behind head, legs stretched out and ankles crossed.	Sit in a 'tiny' pose with your arms and legs tucked in.
Keep your palms open.	Make fists.
Tilt your head towards people.	Tilt your head away from people.
Make eye contact.	Avoid eye contact or blink often.
Mirror other people's body language.	Ignore other people's body language.
Speak clearly without hiding your mouth in any way.	Hold your hand in front of your mouth when you're talking.

PRACTICAL EXERCISE
All this week try to take note of what you're doing with your body, especially when you're feeling tense or nervous. Particularly notice your hands.

Stand in front of a full-length mirror and try to convey the following emotions through your body:

▶ *confidence*
▶ *nervousness*

- *embarrassment*
- *superiority*
- *equality*
- *inferiority.*

Better still, if you have a video camera, set it up on a tripod and film yourself.

As a slightly harder variation, try to visualize how you should be holding your body to convey confidence. Then, with your eyes closed, do it. Now open your eyes and see what you look like.

Let's look at some key points in a bit more detail.

Eye contact

It's very important to make eye contact when you're conversing. Failure to make eye contact signals insecurity, inferiority and, obviously, shyness. Not to mention distaste for the other person. Apart from that, the eyes are an almost infallible sign of someone's reaction to you, so you need to monitor them. On the other hand, too much eye contact – staring – can be unsettling for the other person.

Insight

It's not necessarily true that people look away when they're lying. On the contrary, liars tend to make *more* eye contact because it's important for them to judge whether or not their lies are being believed.

PRACTICAL EXERCISE

1 *If you generally find it difficult to make eye contact, begin by making eye contact with yourself in a mirror. Try using your eyes alone to signal friendliness, empathy and interest.*

2 *All this week, hold eye contact with people you're talking to until you see you've reached the point of making them*

uncomfortable. For the following week, hold eye contact until just before that point is reached.

Matching and mirroring

Matching and mirroring are things we do when we like someone or want to improve the connection. That's to say, we pick up their accents and mimic their body language. It's something that happens unconsciously but you can always accelerate the bonding process by doing it deliberately.

Matching is approximating someone else's body language.

Mirroring means so precisely copying someone else as to seem like a mirror image.

In other words, if someone rests their chin on their hand you might do the same. If the other person clasps their hands behind their head you might follow suit. But don't do it too much or too obviously otherwise the other person might think you're making fun of them.

PRACTICAL EXERCISE

1 *When you're next talking with someone, subtly note the way they're standing or sitting and deliberately but unobtrusively either match or mirror.*

2 *When the other person changes position wait a few moments and then follow suit.*

3 *When you feel you've established rapport try taking the lead by changing your position – if the other person now copies you, then you have confirmation that rapport is strong.*

Reading body language

It's important to know how to 'write' body language but it's just as important to know how to 'read' it. Here are some exercises that will help you improve your skills so you can better judge what effect you're having and what other people are thinking.

1 *Ask a friend some simple questions that require only 'yes' or 'no' answers.*
2 *Note the body language that goes with 'yes' and the body language that goes with 'no'.*
3 *Now put further questions, asking your friend not to reply out loud but simply to think 'yes' or 'no'. From your observations of body language you should be able to say accurately what the correct answers are.*

Insight

Pay particular attention to gestures (especially the little ones known as 'micro movements'), posture, breathing, eyes and tone of voice. Most people will give, at least, a slight nod for a 'yes' and a slight shake for a 'no'. Other signs might be tipping the head forward for a 'yes' and back for a 'no', or warmer eyes for a 'yes' and colder eyes for a 'no'.

PRACTICAL EXERCISE

Once you've mastered 'yes' and 'no' you, too, can become a fortune-teller using a 'crystal ball'.

1 *Conversationally make a few observations that require yes/no answers so you can observe your subject's body language.*
2 *Cup your hands and say that you have a crystal ball there. Move it gently up and down in time with the subject's breathing.*
3 *Now make an opening statement such as 'I see someone very important to you.' Pause to let the subject think of someone then say either 'It's a man' or 'It's a woman'. If the subject's body language shows agreement then move on to the next statement. If the subject's body language shows disagreement, cover yourself by saying, 'No, the mists are clearing and now I see it's … [the opposite].'*
4 *Continue in this way, adding more and more detail.*
5 *Now you're ready for a spectacular finish along the following lines. 'This person has … an important message … for you. Many times … this person … has wanted … to give you … the*

*message ... but never felt able to ... until now ... but within
the next 48 hours ... a situation will occur ... in which their
message ... will be very useful ... to you ... and as you think ...
about this person ... so you will begin ... to understand ...
what the message is ...'*

So now you know how some of those seemingly impossible
'mindreading' feats are carried out. If you find the exercise difficult
you can make it easier by switching from an invisible crystal ball to
palm reading. The procedure is the same but this time you'll receive
subtle yes/no signals unconsciously given by the subject through
their hand. If you can pull this off it will give your confidence a
considerable boost.

Insight

There is a reason for breaking your speech up into small
groups of words when talking about the 'important message'.
Quite simply, this is a 'hypnotic' speech pattern which will
have a powerful effect, especially if you time each group of
words to your subject's inhalations and exhalations.

GIVING A SPEECH OR PRESENTATION

When you're trying to communicate with people from a distance
everything has to be just that little bit more emphatic. A little bit
bigger. Here are a few tips:

▶ *However useful they might be, and however you might
welcome a psychological and physical 'crutch', try not to have
a desk or anything like that between you and your audience.*
▶ *Wear clean, bold lines (see Power dressing).*
▶ *Work the whole audience by keeping your gaze for a time to the
left, then to the centre, then to the right, then start all over again.*
▶ *Memorize as much as possible of your talk and your visual
materials so you don't have to keep looking at them.*
▶ *Hands are important. Make sure they reinforce your message.*
▶ *Have someone video you while you have a trial run. Then
work on all your errors.*

POWER DRESSING

It's a phrase that comes from the 1980s when both women and men wore shoulder pads. And, in fact, shoulder pads do lend an air of authority.

The most important thing is to dress in clothes that make you feel confident. Obviously, the style differs from person to person. But there are certain principles that apply. Most people feel most confident when they fit in with the style adopted by the people they're mixing with.

In other words, if you go to a wedding at which everyone is dressed formally then, unless you're an 'anarchist', you're going to feel very awkward in casual clothes. The way to feel most confident is to 'mirror' their style but personalize it and do it better.

Priming

Psychologists call it 'priming' and it's a very useful technique in every aspect of life. It means preparing someone to respond in the desired way through the use of subtle stimuli. In one experiment, for example, researchers found that leaving a backpack in a room made people feel more co-operative. Wafting in the smell of cleaning fluid made people more willing to clean up after themselves. And a researcher was judged to have either a warm or cold personality according to the temperature of drinks he was handing out.

So never underestimate the importance of the way you dress or the accessories you use. Here I give you some ideas about priming others to perceive you as confident in a business-type setting (and, equally, making you feel more confident). In a different setting (say, mountain climbing) you'd obviously choose quite different clothes and accessories – but the principle remains the same.

TIPS FOR WOMEN
▶ *Designer labels are worth paying extra for, especially where the name of the designer is clear to others.*

- *Well-cut clothes are also worth paying extra for – it's difficult to be confident in clothes that don't fit properly.*
- *For maximum power at work wear suits that mimic men's. In other words, cut for women and in dark colours. Black is best, but you can feminize the look with coloured pinstripes and a coloured waistcoat. Team it with a white blouse.*
- *If you're not wearing a suit, a black dress is always the number one option. Add a splash of colour with a scarf or a belt.*
- *Wear heels – but don't go overboard if you have to be on your feet all day and they should never be so high that you wobble. Heels worn with trousers that come almost to the ground will make your legs look longer – to increase the effect, choose shoes and socks the same colour.*
- *You'll feel just that little bit more confident if you have nice underwear, especially if you're going to be in a situation where you're going to be undressing. If you're a woman, treat yourself to a professional fitting for a bra. It can make all the difference, creating the best possible silhouette and avoiding lumps and bumps.*
- *Never wear patterned or coloured tights.*
- *Make sure your nails are neat and have your eyebrows done professionally – they can make a huge difference.*
- *Good priming accessories include one bold piece of jewellery, a quality briefcase, an expensive pen, an expensive watch and a handbag that complements your body – as a general rule, the larger the bag the smaller you look, and vice versa.*

TIPS FOR MEN
- *Well-cut clothes are worth paying extra for; it's difficult to be confident in clothes that don't fit properly.*
- *In important business situations wear a business suit in a dark colour. It says that you're serious. Team it with a plain shirt, preferably white. Checked shirts say that you're friendly and approachable – but not powerful. Don't*

wear trainers; your shoes should be clean and gleaming.

▶ *Make sure your nails are neat and any facial hair is either neatly trimmed or entirely removed.*

▶ *Priming accessories that can help you feel more confident include a quality briefcase, a handsome watch, a good fountain pen and an expensive aftershave.*

YOUR VOICE

Nothing betrays nerves as quickly and surely as your voice. You can help get it under control using the techniques of suggestion, visualization and self-hypnosis described in Chapter 2, and by rehearsing whatever it is you have to say as much as possible.

In addition:

▶ *Join an amateur theatrical company or some kind of debating society to get experience of speaking in public.*

▶ *Make a conscious effort to speak clearly – don't mumble.*

▶ *Learn to formulate your ideas into logical sequences before speaking.*

▶ *Don't exaggerate (except when telling jokes) or people will learn not to attach too much weight to the things you say.*

▶ *Try not to use too much 'padding' – minimize phrases such as I mean, You know, or Do you know what I mean?*

▶ *Highlight your key points in some way. You could for example say something like: 'I want to underline this point ...', or 'If you don't remember anything else I've said remember this ...'*

PRACTICAL EXERCISE

Practise saying things that make you tense and nervous into a voice recorder, using different rhythms and tones of voice. Try to work out which version works best and why.

Next time you have to make a difficult telephone call record yourself so you can analyse your performance afterwards.

10 THINGS TO REMEMBER

1   Your body language can convey more about you than the things you say.

2   Instead of body language reflecting the way you feel you can learn to make yourself more confident by holding your body in a confident way.

3   Practise body language in front of a mirror.

4   Always make eye contact.

5   Match and mirror other people's body language to accelerate rapport.

6   Observing other people's 'micro movements' will help you work out what they're thinking.

7   When giving a speech or presentation make everything 'bigger'.

8   Black is the ultimate power colour.

9   Choosing the right accessories primes others to see you as you want to be seen.

10 Join an amateur theatrical company or debating society to get used to speaking in public.

HOW CONFIDENT ARE YOU NOW?

- ▶ *Have you developed your very own confident handshake?*
- ▶ *Are you comfortable with kisses?*
- ▶ *Have you been practising your body language in front of a mirror?*
- ▶ *Have you tried matching and mirroring at least one person?*
- ▶ *Have you tried reading a 'crystal ball'?*
- ▶ *Have you practised making longer eye contact?*
- ▶ *Have you bought clothes that will help you feel confident?*
- ▶ *Have you bought accessories that will prime others to see you as confident (and whatever else you wish)?*
- ▶ *Have you used suggestion, visualization or self-hypnosis to get control of your voice?*
- ▶ *Have you joined an amateur theatrical society, debating society, or similar, to give you experience of speaking in public?*

Score:

If you answered 'yes' to most questions, then you've obviously learned to use your body, your voice, your clothes and your accessories to maximum effect. Go straight on to the next chapter.

If you answered 'yes' to between five and seven questions, then you can also go on to the next chapter but revisit this one from time to time and think about the issues it raises.

If you could answer 'yes' to only four questions or fewer, then you're obviously struggling with your body language. Keep working on the practical exercises in this chapter, as well as on the cognitive therapy, visualization and self-hypnosis in Chapters 1 and 2, until you raise your score to five or higher, and only then read on.

6

I'll be me, you be you

In this chapter you will learn:
- *why running away is the quickest route to self-discovery*
- *why you are unique*
- *why you need to enjoy being alone.*

> *For surely anyone who achieves anything is, essentially, abnormal.*
>
> Dr Karl Menninger (1893–1990), American psychiatrist

One of the greatest gifts you can give other people is the permission and encouragement to be themselves. And one of the greatest gifts they can give you is the same.

You can't feel confident when you're pretending to be something you're not.

But here's the first problem. Who are you? It's the question many of us wrestle with for years, sometimes our whole lives. The only way to find the answer is to try different things and experience different ways of being. Experimentation is something associated with teenagers but, in fact, you should continue it all your life. Which is why relationships and friendships should never be stifling. On the contrary, they must allow for the possibility of change. If you're not allowed to change, or if you don't allow another person to change, then that relationship is doomed to failure at some point.

Which brings us to the second problem. Okay, you're going to try new things. But what new things? In all probability, you'll still be operating within the same old straitjacket if you only make conscious choices. In fact, the only way you're going to discover something exciting about yourself is to allow chance to enter your life.

RUNNING AWAY IS GOOD

In our culture we're discouraged from running away from things. We're told: You can't run away from yourself. We're told: You'll just have exactly the same problems somewhere else. We're told: You've made your bed, now you've got to lie in it.

There's not a word of truth in it.

Well, hardly a word. On the contrary, running away is good.

Okay, maybe I've exaggerated a little for effect. I'm not saying you can just walk away from your responsibilities and to hell with everyone else. But I am saying that it's bad for you and everyone else to stick at something that's wrong for you.

Just think about it. Would it really make sense to remain with the first boy or girl you ever went out with, merely on the grounds that you shouldn't ever run away? Would it make sense to stick at your first job, even though you hate it and you're hopeless at it? Is it really true that if someone is picking on you at school or at work that you'll automatically have another person pick on you if you move? The answer in all these cases is 'no'.

Now I'm going to share an important secret with you. The only way you're ever going to find out what's right for you is by trying lots of different things. But not just the things you choose to try. You see, you need to try things you haven't even thought of yet. When you make a conscious decision to try certain things, you still run the risk that you're restricting yourself because of society's conventions and other people's opinions of you. It's only when you allow chance to enter the picture that you introduce the possibility of making a discovery you'd never dreamed of.

In other words, by 'running'.

Insight

I could give you hundreds of real examples from other people's lives and my own. The way I live now, where I live, how I live, with whom I live – none of this is how I would have imagined a few years ago. It happened by accident because I allowed the possibility of chance to enter my life. And in that way I discovered much more about who I am than I ever would have done otherwise.

Once you know who you are you will have more confidence than you ever imagined. That's something that can never be taken away from you.

▶ *You will be you.*

That may sound a rather silly, meaningless thing to say but, in fact, it's vitally important. You may have many things in common with many other people but you will not have everything in common with any other person on the planet. You are unique. When you go for an interview, when you go to a social event or when you go on a new date say this to yourself:

▶ *They're going to be meeting a unique human being, they want to meet a unique human being, and I shan't hide the ways that I'm unique.*

And whenever you're not sure about something just stop for a moment and remind yourself of this:

▶ *I am unique. I cannot follow anybody else's path. I must make my own path.*

BEING NORMAL AND BEING DIFFERENT

Most people want to be 'normal'. And if that's how you feel, too, then that's fine. But if you feel you're different to other people, and if that worries you, then don't let it. Most of the people the world looks up to have been 'different' in some way. Being different doesn't automatically make you superior but nor does it automatically make you inferior, either. Different is simply different.

It may be that because you're different you feel you don't 'measure up'. But who's doing the measuring? Remember, measuring up to other people's standards is not important. The important thing is to measure up to your own. You don't have to prove anything to other people. If, as far as other people are concerned, you don't 'measure up', then that's a fact of life about which there's no point getting upset. Let's hear it again: That's their problem.

▶ *There's no point in striving to be something that, in your essence, you're not.*

In fact, many of us suppress our individuality in order to feel comfortable among other people and be accepted by them. But, when you think about it, it's a shame. Because it robs us all of the stimulation of diversity. It robs us all of new ideas. So if you feel different, don't hide it. Celebrate it. And celebrate it in other people. Don't fear it.

Here, to encourage you, are the names of people who were or are very different, picked at random and in alphabetical order. If they'd striven to be 'normal' we'd have missed a great deal:

William Blake, David Bowie, Byron, Christopher Columbus, Salvador Dali, Daphne Du Maurier, Isadora Duncan, St Francis of Assisi, Sigmund Freud, Mahatma Gandhi, Paul Gauguin, Howard Hughes, Elton John, Carl Jung, George Bernard Shaw, Mark Twain, Leonardo da Vinci, Vivienne Westwood.

PRACTICAL EXERCISE

1 *List ten things that you think help define who you are. Then, in a few months' time (after following Exercise 2 below) make a new list and see how it compares. Your list might include things like career, political beliefs, outlook, lifestyle and ambitions.*

2 *Every day, at random, try something new. It could be something you've dismissed without ever actually having experienced it. Or it could be something you've never previously thought of. Most days it will have to be something 'small' – although psychologically it could be highly significant. And then at weekends and on holiday aim for some 'big' experience. Obviously don't waste time on something you already know you don't like (assuming, that is, you've already tried it and proved you don't like it).*

   Here are some suggestions for daily experiments:
   ▷ *Buy a different newspaper to your usual.*
   ▷ *Read a genre of book you've always dismissed.*
   ▷ *See a film you normally wouldn't bother with.*
   ▷ *Try a type of entertainment that's new to you (opera, ballet, theatre, disco or whatever).*
   ▷ *Try a style of clothing you've always assumed wouldn't suit you.*
   ▷ *Go out somewhere you've never been before.*
   ▷ *Prepare a meal that's entirely new to you.*
   ▷ *Talk to someone about a subject you're normally reticent to discuss.*
   ▷ *Consider the opinions of a politician from the opposite end of the spectrum to your own.*
   ▷ *Read the biography of someone whose lifestyle is or was totally different to yours.*
   ▷ *Enrol in an evening class to learn a new skill.*

   And here are some suggestions for weekends and holidays:
   ▷ *Try activities you've assumed you wouldn't like (riding, climbing, hiking, cycling, golf, archery, orienteering, sailing, wind surfing ...).*
   ▷ *Try a new style of holiday in a location you've never visited before (sightseeing, beach, skiing, activities, wildlife, volunteering ...).*

> ▷ *If you're single and looking for a partner, try dating people who are different to the 'blueprint' you have in your mind (taller, shorter, more serious, more frivolous, more introverted, more extroverted, more artistic, more logical ...).*
> ▷ *Apply for work experience in a different kind of job.*
> ▷ *Rent a holiday home in a different environment to see if you might like to live there (city centre, village, countryside, seaside, further north, further south, another country ...).*

3   *At the end of every day, review the day's events. When you're in bed, just before going to sleep, can be a good time. (In fact, this exercise can double as a treatment for insomnia!) Just run through them, without being self-critical at all, and ask: 'When such-and-such happened was I me?' If not, try to work out why you behaved in a way that wasn't really you.*

Those are just a few ideas to get you started. Remember the object isn't so much to have fun – although you will – but to challenge your preconceived ideas about the kind of person you are and the life you want for yourself. And what's the connection between that and self-confidence? Because you can't feel confident if you're living a lie – even unwittingly.

LOOKING AT YOURSELF FROM THE INSIDE

Interacting with all kinds of different external experiences is of major importance. But that's only half the story. You also need to take a look at yourself from the inside. How? By meditating.

Don't go thinking that meditation is some kind of Oriental, quasi-religious mumbo jumbo that has no relevance to your everyday life in the West. Meditation is simply another way of trying to understand yourself and your place in the world If not, indeed, the universe. There's nothing weird about that. And meditation has direct benefits in terms of self-confidence.

Benefits of meditation

Meditation teaches you to take control of your mind so you can keep out all those stupid negative thoughts that lead to self-doubt and undermine your resolve. It also gives you a strong sense of self through a deep insight into your true nature and makes you more optimistic (researchers have monitored the brains of people who begin meditating and found that, over a period of months, activity tends to increase in the frontal lobe of the left brain – the part associated with higher moods and a positive outlook).

Meditation also has a number of other benefits, including:

▶ *refreshing and revitalizing yourself after your day's work*
▶ *forgetting, for a while, your cares about the past and your worries for the future*
▶ *cultivating a calmer mind and a more tranquil outlook*
▶ *developing a more balanced mental state in respect of a particular issue.*

Technically speaking, meditation means entering a state of consciousness that is neither the normal, everyday state of being awake nor the state of being asleep. There are four categories of brain waves:

▶ *Beta: 13–40 Hz. The fastest frequencies, associated with normal waking consciousness and being alert.*
▶ *Alpha: 7–13 Hz. The next fastest frequencies, associated with feeling relaxed, daydreaming, reverie and light meditation.*
▶ *Theta: 4–7 Hz. Slower again, associated with dreaming sleep and deep meditation.*
▶ *Delta: Under 4 Hz. The slowest, associated with deep sleep.*

Notice the use of the word 'associated' because, in fact, it's possible for two or three or even four frequencies to be present at the same time. Although 'light' meditation is normally said to be in alpha mode and 'deep' meditation in theta mode, in practice deep meditation can involve not just alpha but also beta and theta and, in rare cases, all four. That is normally the preserve of a 'master' possessing what some call 'the awakened mind'. But everyone who meditates will combine frequencies in a way which is different to sleeping.

Meditation routine
So here's a quick course in meditation:

1 *Choose a time of day: Some teachers recommend first thing in the morning, especially before dawn, as a way of setting you up for the day. Others recommend the late evening, when everything has been done, as a way of unwinding from the day. Find out what works best for you and then try to stick to it. Your body and mind will adapt accordingly and you'll find it increasingly easy to get into a meditative state at the same time every day.*

2 *Choose a place: You can meditate anywhere. But most people like to have a special place and some also like to have special 'props' to help them get into the meditative state. As a beginner you're probably best to have a quiet place where you won't be disturbed. Except for open-eyed styles of meditation, it will help if the room is dim or even dark or you could wear an eye mask. Make it a nice place so that you look forward to going to it and come to associate it with meditation.*

3 *Choose a position: The pose traditionally associated with meditation is the lotus. The idea behind it is that it's extremely stable so that, in deep meditation, you won't topple over; at the same time, it's not a position in which it's easy to fall asleep. But when you meditate you need to be comfortable. That's vital. You don't want to be distracted by thinking how painful your ankles or knees are. So if you can't do the lotus but can easily manage the half-lotus (only one foot resting on the opposite thigh, the other foot going under the opposite thigh) all well and good. And if you can't do the half-lotus, just sit cross-legged or sit upright in a chair or even lie down. Many teachers frown on this as not being 'proper' and because of the danger of falling asleep. But, in fact, it's an excellent position for meditating because it automatically reduces beta waves. In the last analysis, the important thing is the meditation not the pose. Whatever works for you is fine.*

4   *Choose a length of time: You could meditate all day, although
    in the context of a busy modern life 20–30 minutes is the
    longest most people can aim for. But the more time you can
    devote to it the more likely you are to reach a deep state.
    Some people like to set a timer. That can work well because
    it removes any anxiety about not meditating for long enough
    or, on the other hand, taking too long and being late for the
    next thing you have to do. But others prefer to let whatever
    happens happen.*

5   *Choose a technique: You can learn various techniques from
    teachers or books. To get you started here's a simple but
    effective way of meditating for self-confidence:*

    ▷ *Sitting or lying down with your eyes closed, notice your
      breathing.*
    ▷ *Without forcing anything, gradually slow down your
      breathing.*
    ▷ *Empty your mind of any thoughts of past or future.*
    ▷ *Just concentrate on experiencing the present moment
      which is your breath.*
    ▷ *If any thoughts push their way into your mind, just let
      them drift past; don't pursue them.*
    ▷ *When your breathing is slow and relaxed, notice your
      heartbeat.*
    ▷ *Without forcing anything, gradually try to think it slower.*
    ▷ *Next notice the sound of your blood in your ears.*
    ▷ *Without forcing anything, gradually try to think it slower.*
    ▷ *In the same way, visit any other parts of your body that
      you choose.*
    ▷ *Now notice the little dots that 'illuminate' the blackness
      of your closed eyes.*
    ▷ *Imagine the dots are stars and that you're floating in
      space towards them.*
    ▷ *Relax your jaw and let your mouth open into a smile.*

Insight

If you can't seem to get into a meditative state at all,
try lying on the floor rather than sitting (but don't fall
asleep). Gradually slow down your breathing, making your

(Contd)

exhalation longer than your inhalation, and let your mouth fall open so that your tongue relaxes and drops out. You could also try touching the tip of the ring finger of your left hand against the fleshy base of your thumb as you breathe in and moving it away as you breathe out. As you breathe in think 'So' and as you breathe out think 'Hum' – it's a classic mantra.

Beginners often wonder if they're meditating correctly or even at all. What should it feel like? In fact, there is no precise definition but the stages of increasingly deeper and deeper meditation should go something like this:

▶ *Stage 1 Your mind is no longer filled with everyday matters and you sense that you're drifting towards sleep; you're on the very fringe of the meditative state.*
▶ *Stage 2 As you go deeper, images may come at you from nowhere. You don't actually fall asleep but start to feel as if you're floating. You may feel like rocking and swaying; that's fine at this stage but you'll need to stop moving to go deeper.*
▶ *Stage 3 You become intensely aware of the functioning of your body – breathing, heartbeat, blood flow – but at the same time you no longer know where your body ends and other things begin. Parts of your body may feel very heavy.*
▶ *Stage 4 You feel 'spaced out' and quite detached but, at the same time, alert.*
▶ *Stage 5 You feel in touch with the universe and nothing else matters at all.*

The deepest meditative states are usually only reached by those who have been practising for a long time – perhaps two or three years. But you may occasionally experience moments of those deeper states even as a beginner.

Insight

Meditation is not a competition. Every experience of meditation is slightly different. Don't set out with a goal and then consider the session a failure because you didn't achieve it. Just experience and enjoy whatever occurs.

USING COGNITIVE THERAPY

Cognitive therapy, as we saw in Chapter 1, is all about distorted thought patterns. And there can be no greater distortion than having a misconceived idea of who you are. Where this is concerned the most significant distortion is often:

▶ *I feel guilty that I'm not doing the things I should.*

Let's forget about minor issues such as washing up or cutting the grass. There are big, life-changing themes to be considered, such as:

▶ *I should get married to (whoever).*
▶ *I should dress my age.*
▶ *I should do what my father/husband/wife (or whoever) thinks best.*
▶ *I should stay in my present job.*
▶ *I should stay with my partner.*

In fact, you shouldn't have any 'should' statements other than this one:

▶ *I should be true to myself.*

I'm not advocating selfishness. Obviously, there are times we all have to do things we'd rather not. We have responsibilities. But you can still be true to yourself even when you're doing things you dislike. Confidence comes from being yourself and not from doing things other people say you should. When you're truly yourself you'll be full of confidence because that's something that can never be taken away from you.

PRACTICAL EXERCISE

Take a sheet of paper and divide it down the middle. On the left-hand side head it up 'Reasons why I should' and on the right 'Distortions in my thinking'. As an example, let's say you're not happy in your relationship. You've developed and grown over the years but your partner hasn't. Nevertheless, you feel you should stay together. Here's how you might start to fill it in:

Reasons why I should stay	Distortions in my thinking
My partner will be very upset if I leave.	My partner deserves happiness, too, and isn't going to find it with me if I'm miserable.
We've been together a long time and it would be a tragedy to throw all that away.	The happy times can't be taken away from us. But the past has passed. I now have to think about my present and my future. The real tragedy would be throwing that away.
We'll both be financially worse off.	Money isn't everything – and it's certainly far less important than my being true to myself.
Our parents will be very upset.	We can't live for our parents. In reality, they probably won't be at all surprised. They'll get used to it.

Now you do the same for the things you 'should' do in your life.

USING SELF-HYPNOSIS

It's obviously impossible to visualize 'being yourself' if you don't yet know what 'being yourself' truly means. But what you *can* do is use self-hypnosis to make yourself more open to new experiences, less inhibited, and less frightened of change.

PRACTICAL EXERCISE
1 *Complete the 'external' phase of the process of self-hypnosis described in Chapter 2, stating the aim of the self-hypnosis as follows: 'I am entering into a state of self-hypnosis so that I can hand over to my unconscious mind the task of liberating my true personality.'*

2 *Having completed the 'external' phase, close your eyes and wait for a scene to present itself to you.*

3 *Using the visualization that's been presented, continue with the 'internal' phase as described in Chapter 2, to deepen the trance.*

4 *Come out of trance, as described.*

5 *Repeat the process from time to time until you feel you have 'become yourself'.*

Insight

Although the visualization presented to you may not seem to have much to do with becoming your true self, you will nevertheless find that your unconscious will work away at achieving your goal. In subsequent sessions of self-hypnosis you may have a clearer idea of how you want to be and can deliberately visualize that.

CELEBRATING THE REAL YOU

Okay, so you're starting to fit the bits of your personal jigsaw together. Now what? Well, one thing you must do is express the real you. Whether it's a new you or the same you, be creative about it.

Show who you are

Let's start with one of the most obvious ways. The way you look. Your clothes and your hair. This is one of the clearest ways you can, as it were, show solidarity with yourself, and signal to other people what kind of person you are.

Don't ask yourself:

▶ *Do I fit in with everybody else?*

Instead, ask yourself this:

▶ *Do I look like me?*

Do you, in fact, even know what you look like? If your essence, your soul if you like, could walk and talk and dress would it look the way you look now? Or would it be something different? Would it have longer hair? Shorter hair? A moustache? Bolder colours? A longer skirt? A shorter skirt? A younger style? A more classic style? What? Experiment and find out.

PRACTICAL EXERCISE

1 *Go clothes shopping. Yes, I know, that's going to be such a tough thing to do! But don't go to your usual shops. Seek out styles, cuts, colours, patterns, combinations and 'looks' you've never previously gone for. Maybe you won't find anything you like and will stick with what you've got. That's fine. At least you don't have to buy anything. On the other hand, maybe something will suddenly click and you'll look in the mirror and see, in astonishment, the real you for the very first time. That can be a wonderful moment – with an expensive aftermath. Another way of trying lots of different clothes is to go swishing – that's to say, to clothes swapping parties. You can find details of UK events at www.swishing.org. Or organize your own – it's a great way to interact with other people.*

2 *Play around with your hairstyle. You'll have to be a little inventive here. You don't, after all, want to shave your head to see what you look like and then decide you can't stand the result. But you can get an idea of things using swimming hats, wigs, pins, scrunchies, water and gel. You can also get computer programmes that, once you've loaded a photo, will let you test different styles.*

3 *Play around with your facial hair (this one is for men only). It's amazing the variety of effects you can achieve. More, probably, than with the hair on your head. Short moustaches, long moustaches, designer stubble, full beards, goatee beards ... The permutations are almost endless and can provide weeks of fun.*

Live the way you are

Next take a look at your home and where you live. Ask yourself this question:

▶ *Why am I living here?*

If you've made a deliberate choice to stay where you grew up, having taken a good look at all the other possibilities, that's fine. But if you're merely living in the place in which you grew up for no reason other than the fact that you're already there, then start thinking about the other possibilities. Would you be happier in the countryside? In a bigger town? What about the climate? Do you like it or would you prefer more sunshine? More snow? Can you pursue the lifestyle you hanker after – the theatre, café life, hillwalking, sailing, or whatever it might be?

Wherever you live, your home should say as much about you as your clothes. Does it? Take a look at the décor. The furniture. The objects. The paintings and posters. Is it as unique as you are?

PRACTICAL EXERCISE

In fact, the only real way to express yourself is not to buy things conceived by others but to design your own. And, if possible, make them. Why not?

1 *You can certainly produce your own paintings, for example. Don't be put off by a lack of technical skill. Just use abstract forms and colours to make a statement.*
2 *Collect 'found' objects and arrange them in a way that pleases you – pieces of driftwood, pebbles, rocks, scrap iron and so on.*
3 *Design your own chairs, tables, beds and cupboards and have them made up by carpenters or wrought iron craftsmen.*

A job you'd do for nothing

You're probably going to spend a huge chunk of your life at work. So it's pretty obvious it should be something you can enjoy. But, more than that, it should be an extension of your personality. Ask yourself:

▶ *Do I wake up in the morning eager to get into work?*
▶ *Is it something I genuinely want to do rather than, in some way or another, having been forced into?*
▶ *Do I have an aptitude for this job?*

If you can't answer 'yes' to those questions you're in the wrong job. And that's very bad for self-confidence. Because you can't feel confident in a job which doesn't match your personality. In which you have to struggle. A job that's a chore. You want a job you can be good at because it inspires and fascinates you. A job you're proud to do. Something you'd do even if you didn't get paid for it. If you think there is no such job for you, you're completely wrong. There are thousands of jobs you've never even dreamed of.

PRACTICAL EXERCISE
Over the next month research as many different jobs as you can. Think carefully about the lifestyle that goes with the job. Don't just focus on the actual job itself. For example, is it indoors or outdoors? Active or sedentary? Social or solitary? Nine to five or flexible? Close to home or a long commute away? Five days a week or six? Employed or self-employed? Stressful or tranquil? All these things need to be taken into account. Then organize some work experience to see what your dream job is really like.

IF YOU WANT FRIENDS, LEARN TO BE ALONE

As you learn more and more about yourself and discover the person you genuinely are so you should become increasingly happy with your own company. And that's important. After all, if you're not, how can you expect anybody else to be?

I'm not saying you should love being on your own. Human beings are social creatures. Being pleased and happy to meet other people is good. But being desperate to meet other people is bad. The problem is that your desperation – if that's what you feel – communicates itself to everyone else. And nobody likes it.

Those other people also want friends, of course, but for positive reasons. They want friends who make them happy, energized and carefree. They don't want friends who:

▶ *drain energy away from them*
▶ *seem to offer nothing in return*
▶ *threaten to be a burden.*

If you feel desperate, that's how you'll come across.

But how can you not feel desperate if you don't have any friends? The solution is to learn to be happy on your own. When you're happy in your own company that transmits itself to everyone else. And everyone else then feels more relaxed and more positive towards you.

In fact, you need time on your own. Everyone needs time on their own. Being alone doesn't have to mean being bored. On the contrary. Being alone means being free to:

▶ *indulge yourself*
▶ *pursue 'non-social' activities*
▶ *experiment with new things*
▶ *discover who you really are*
▶ *let your creativity rip.*

Insight

When you have periods on your own don't mope around. Take advantage of them to do things you wouldn't otherwise be able to. Welcome them. Maybe you think you can only enjoy yourself if you have someone special with you. Well, it's just not true. Below are some of the things you can do far better on your own.

Experiment with your appearance

I've already suggested you should experiment with your appearance. But that can be difficult when you're being watched by people who think they know you very well. It's so easy to get trapped by other people's expectations. When everyone has become used to the business suit it's very difficult to suddenly turn up in a kaftan. If you live alone right now, or have a lot of time on your own, you're in the perfect situation to experiment.

Meditate

Although you can meditate together with other people it's not really a very sociable activity. So periods when you're alone are ideal for experimenting with the meditation exercises described earlier.

Study

It's not a lot of fun being around someone who's studying. So take the opportunity to study now, while you have time alone. Later, the situation might be very different. Maybe there are exams you could take to further your career, maybe you'd like to follow an Open University course or maybe all on your own you'd just like to study a subject that interests you. In turn, this is all going to give you something to talk about when you do meet up with other people.

PRACTICAL EXERCISE
To begin with, sign up for a short course in something that, for you, would be a little bit unusual. Painting, bricklaying, car mechanics, photography, gardening, Chinese ... there's so much to choose from. In the UK see www.direct.gov.uk/en/EducationAndLearning/AdultLearning/index.htm. Or simply put 'adult education' into your search engine, together with the name of your town.

Be creative

Being alone is a wonderful opportunity to explore your creativity without being constrained by other people's views.

PRACTICAL EXERCISE
Maybe you're already alone a lot. But if you're not used to it, don't panic the next time loneliness threatens. Don't immediately reach for your mobile. Instead, start thinking positively about all the things you could experience and enjoy on your own. Then try some of them out, such as:

- *playing a musical instrument*
- *drawing, painting or sculpting*
- *photography*
- *creative writing*
- *starting a blog*
- *designing your own website*

- *making clothes*
- *making jewellery*
- *woodwork.*

In fact, there are endless ways to be creative and, given enough time to explore on your own, you'll find at least one medium that will suit you.

10 THINGS TO REMEMBER

1 *You can't be confident if you're pretending to be something you're not.*

2 *Be yourself and let other people be themselves.*

3 *You'll never know who you really are if you don't experiment with lots of different things.*

4 *It's right to 'run away' because it's then you allow chance to enter your life.*

5 *Don't try only things you think you'll like; experiment with things you've never even considered before.*

6 *If you want to be 'normal' that's fine, but don't be afraid to be different if that's how you feel.*

7 *Meditation can increase your sense of self and therefore your self-assurance; it also helps you take control of your mind, so self-defeating, negative thoughts can't enter on their own.*

8 *Be true to yourself; don't do things against your beliefs just because you think you 'should'.*

9 *Express your personality in your clothes, your hair, your home and your work.*

10 *Don't be afraid to be alone – it's a wonderful opportunity to explore who you are, experiment and express yourself in new creative ways.*

HOW CONFIDENT ARE YOU NOW?

- ▶ *Have you 'run away' and tried some new things?*
- ▶ *Have you succeeded in reaching a meditative state on a regular basis?*
- ▶ *Have you been able to rid yourself of the belief that you 'should' do things you don't want to?*
- ▶ *Have you been able to liberate your true personality?*
- ▶ *Have you experimented with different clothes and different styles?*
- ▶ *Have you expressed your personality through the way you decorate your home?*
- ▶ *Have you identified your dream job, organized work experience in your dream job or clinched your dream job?*
- ▶ *Have you learnt to enjoy and benefit from time spent alone?*
- ▶ *Have you signed up for any adult learning?*
- ▶ *Have you unleashed your creative abilities?*

Score:

If you answered 'yes' to most questions, then you're obviously 'yourself' or, at least, well on the way to unleashing your true personality. Go straight on to the next chapter.

If you answered 'yes' to between five and seven questions, then you can also go on to the next chapter but revisit this one from time to time and think about the issues it raises.

If you could answer 'yes' to only four questions or fewer, then you're obviously struggling to discover who you really are. Keep working on the practical exercises in this chapter until you raise your score to five or higher, and only then read on.

7

How to win arguments by being assertive, not aggressive

In this chapter you will learn:
- *the three-step formula for being assertive*
- *why you should always be willing to make concessions*
- *how to seed your ideas in other people's minds.*

Anger leads to ill feeling and hatred.

HH Dalai Lama

People often confuse being assertive with being aggressive, but the two are completely different. Assertive people are calm, considerate and polite but, nevertheless, tend to get what they want. And they seldom get pushed into doing things they don't want.

Aggressive people, on the other hand, often fail to get what they want because they goad other people into being aggressive in return. Remember the adage:

▶ *Every force creates an equal and opposite force.*

Even when aggressive people do get what they want they lose out in many other ways because (a) nobody wants to have any dealings with them and (b) nobody likes them.

So you want to be assertive, not aggressive.

THE THREE STEPS TO ASSERTIVENESS

The secret is in learning to express your opinions and requirements in a non-confrontational manner. The key to that is the three-step response:

▶ *Step 1 Acknowledge the other person's point of view.*
▶ *Step 2 Introduce your own point of view.*
▶ *Step 3 Suggest a reasonable way in which the conflict might be resolved.*

These are the kinds of situations in which you may want to say 'no' but feel pressured or embarrassed:

▶ *your boss wants you to take on extra work*
▶ *a friend wants to borrow something that's very precious to you*
▶ *a new boyfriend or girlfriend wants to forge ahead too quickly*
▶ *your partner wants to move but you want to stay put.*

These can all be very delicate situations. Let's take that extra work as an example. Your three-step response might be something like this:

▶ *Step 1 I realize the company is short-staffed at the moment.*
▶ *Step 2 However, I'm already finding it difficult to get through my own workload.*
▶ *Step 3 Do you think it might be possible to provide me with some more powerful software?*

Obviously, you'll have to adapt the formula to the specific circumstances you're in. But you get the idea. Of course, the other person may persist. In which case, you parry the other person's response with a new and appropriate three-part formula. Let's say, your boss answers your first three-step response by saying that new software will take too long to install. You might then respond like this:

- ▶ *Step 1 I agree that new software wouldn't be an immediate solution.*
- ▶ *Step 2 However, I think it should be ordered now to tackle the problem in the medium term.*
- ▶ *Step 3 In the meantime, maybe you could take on temporary staff.*

As long as the other person persists, so you keep using the three-step response. Eventually, however, you may reach a point at which you've run out of arguments and the other person still won't give up. Your best course of action then is to ask for a 'breather'. Say something like this:

- ▶ *You've made some very interesting points and I'll need time to think them through. Can we talk about the situation again tomorrow?*
- ▶ *I just don't know how I feel until I've had the time to let this sink in. Please can I give you a reply next week?*

By doing this you achieve several things:

- ▶ *First of all, you do give yourself time to consider what you feel. When confronted with a new idea – something you've not experienced before – you genuinely need time to work out what you truly think.*
- ▶ *Secondly, the other person may go away and reconsider things in the light of the comments you've already made (see Planting a seed later in this chapter).*
- ▶ *Thirdly, you give yourself the opportunity to marshal new arguments and stiffen your resolve (possibly with the help of a friend).*

It may be that, in the end, you're going to have to give way to a certain extent. That can be okay. Making concessions is a normal part of negotiating and it certainly doesn't mean you're weak or insufficiently assertive, provided the other party also makes concessions (see later).

PRACTICAL EXERCISE

1 *Here are some difficult requests. In each case, frame a three-part reply to turn the request down.*

   ▷ *Someone you don't much like asks: 'Will you go out with me on Saturday night?'*

   ▷ *A friend asks: 'I'm in a bit of a fix. Can you lend me some money?'*

   ▷ *A friend asks: 'Can I borrow your necklace to wear to a party?'*

   ▷ *A relative asks: 'Can I stay with you until I find somewhere to live?'*

   ▷ *Your boss asks: 'Can you work on Sunday to clear the backlog?'*

2 *Now we're going to make things a little bit harder and a little bit more interesting. I want you to role-play with a friend. Make sure your friend understands what's required. That is, to persist and not to accept 'no' for an answer. Your task is to continue to be assertive but not aggressive and not to give in.*

Here's some dialogue to get you started:

PARENT (played by your friend): I'm going on a week's holiday next month and I'd like you to stay at the house to keep an eye on it.

YOU (playing yourself): I understand it would be reassuring to have someone stay at the house. However, that would mean me leaving my house. I suggest you ask a neighbour to keep an eye on things.

PARENT: You know I can't rely on the neighbours. And there's Tiddles to feed.

YOU: I understand your anxiety about the neighbours feeding Tiddles properly. However, I just can't drop everything here. Couldn't Tiddles go into the kennels for the week?

PARENT: After all the things I've done for you can't you do this for me?

YOU: You know how much I appreciate the things you've done and I would do anything reasonable to help you enjoy your holiday without anxiety. However ...

Now you continue the dialogue.

Dealing with the aftermath
Sometimes you just have to accept that if you say 'no' the other person may feel differently about you. It may be that's what you want. But if you want to try to keep the relationship as it was, then avoid the following traps:

▶ *Don't hide away afterwards or become withdrawn.*
▶ *Don't try to compensate by acting with abnormal friendliness.*

Instead, just behave normally. The other person will be watching you for signs that you're upset, angry or resentful at being asked. So it's important you show that, as far as you're concerned, nothing has changed between you (unless, of course, you want something to change).

> **Insight**
> Once you've made your decision, once you've said 'no', try not to agonize over it. Just put it behind you and move on. It's a closed issue.

DO YOU FIND IT HARD TO SAY 'NO'?

Stella has two young children who wake up every night asking for various things. As a result she often feels exhausted.

She considers she's being a good and caring mother. But is she really? They don't get a proper night's sleep and neither does she.

If Stella would only admit it, she actually likes her children to come to her in the night. She likes to know she's needed. It makes her feel more valuable. That's why she doesn't tell her children, 'No, you may not get out of bed'. Consciously she believes she's doing her best to stop them but, unconsciously, she encourages them.

Maybe you also find it difficult to say 'no' because, consciously or unconsciously, you want to be popular.

PRACTICAL EXERCISE
Next time you find yourself in a situation in which you find it hard to say 'no', ask yourself the following question:

▶ *Do I achieve a better outcome by saying 'no' or by saying 'yes'?*

If the answer is 'no' then focus your mind on that better outcome. You'll find the word 'no' will come much more easily.

MAKING REQUESTS

Okay, so far we've dealt with people wanting something from you and you asserting your right to refuse. Now let's turn things round. In this case it's you who's doing the asking and the other person who's doing the refusing. Nevertheless, once again, you employ the three-step technique.

YOU (playing yourself): I know you usually charge more. However, I'd like to buy the very large quantity of 1,000 units and for that reason I think a fair price would be £500 (US $790 approx.) each.

COMPANY DIRECTOR (played by your friend): You must be joking. We usually sell those units for £749 (US $1,185 approx.).

YOU: I realize I'm asking you to accept well below list price. However, 1,000 units would be a very substantial order. I suggest that if you look at your costings, you'll see you can still make a good profit.

COMPANY DIRECTOR: What profit we make is our affair.

YOU: Of course it is. However, cutting profit margin to win such a large order makes good business sense when machinery is idle. Why not see if you have the spare capacity for this?

COMPANY DIRECTOR: It's not our policy to sell below list price otherwise everyone will want a discount.

YOU: I can understand why you say that. However ...

Now you continue the business negotiations. Of course, the same principles apply in other spheres as well, from asking someone to do a household chore you know they don't like, right up to discussing an international treaty.

USING COGNITIVE THERAPY

Sometimes it can be difficult to feel assertive. You understand the principles but you can't put them into practice because you lack the resolve. Basically, you anticipate failure before you even begin. That saps your will. Well, our old friend cognitive therapy can help. Maybe you feel you won't be able to hold your ground because:

▶ *They're better than me.*

Do you remember that one from Chapter 1? It's the style of thinking psychotherapists call 'mental filter'. You focus on one area in which you're weak, ignore your strengths and then become overwhelmed by doubts. It's like being a golfer who expects to lose every game on the putting green despite being brilliant with all the other clubs. Well, every golfer has weaknesses. Work on yours but don't dwell on them. Play to your strengths.

If you're thinking negatively at the start then you're undermining yourself. Get rid of those negative thoughts in the way that should now be second nature. Divide a blank sheet in two from top to bottom. Head up the left-hand side 'Negative thoughts' and the right-hand side 'Why those negative thoughts are wrong'. Like this:

Negative thoughts	Why those negative thoughts are wrong
I'm no good at arguing and am bound to be beaten.	I'm not going to argue. I'm simply going to express my point of view clearly, using the three-step technique. For that I shall prepare using role-play. Nothing the other side says can alter the validity of my position.
But he's a trained lawyer. He'll just bamboozle me. It's hopeless.	Being a lawyer has nothing to do with it. I know what I'm willing to agree to and what I'm not willing to agree to. I shall stand my ground.

Now do the same for any issues that are undermining your resolve.

USING VISUALIZATION AND SELF-HYPNOSIS

Visualizing yourself being more assertive is a good way of becoming more assertive. Simply close your eyes and imagine the scene as you would like it to be. For a stronger effect, the visualization technique known as the *Circle of Confidence* (turn back to Chapter 2 if you've forgotten about it) can easily be adapted.

PRACTICAL EXERCISE
1   *Something challenging is coming up for which it's important you feel assertive. Search your memory for a past situation in which you felt that way. It doesn't have to have been an*

especially difficult situation. Relive that assertive feeling, seeing and hearing everything in as much detail as possible.

2 *Imagine a circle on the floor. Take the assertiveness you feel and pour it into the circle. Immediately the circle takes on a colour – the colour that, to you, is the colour of assertion. It also makes a noise. Maybe it's a buzzing sound or even music – again, it's whatever expresses assertiveness to you.*

3 *Turn your thoughts to the future occasion when you'll be wanting to feel assertive. Select a cue to that moment. For example, if you're going to visit a company to negotiate a contract, it could be a secretary calling your name. (But don't make it too specific otherwise you might never get the cue you envisaged.)*

4 *Holding that cue in your mind, step into the circle and visualize assertiveness rising up from the floor, permeating and enveloping you. As you move around so that cocoon of assertiveness will move with you.*

5 *Visualize the future unfolding from that cue moment. See yourself being assertive but not aggressive (for example, employing the three-step formula).*

6 *When the cue moment arrives for real, visualize the circle on the floor, step into it and go and do what you have to do.*

Insight

NLP, from which this is adapted, makes the presupposition that people already have all the resources they need. You should try hard to find the necessary assertiveness within you. However, if you can't recall any occasion on which you were assertive (as required by Step 1) then visualize another person you've seen being assertive, perhaps a character in a film.

As we've seen before, self-hypnosis is simply an enhanced form of visualization. Here's a way of using it to become more assertive.

PRACTICAL EXERCISE

1 *Complete the 'external' phase of the process of self-hypnosis described in Chapter 2, stating the aim of the self-hypnosis as*

follows: 'I am entering into a state of self-hypnosis so that I can hand over to my unconscious mind the task of making me more assertive.'

2 *Having completed the 'external' phase, close your eyes and move on to the 'internal' phase. As in the visualization exercise above, imagine a future occasion on which you'll need to be assertive. See and hear yourself behaving assertively and feel what you would feel. Select examples of each 'representational system' exactly as described in Chapter 2, in order to deepen the trance.*

3 *Come out of trance, as described.*

4 *Repeat the process from time to time until you feel you have become assertive.*

MAKING CONCESSIONS

Settling a dispute in an assertive way doesn't mean getting everything you want while the other person gets nothing. That only causes resentment and stores up trouble for the future. Being conciliatory means both parties get something – hopefully what they truly need – even if it's less than they thought they wanted. This is the 'win – win' situation.

Let's take Mary and Mark. Mark works hard all day and comes home tired. In the evenings and at weekends he just wants to eat and relax. Mary doesn't go out to work but she does look after their two young children and she thinks that when Mark is at home it should be her chance to take a break. But it never works out like that and they argue.

Mary goes on the attack like this: 'Why won't you ever take any responsibility for looking after the children and doing things round the house?'

Mark goes on the attack like this: 'I've had a hard day at work earning the money to pay the bills and surely the least I can expect when I get home is to find dinner ready.'

Neither is acknowledging the other's position. And that only makes for resentment and a hardening of attitudes. This is where the three-step approach once again comes in.

Mary could say something along these lines: 'I realize you've had a really tough day at work. However, my day has been pretty hard too. Supposing I bring you a cup of tea and some biscuits and then we fix dinner together.'

And Mark could say something along these lines: 'I know how tiring it is having to look after two small children all day. However, I've had a really hard day at work too. Supposing I get the kids into bed while you fix dinner.'

In each case concessions are being made. Mary is offering to provide tea and biscuits. Mark is offering to take responsibility for putting the children to bed.

Insight

Don't express your concessions as a sort of ultimatum. In other words, don't say that you'll 'only' do your part if the other person does something else. That's not assertive. It's downright provocative. The other person may well become angry and less likely to agree. Instead, as in the examples above, use the word 'supposing' or phrases such as:

▶ *Can I suggest ...?*
▶ *What do you think of ...?*
▶ *I'm wondering if ...?*

ARGUING WHEN THERE'S NO NEED

Most of us like to 'win' arguments. And it's not just a question of getting the desired outcome. Once the blood is up we want the other person to acknowledge that we're right and they're wrong. In fact, it's possible to get so charged up that we carry on arguing even when there's nothing to be gained from it.

So it's sometimes a good idea to step back from an argument and do a 'reality check'. It's what professional negotiators sometimes call a 'cooling off period'. Ask yourself:

- ▶ *What am I hoping to gain?*
- ▶ *Am I only arguing to bolster my own ego?*
- ▶ *Am I giving proper consideration to the opposing arguments?*
- ▶ *Is continuing the argument now going to achieve anything?*
- ▶ *Would it be more productive to discuss this again later?*

Once you've done that, ask yourself the same questions regarding the other person. If you think the other person is just arguing for the sake of it then a cooling-off period is essential. You could suggest this by saying one of the following:

- ▶ *I think we're generating more heat than light. Can we talk about this again tomorrow?*
- ▶ *I think we both need time to think this through. Shall we discuss it again tomorrow?*
- ▶ *You've really opened my eyes and I'm going to need time to take in these new ideas. Let's return to this subject tomorrow.*

LEARNING TO AGREE

One way of ending a dispute – the way most of us hope to – is by winning it. But there is another way. And that's by losing it. Just think about it for a minute. If you come to agree with the other person's point of view there's no longer any disagreement. End of problem.

I can already hear your objections. How, you ask, can that be assertive? What will that do for my self-confidence? But let's just carry on this line of thought for a moment. Let's assume the other person sincerely believes in their point of view. Let's suppose they're normally reasonable, intelligent human beings. That should tell you something. What? That there's probably some validity to what they have to say.

So your first step is to try to agree. Now, since you're reading this book, you're probably objecting that you usually do 'give in' anyway. And that you want to stop.

But there's a world of difference between 'giving in' when you think you're right and, on the other hand, coming to understand and accept the other person's point of view. It requires considerable strength to be able to say, 'You're right'. In fact, it's a sign of weakness not strength to try to bulldoze other people's opinions out of the way. It's what people try to do when they know their arguments don't stand up to scrutiny.

So your first step is to try to find things to agree with. Of course, the other person may be wrong or in the wrong or may be making a suggestion you won't like. But don't begin the process by making that prejudgement.

Consider these questions for example:

▶ *Will you invest in my business venture?*
▶ *Will you accept the job I'm offering you if it means moving abroad?*
▶ *Will you marry me?*
▶ *Shall we have children together?*

Anyone who answers 'yes' is assuming a degree of risk that calls for a good measure of confidence. It's strange, then, that 'yes' has such a bad reputation when it comes to assertiveness. Answering 'yes' to those and many other questions isn't for the faint-hearted.

What is it about 'yes' that unnerves such a lot of people? Well, clearly, 'no' is the safe option. When you say 'no' you can usually predict the outcome with certainty. 'No' means that everything stays as it is. 'Yes' is the unsafe option. When you say 'yes' you embark on a journey whose outcome is unknown.

Insight

Of course, we have to get this business of 'no' and 'yes' into perspective. There are many things to which we must say 'no'. But some people say 'no' to almost anything that's new. They say 'no' to whatever threatens to disturb their routine and their security, 'no' to new ideas, 'no' to new situations. The fact is that lots of people say 'no' but regret it afterwards. If that sounds like you then you need to learn to say 'yes' just as much as you need to learn to say 'no.'

PRACTICAL EXERCISE

Next time you're in disagreement with somebody:

1 *Say nothing contradictory.*
2 *Instead say something like: 'That's an interesting point. Let's examine it for a moment.'*
3 *Try to find as many things to agree with as possible.*
4 *Only when you've done that should you then raise your objections.*

Here, to get you started, are some statements you may initially disagree with. If you do, try nevertheless to find five reasons for agreeing.

▶ *George Bush accomplished some good things while President of the United States of America.*
▶ *Most terrorists think their actions will make the world a better place.*
▶ *Native peoples all over the world should have their lands restored to them.*
▶ *There can be bigger differences between two women than between a woman and a man.*
▶ *The reason so many people are poor is that society doesn't reward them fairly for the work they do.*

TIME FOR CHANGE

Human beings generally find it very difficult to admit they were wrong about something (even to themselves) and even harder to change their minds. You only have to listen to politicians in the Houses of Parliament or in Congress to know that. You won't very often hear one of them say: 'Your speech has made me realize I was completely wrong.' That's rare.

In fact, very few of us are capable of making what you might call a quantum leap. That is, a dramatic change of view. A U-turn, if you like. We change our opinions by degrees, not all at one go. It takes time.

So when you have a disagreement about something it's way too optimistic to imagine, that just because you've put forward some compelling arguments, the other person is going to experience a change of heart then and there. The best you can hope for is that you've planted a seed.

Planting a seed
Do what farmers do. They don't start out with a finished product. They plant a seed and leave it to grow. But even before they do that they first have to prepare the ground. You should do the same.

I know that can sound a bit manipulative. But it isn't at all, really. It's just a question of being realistic and acknowledging how the human mind works.

Preparing the ground means making it more likely that people will come to the conclusion you want rather than you telling them what conclusion to draw. In other words, don't say: 'You should decide on the following course of action and here are the facts to support that.' Instead, say: 'Here are the facts.' Then let them draw their own conclusion.

If you present the right facts in the right way people will probably even get ahead of you. That's perfect. Because when people decide things for themselves, their commitment to the ideas tends to be stronger. It becomes, in fact, their idea as much as your idea. If it's only your idea, it's more easily jettisoned if someone else comes along with a different idea.

IN FACT, PLANT SEVERAL SEEDS

As every farmer or gardener knows, only a proportion of seeds ever become mature plants. Some don't germinate. Some get eaten. And of those that do germinate, many of the plants will die for various reasons. There's really no point in fretting over it. That's just how things are. You can never achieve 100 per cent success. The only solution is to sow more seeds than the number of plants wanted.

You, too, need to plant extra seeds. In other words, don't just apply for one job and then feel despondent if you don't get it. That would be aiming for 100 per cent success. It's unrealistic. You're setting yourself up for a severe blow to your self-confidence. Be more like the farmer. Apply for ten jobs. Then you only need a success rate of 10 per cent. Or 100 jobs. Then you only need a success rate of 1 per cent.

Now water the plant

Things are moving. But they're still a long way from where you want to be. So now you water the plant. Create the conditions for growth. In other words, once you've planted the seed you have to let the idea grow day by day. Just as a plant may take weeks or even years to reach its full size, so it will take time for your idea to be fully accepted.

Let's say you want to persuade your partner to move abroad to start a new life in the sun but you already know he or she has no such thoughts. So you plant the seed and then you water it, week by week, until maturity.

The stages might go something like this:

- ► *Week 1: It's nice here but there are a few drawbacks.*
- ► *Week 2: Do you think we could afford a bigger house if we moved to a cheaper area?*
- ► *Week 3: I've just been reading that property prices are much lower in Spain.*
- ► *Week 4: Don't you find the British winter depressing?*
- ► *Week 5: We could easily get work in Spain.*

Don't take that as the exact blueprint to follow. It's just to give an idea of how a concept can be nudged along. Don't be too heavy-handed. If someone thinks they're being 'got at', then, of course, it won't work. And if someone is already very sensitive about an issue, go all the more carefully.

Insight

Notice that some of the ideas are phrased as questions. I find that questions get other people thinking and provoke less resistance. Then they may come up with their own versions of your idea.

ADVANCED TECHNIQUES

Just as a farmer uses fertilizer so there are a few special techniques you can also employ to improve your chances of success. Getting other people to develop variations on your proposal is one of them.

People prefer their own ideas

We all prefer our own ideas. That's normal. So if you let other people think your ideas actually are their ideas, you'll do better. Don't be too possessive about them. You're interested in the end result. When other people take over your ideas be glad. Congratulate them on coming up with such brilliant solutions.

▶ *The 'seeding' technique will often lead to people taking over your ideas.*

Similarly, it can be a good tactic to accept variations on your ideas. If you do, you've undoubtedly got the other people hooked. They've now got an 'investment' in the project. They've contributed an idea and they'll want to see it succeed. If no variations are forthcoming, you could fish for them like this:

▶ *I don't quite see the solution to this ...*

The other person may then come up with a suggestion. With luck it will be more or less the course of action you'd already decided upon. But rather than you imposing it, you've allowed the other person to become a part of the concept.

If it's not quite the solution you favour then you could try nudging it in the right direction:

▶ *That's a really great idea. I'm just wondering if there's a way of ...*

Insight
If you're bothered that all this may sound a little devious, think of it simply as working with human nature rather than against it.

The politicians' trick
This next one really is a bit tricky. Politicians are masters of it. They let it 'leak' in some way that a certain very severe policy is under consideration. Let's say, for example, that a 5 per cent increase in the rate of a certain tax is considered essential. The politicians know it would be hugely unpopular. So what do they do? They 'leak' that a 10 per cent increase is under consideration. When the 5 per cent plan is actually announced, instead of being angry everyone is relieved because it's less than they'd feared.

The Muhammad Ali trick
When Muhammad Ali, the three-time World Heavyweight Champion, was up against the immensely powerful George Foreman in the famous 'Rumble in the Jungle' he used a tactic he later called 'rope-a-dope'. He lay back against the ropes, covered up and let Foreman punch himself out. When Foreman was exhausted Ali launched his real attack. Again it's a device frequently used by politicians. They announce an unpopular project. Opposition mounts. The politicians announce the plan is being dropped. And then, when the protesters have packed up and gone home, they introduce a variation to the original

plan, knowing the opposition will be too exhausted to do anything further.

PRACTICAL EXERCISE
1 *Think of six ideas about which you wish to persuade other people.*
2 *Set yourself a realistic timescale – don't be impatient.*
3 *Prepare the ground.*
4 *Plant the seeds.*
5 *Water them.*
6 *If one of your seeds grows to fruition, consider that a success.*

THE NLP 'MILTON MODEL'

In the early days of their collaboration on Neuro-Linguistic Programming (NLP), Richard Bandler and John Grinder studied – or, as they called it 'modelled' – the techniques of America's most famous hypnotherapist, Milton H. Erickson. As a result they developed what they called the 'Milton Model' – a method for being more persuasive, changing people's minds and getting them to do what you want.

Erickson believed that the unconscious mind was always alert and therefore always accessible but that it couldn't be given direct instructions. That's why simply telling someone what to think or do is often completely ineffective. Instead, he would be deliberately vague – 'artfully vague' Bandler and Grinder called it – so his clients would have to *think*. People who have to work things out for themselves:

▶ *remember better than when someone else tells them*
▶ *believe in their conclusions more than in those they are told*
▶ *prefer the ideas that result over other people's, because they are their own*
▶ *use a so-called transderivational search (TDS) of the unconscious mind, which can result in changes at a deep level*
▶ *are distracted while they're thinking, which can be an opportunity to plant a suggestion in the unconscious mind.*

If you're a very direct sort of person you may find it hard to adopt the Milton Model. Indeed, there are times when precision – the very opposite of the Milton Model – is essential. But we're not concerned here with something like flying an aeroplane. We're talking about changing the way people think and feel. That change comes about more easily when people do it for themselves *from within*. Your role, then, is to prompt them into beginning that process. By making vague, confusing and ambiguous statements you force people to use their own minds to unravel the meaning. That process of discovery means that the ideas they develop are perceived as their own. And because the ideas are 'their own' they obviously cause no resistance. Here, then, are some of Erickson's little 'tricks':

Using questions

Rather than giving instructions, which might meet with resistance, you can often get a better result by asking a question. For example, you might ask, 'How far are you willing to go?' By posing that question you make it harder for the other person to say anything less than 'all the way'. And once they've said 'all the way' then they're committed.

The power of questions was vividly illustrated in an experiment (Barber, Dalai and Calverley 1968) in which people who had been hypnotized were later asked one of two things. Of those asked 'Did you experience the hypnotic state as basically *similar* to the waking state?' 83 per cent said they did. But of those asked 'Did you experience the hypnotic state as basically *different* to the waking state?' 72 per cent said *they* did. In other words, merely posing the question changed people's perceptions of their experiences.

PRACTICAL EXERCISE
See if you can find a way of rephrasing this instruction as a question that, in the face of resistance, might have a better chance of getting the result you want:

▶ *Give up smoking.*

Don't look at the next bit until you've come up with at least one question. Okay? Well, you could ask something like: 'Do you think it's possible for a strong-willed person to give up smoking just like that?' Or: 'How much better do you think you would you feel if you gave up smoking?' Or: 'What would you do with the extra 21 years of life that half of all smokers miss out on?'

No one is suggesting that the asking of such questions will immediately make anyone give up smoking, but the ideas planted will continue to work on the unconscious in a way that direct instructions do not.

Using negatives

When people are feeling negative about something it's important for rapport to show that you understand their feelings:

- ▶ *I understand how you feel.*
- ▶ *Everyone finds it difficult the first time.*

In fact, you can simply repeat back to people the negative things they've said. 'So you're saying you feel you're not ready to take this step ...' You can then overcome resistance by using more negatives to discharge their feelings. For example, you might say: 'You won't have to sign anything until you're quite sure.'

PRACTICAL EXERCISE

Cover up my suggestions below and see if you can come up with a 'discharging negative' for:

1 *someone who doesn't want to go on*
2 *someone who is wavering over a decision*
3 *someone who doesn't know who to vote for.*

Well, you could simply say:

- ▶ *You don't have to continue if you're not enjoying it.*
- ▶ *You don't have to make a decision until you're completely convinced.*

▶ *You shouldn't vote for my candidate until you've fully examined her record.*

Cause and effect

We're all used to statements which link a cause and an effect. You might say, for example, 'Prices are going up next month so it would be a good idea to order now.' In fact, we're so used to them that any compound statement that begins with something obviously true tends to make us feel that the second part will also be right. The truth of the first part rubs off on the second.

A variation is what's known as 'implication' using an 'if' construction:

▶ *If you want a great weight lifted from your shoulders, you should sign this.*

Most people would, indeed, want a weight lifted and be inclined to sign.

PRACTICAL EXERCISE

See if you can create some compound statements for the following circumstances. Remember, the first part of your sentence has to be something that's obviously right. The second part – your real aim – should appear to be a logical consequence, even though it may not be.

1 *You want someone to donate money to charity.*
2 *You would like a raise at work.*
3 *You want someone to accept a lower price for something.*

Pacing and leading

Pacing and leading together form a powerful technique in hypnosis but can also be used effectively on people in their normal waking state. Essentially, you feed their experience back to them (pacing) and once you've established rapport you then guide them in the direction you want to go (leading). If you watch mentalists like Derren Brown and hypnotists like Paul McKenna on TV or YouTube you'll see them using this technique a lot.

Pacing can be:

- ▶ *physical – you match the other person's posture, mannerisms, tone of voice, breathing and so on*
- ▶ *verbal – you tell the other person the things they're experiencing at that moment.*

This pacing not only creates rapport but it also establishes a positive momentum which the other person may find hard to resist. Let's hear a good salesman in action: 'You have a very nice car there. It's a recent model with only 20,000 miles on the clock and silver is a popular colour so in part-exchange I can offer you ...' The customer knows everything the salesman has said is true. It *is* a nice car, it *is* a recent model, it *is* low mileage and it *is* silver. So when the salesman makes a low offer the customer, carried along by the momentum, is inclined to accept.

PRACTICAL EXERCISE
Today, try feeding people's experiences back to them before going on to make a request and see if it makes a difference. (Top tip: don't make it too obvious.)

Presuppositions and binds
The idea of presuppositions and binds is to make it necessary for the other person to summon up a certain strength of will to resist you. If they don't have that mental strength then you will persuade them.

Let's look at some simple presuppositions:

- ▶ *Would you like to pay by credit card?*
- ▶ *You've definitely chosen the best one.*
- ▶ *You're so right to go for the pink.*

If these are said *before* any buying decision has actually been made, then they have the effect of bumping the customer into doing what you want. Essentially, you're *presupposing* that they've decided to buy and they now have to actively resist you if they want to get out of the purchase. Now let's have a look at something more sophisticated:

▶ *Would you like to do this now or would you like to do it in an hour?*

This presupposes that the person would like to do it *at all*. He or she now has to, as it were, overturn the presumption ('Neither') or opt for one of them. For that reason, this type of presumption is also known as a 'bind' because it puts the other person in the artificial position of having to choose between two things when, in reality, the range of choices may be much larger. Quite often, the other person won't even notice that their options have been restricted.

▶ *We're going to have to choose between two courses of action.*

This presupposes that there *are* only two possibilities (both of which are favourable to you) and tends to prevent anyone coming up with a third or fourth (that might not be favourable to you).

▶ *You've done incredibly well, so you're not going to have any problem with the next step.*

This presupposes the person has already agreed to the next step.

Stories and quotes
It was probably his use of stories that was Erickson's most distinctive skill. Rather than say, 'Do this' or 'Don't do that' (although he was also quite capable of giving orders when appropriate) Erickson would instead relay an anecdote that would go directly to the unconscious and bypass the resistance of the conscious mind.

Suitable stories:

▶ *entertain and capture the other person's attention*
▶ *bypass resistance because they are non-threatening*

- ▶ *allow the other person to deduce the meaning*
- ▶ *carry on 'working' indefinitely*
- ▶ *are less likely to be forgotten than straightforward statements.*

If you've always been a fairly direct person then, initially, you'll struggle to come up with anecdotes that suit the circumstances. But if you work at it then over time you can build up your own personal 'library' and have an anecdote for every occasion. It will help if you think in terms of universal experiences, which could apply to just about everybody.

Let's look at a practical application. Your teenage son won't study. So you concoct a little story which you tell to your partner, knowing that your difficult teenager is within hearing. 'I bumped into Joe Brown today. He's really concerned about his son Harry because, apparently he's a magnet for the girls. It seems they all want to go out with someone who's got good prospects. He gets top marks in everything and the girls like that …' And so on. You could lower your voice now and then to make it clear you don't want to be overheard. The unconscious usually pays attention to lowered voices.

Insight
In dealing with a situation in which resistance is almost inevitable (for example, when talking to your own children) it's generally better not to make yourself the subject of the story, but to talk about someone else. It can help to use quotes. For example you might say 'A very wealthy man once told me, "Money never made me happier …"'.

If you're not convinced by the power of stories, think back to the things that have shaped your own outlook. What about the story of Robin Hood, for example, who stole from the rich to give to the poor? Did that mould your views in any way? Or maybe real-life stories of heroism or success or sacrifice? And, of course, the parables told by Jesus have had an immense effect on Western culture.

Phrasing

The pace at which you speak and the way you separate groups of words by pauses are crucial to your powers of persuasion. Most of us speak too quickly. If you think of the politicians whose words you give weight to (even if you don't necessarily agree) they'll probably be people who speak slowly and use plenty of pauses. Barack Obama immediately comes to mind. Long pauses are a signal of dominance. And words delivered slowly give the impression of being well-considered and important, even if they're not. But there's another aspect to phrasing and that's its hypnotic effect. When you're up close to someone, attuning your speech to the rhythm of their breathing can be very powerful.

Compare this sentence with the first sentence of the above paragraph, for example:

▶ *The pace ... at which you speak ... and the way ... you separate ... groups of words ... by pauses ... are crucial ... to your powers ... of persuasion.*

Do you see the difference?

PRACTICAL EXERCISE
Ask a friend to help you. Try speaking to him or her in this new way. And ask your friend to speak to you in the same way. Then discuss the effects.

Using amnesia

Amnesia is a rather frightening word but, in fact, it simply means a loss of memory. Most people associate it with the word 'total' which, fortunately, is rare. Partial amnesia, on the other hand, is common and can work to your advantage when, for example, you don't want someone to think things over in case they change their mind or develop a resistance later.

Here, then, is a way of encouraging partial amnesia. Change the subject the *instant* you've planted your idea and then talk about the new subject quickly, at length and in detail. The planted idea will remain in the unconscious but may be forgotten by the conscious mind.

HOW TO COMPLAIN

'Complain' sounds such a belligerent sort of word. So it's not surprising that millions of us are reluctant to have anything to do with it. One dictionary definition is 'to express resentment, displeasure, etc'.

In fact, it's not necessary to be aggressive in order to complain. Nor is it even necessary to express displeasure. All you have to be is assertive – which, as we've seen is not the same thing at all.

Quite often, probably in the vast majority of cases, people will be only too happy to put things right on the merest mention from you that something is wrong. Very likely they'll be embarrassed about it and anxious to make you happy.

Let's face it. We all make mistakes. And that includes you. Now, it might seem strange that, when I'm supposed to be giving you the confidence to complain, I'm undermining your resolve by pointing out that you, too, make mistakes. But that's exactly the point. I'm trying to get you to see that complaining should be an everyday sort of thing. Making mistakes is normal. Correcting mistakes is normal. It doesn't have to be a big drama. So, initially, just draw attention to the problem in a low-key, unaggressive, discreet sort of way.

Getting ready to complain
The first thing is not to build the situation up in your mind. Just look upon it as providing information. Sometimes you provide people with information about the weather, sometimes about how to get somewhere. In this case, you'll be providing information about a product or service that wasn't as it should have been.

If you're nervous about it, enlist the help of your unconscious, as described in Chapter 2. The night before, as you're laying in bed, you can prime your unconscious by thinking something like this:

▶ *Everyone is entitled to goods that work properly. Tomorrow I shall return to the shop. I will be composed, relaxed and friendly. I will ask for the item to be replaced and it will be replaced.*

You can reinforce that with visualization:

▶ *See yourself strolling calmly to the shop. See yourself catching the eye of a sales assistant and explaining the problem. See the assistant immediately apologizing and replacing the item for you. See yourself leaving the shop with the new item, smiling happily.*

Insight

Here's the usual warning: Don't allow any negative images to enter your visualization. Don't start thinking 'Yes, but supposing …'. If you visualize anything negative you'll create the opposite effect to the one you want and make yourself tense.

If you know the situation is going to be challenging, because of things that have already been said, you may want to employ some additional techniques to prepare yourself mentally. If appropriate, try:

▶ *going for a brisk walk beforehand to calm yourself down*
▶ *going through your exercise routine beforehand to give your spirits a lift*
▶ *listening to some music that inspires you.*

You might also like to have a go at role-playing (also in Chapter 2). Whether you do it with a friend, or just in your own mind, make a note of all your best arguments as you come up with them, so you can use them in the real situation.

In simple cases the three-step formula can be reduced to just two steps:

1 *Excuse me. My soup is cold.*
2 *Please can you have it heated up for me.*

A perfectly reasonable request which will undoubtedly be met. However, if you encounter resistance, or the situation is a little more involved, you may need the full three-step formula:

1 *I realize you've worked hard to try to correct the problem.*
2 *However, the gearbox still isn't functioning as it should.*
3 *I'm therefore asking you to replace the entire gearbox under guarantee.*

Here's the beginning of a role-play to get you started:

YOU (playing yourself): Who am I speaking to?

CLERK (played by your friend): Melanie Brown.

YOU: Melanie, I have a problem. This electricity bill is about ten times higher than it should be.

CLERK: That's not possible.

YOU: I'm sure you'd normally be right to say that. However, mistakes sometimes do happen in the best of organizations. Please could you look into it for me?

CLERK: I think you'll find you've just used far more electricity than you thought.

YOU: I can see why you might think that. However, I've been living in the same apartment for three years and all my previous bills have been a tenth of this one. I'm wondering if there's any procedure for checking this.

CLERK: Probably the earlier bills were just estimates.

YOU: If they had been estimates that would be a possible explanation. However …

Now you adapt the scenario to suit your circumstances and carry on with it for a couple of minutes.

Insight

When complaining:

▶ *Have a clear idea of what you want to achieve.*
▶ *Make notes of the points you wish to make and tick them off as you go.*
▶ *Make sure you're complaining to the right person.*
▶ *Don't be abusive or aggressive.*
▶ *Keep the emotional temperature down.*
▶ *Never say 'I don't know anything about this, but …'. (You're just making it too easy for the other side to bamboozle you.)*

Complaining to large organizations

Many large organizations have whole departments to deal with complaints where staff are specially trained and there are clear but rigid procedures. Initially, the best thing is to be empathetic and polite and to work within their rules. Neither exaggerate nor minimize the situation but provide clear and precise details so the other person can make an accurate assessment.

In all probability, the complaints staff will have different levels of remedy at their disposal. Naturally, they'll begin with the one that costs the company the least. They'll not get promoted for giving away too much of the company's money (and probably have a target time for dealing with each customer, which may make them brusque). But if you're persistent they'll eventually increase their offer up to the highest level.

And that's as far as you can get without a lot of aggravation. You see, the complaints staff are not usually empowered to deviate from those standard procedures, no matter how loudly you shout. Indeed, shouting will only give the other person the excuse to terminate the conversation. It's a frustrating situation all round. The staff in the complaints department are abused for things for which they have no responsibility at all. It's a stressful job for which they're probably not paid enough. Meanwhile you're prevented from speaking to the person who actually is responsible.

Insight

When complaining over the telephone or in person, always make a note of the time and date, the name of the person you're speaking to and the details of any offer made to you. This information may be useful in later negotiations and possibly crucial if the dispute goes to court. If the matter is especially contentious, send the other side a letter or email setting out what's been said – and ask for its receipt to be acknowledged.

If you can't get satisfaction by telephone, letter or email and the organization isn't far away, it may help to make a personal visit. It isn't good public relations to have someone complaining on the premises – but make sure you don't do anything against the law or open yourself up to a charge of slander. Just stick with the assertive but non-aggressive techniques that you've learned. Ask someone to come with you as a witness and take notes.

A CAUTIONARY TALE

Mrs L was astonished one day to see a strange man looking at the cars in her driveway. Naturally, she went out to ask him what he was doing. He explained that he was going to take one of the cars away under a court order. Mrs L was apoplectic. It all had to do with a dispute with a large organization over a mistaken bill. The organization had verbally accepted several weeks earlier that they'd got it wrong. But no one had told the legal department. The moral: Always get it in writing.

IS IT WORTH IT?

At some point you have to decide whether it's worth carrying on. If a utility company has got a decimal point in the wrong place and sent you a bill ten times higher than it should be, then you have no option. But in many other cases you may decide 'life's too short'. That's okay. That's a perfectly rational and sensible decision in many cases.

Here's why:

▶ *Disputes played out in court can be highly costly both in terms of money and stress.*

The fact is that lawyers are expensive and court costs could be ruinous. It's just uneconomic to employ a lawyer in a dispute involving small sums of money. You can represent yourself in court but the stress factor remains.

Relationships and marriages have been destroyed by the pressure of long-running disputes. Backing away from a court case does not mean you're lacking in confidence or are weak. Draw a line down a sheet of paper. On one side put all the benefits of winning your case. On the other side list all the possible drawbacks of the litigation. Weigh the two sides up very carefully.

Insight

If you decide not to proceed just put the whole episode down to experience. Experience sometimes costs money. Then close your mind to the whole affair and put it behind you.

10 THINGS TO REMEMBER

1 *The three-step formula will help you behave in a way that's assertive without being aggressive – use 'however' rather than 'but'.*

2 *After turning down a request, behave normally.*

3 *Difficulty with saying 'no' may indicate a contradictory unconscious desire.*

4 *Cognitive therapy, visualization and self-hypnosis can all be used to help you overcome doubts and be more assertive.*

5 *Being assertive doesn't mean you getting everything you want and other people getting nothing – it's wise to make concessions that avoid feelings of resentment and, thereby, problems in the future.*

6 *If either you or other people are arguing just for the sake of it, ask for a 'cooling off' period.*

7 *Don't be afraid to agree with other people if you realize they're right – 'yes' can sometimes be as assertive as 'no'.*

8 *It takes time for people to change their minds so 'seed' your ideas early and give them time to grow, even letting other people think your ideas are their ideas.*

9 *Many techniques from hypnotherapy, such as binds and pacing/leading can be used in everyday life.*

10 *Don't be intimidated by the idea of complaining or standing up for your rights – but it's not weak to decide that 'life's too short' for a big 'battle'.*

HOW CONFIDENT ARE YOU NOW?

▶ *Have you used the 'three-step formula' in real life?*
▶ *Have you been able to say 'no' in the kind of situation in which you'd previously felt intimidated into saying 'yes'?*
▶ *Have you genuinely worked through some role-playing as suggested in this chapter?*
▶ *Have you employed the 'two-column' cognitive therapy technique to eradicate negative thoughts?*
▶ *Have you employed visualization or self-hypnosis to become more assertive?*
▶ *Have you made a concession in a real-life situation to achieve a greater goal?*
▶ *Have you given up arguing for the sake of it and been willing to change your mind after hearing a genuinely persuasive argument?*
▶ *Have you used the NLP Milton Model to help you get what you want?*
▶ *Have you planted seeds ... and watered them?*
▶ *Have you complained about something in real life in a way that was assertive but not aggressive?*

Score:

If you answered 'yes' to most questions, then you've obviously succeeded in becoming assertive. Go straight on to the next chapter.

If you answered 'yes' to between five and seven questions, then you can also go on to the next chapter but revisit this one from time to time and think about the issues it raises.

If you could answer 'yes' to only four questions or fewer, then you're obviously struggling to assert yourself. Keep working on the practical exercises in this chapter until you raise your score to five or higher, and only then read on.

If you're afraid of it, do it

In this chapter you will learn:
- *how to take control of your imagination*
- *techniques for cutting your fears down to size*
- *why you need to challenge yourself – just a little*

> *Do the thing you are afraid to do, and the death of fear is certain.*
>
> Ralph Waldo Emerson

That's very good advice from the nineteenth-century American poet. But, unfortunately, it doesn't tell you how. After all, if you could do the thing you're afraid of, you probably would. Luckily, I can tell you. Just read on.

When we're afraid of something most of us steer well clear of it. Sounds pretty sensible. After all, that's what fear exists for. To keep us out of trouble.

But sometimes the fear mechanism goes wrong. In fact, all of us are capable of feeling frightened when there's no real danger at all. Just think of the reaction to horror movies and thrillers. We know it's just a film. We know the nasty man can't climb out of the screen and get us. But we can't easily control our imaginations.

Even when fear is appropriate, it's a mistake to see it as a kind of policeman holding up a big No Entry sign. Fear can also be a warning sign saying merely Proceed With Caution. If your reaction to fear is always to turn back, then you're never going to learn anything and you're never going to grow. You're also going to miss out on an awful lot.

Developing self-confidence is all about learning to:

> ▶ *Overcome situations in which you feel anxious or afraid.*

It's obvious when you think about it. If you're scared of that dark cupboard under the stairs and you never go in it, then you're going to be afraid of it for the rest of your life. Go in the cupboard and you slay your fear.

Here we're not so much concerned with cupboards as with things like initiating a conversation with strangers, getting onto the dance floor at a party, contributing suggestions at a business meeting, or having the confidence to take some of those bold steps in life like getting married and becoming a parent.

THE THREE-STEP PLAN

The fact that horror films can make people scared should give you a clue. Our fears are so often caused by our imaginations. And our imaginations have no limits. In our imaginations we can fly like Superman, be looked up to by everyone we meet and be successful in everything we do. We can also fall from the highest building, be booed off the podium, and fail abjectly as partners, parents and everything else.

So overcoming anxieties and gaining self-confidence means taking control of the twilight world of the imagination.

Step 1 Change the name, reduce the fear

There was a blue on blue incident yesterday and a couple of guys bought the farm. Doesn't sound too serious, does it? Even if you know that 'blue on blue' is a euphemism for being shot by your own side and 'bought the farm' means to be killed.

You see, it's one of the quirks of the human mind that changing the language we use to think about or talk about something can actually change our attitudes.

Euphemisms can certainly add a lot of colour and humour to language, but there is another far more important reason that's connected with fear. It's this. When you substitute a euphemism for the name of something that frightens you, so you also reduce its power. Think about these words and phrases for example:

Normal term	Euphemism
Accidental killing	Collateral damage
Bottom	Derrière
Dead	Fallen off the twig
Drunk	Merry
Old	Mature
Pornography	Adult entertainment
Second-hand	Pre-owned

There's an astonishing mental trick here. The normal word and the euphemism mean exactly the same thing. And yet, somehow, the euphemism softens the impact. Falling off a twig sounds almost charming.

You can use exactly the same mental sleight of hand when dealing with situations in which you lack confidence. Let's say you have to give a speech and the whole idea unnerves you. Well, instead, how about calling it a 'chat'? Does that seem less threatening? Or how about a 'prattle'? Or a 'jabber'?

Below, as an exercise, I suggest you invent your own euphemisms. It might seem silly but it definitely helps.

PRACTICAL EXERCISE

Draw a line down the middle of a sheet of paper. On the left-hand side head it up 'Situations in which I lack confidence'. On the right-hand side head it up 'Euphemisms'. For example, instead of 'asking a girl for a date' you could substitute 'talking to a girl about the weather'. That sounds a lot less daunting. Now you invent your own euphemisms – anything you like that makes you feel more relaxed. Once you've prepared your list, always use your euphemisms whenever you're thinking about or talking about one of the situations that makes you anxious.

Step 2 Imagining a different outcome

When we're disproportionately afraid of things it's partly because we imagine a terrible outcome. When we go up somewhere high we imagine falling off and going splat. When we get on a plane we imagine it crashing. When we want to talk to an attractive man or woman we imagine them treating us with disdain. When we have to give a speech we imagine the audience yawning.

But if we can imagine those things, we can equally imagine completely different outcomes. Nicer outcomes. Quite frankly, far more realistic outcomes. How often do people accidentally fall from high places? Very seldom. Of all the flights taking place all over the world every year, what percentage end in crashes? The number is so small it's practically zero. How often does a woman, or man, respond to a pleasant invitation with a show of disdain? Rarely. And what's the actual likelihood of your speech being met by a show of boredom? It's just not going to happen.

So why not rewrite those scripts you've implanted in your head and replace them with more positive ones?

PRACTICAL EXERCISE
Write down a situation in which you lack confidence. Then answer the following two questions:

▶ *Is the outcome I'm imagining really very likely to happen?*
▶ *What is a more likely outcome?*

Stop thinking of the unrealistic negative outcome and imagine the realistic, positive one instead. For example, let's suppose you're anxious about meeting your future father-in-law. You imagine falling up the steps, spilling your coffee over the carpet and being thought entirely unsuitable. But how often do you fall up steps? Or spill coffee on the carpet? And why should you be thought unsuitable? There's really no basis to any of it. It's far, far more likely everything will go perfectly well. So erase that ridiculous old film from your mind and replace it with the new one. Keep playing the new one and never give the old one a screening ever again.

Step 3 Gradual exposure

Let's take a fear of heights as an example, because it makes the whole process of gradual exposure very easy to understand. But the principle can apply to just about any fear.

Everybody is 'afraid' of heights in the sense of understanding that to fall from a great height would be a lethal experience. But for some people it goes far beyond that. They're overcome by fear at the idea of dining at, say, the rooftop terrace of a tall building. The logical part of the brain knows there's no real danger whatsoever and yet they're still terrified. Does that sound like you in any way?

Gradual exposure is the solution. But before you can implement it you first need to learn a particular skill – the skill of relaxation. I'm not talking about knowing how to lie on a sofa. I mean, deliberately taking control of your body and calming it down whenever you're facing a stressful situation.

Here are some exercises you'll need to master before administering the 'fear vaccine'.

PRACTICAL RELAXATION EXERCISES

Breathing leads the body and the mind. Which means that if you can only learn to harness your breathing, you have a physical way of taking control of your mind.

1 *Rapid breathing is associated with agitation. If you can just slow your breathing down then you'll also calm down. Here's the key:*
   ▷ *You must breathe out for longer than you breathe in.*

A ratio of about 7:11 has been found to be effective. That's to say, breathe in while slowly counting to seven and breathe out while slowly counting to eleven. Keep that up for as long as you need to, getting slower and slower. It will help enormously if you can close your eyes. At the same time, touching the tips of your fingers together in a 'steeple' will reinforce the feeling of calm. As an added refinement you can hold your 'steepled' hands over your navel and feel your belly going slowly up and down. Test it for yourself the next time you're at the dentist.

2 *You can use the first technique just about anywhere. But this one might get you some strange glances if you do it in a public place. You're going to play with a balloon. Not only that, it's an invisible balloon! It's best done sitting upright. Hold your hands out about six inches in front of your mouth, six inches apart and slightly curved. Now breathe out through your mouth and let your hands move apart as if the invisible balloon is inflating. Don't force the breath, as you'd have to for a real balloon. This one just requires a steady, gentle exhalation. Then breathe in through your mouth and let your hands come back to the starting place. Keep that up for a couple of minutes, your hands coming closer and closer each time. Finally, let your hands touch. That's the first stage. The second stage is to keep your hands together and your eyes closed, as if praying. Now breathe slowly in and out through your nose. As you breathe in, imagine that you're sucking energy (what the Japanese call ki) up through your fingertips, and as you breathe out imagine the energy is discharging from your fingertips. Some people find it helps to think of the ki as water being sucked up through the fingertips into the body and then spurting out like a fountain. Others envisage ki as sparks. When you've done all that for a few minutes you should feel relaxed but also energized.*

3 *If you ever suffer from panic attacks in which you breathe rapidly and feel faint, here's an emergency method for getting them under control. Have a paper bag with you and when an attack comes on hold it over your nose and mouth so that you're rebreathing your own breath. How does it work?*

It increases the carbon dioxide content of the air you're breathing in, thus countering the effects of anxiety-induced hyperventilation.

Insight

When you breathe faster and deeper than necessary (hyperventilation) you not only flush out carbon dioxide but reduce the level of carbonic acid in the blood (the form in which carbon dioxide is carried). That in turn means the blood becomes less acid. When the blood is less acid (more alkaline) the blood vessels in the brain (and elsewhere) constrict, thus reducing the blood flow. As a result you feel lightheaded and, in an extreme case, you might faint.

THE FEAR VACCINE

The principle of gradual exposure is very simple to understand. It works a little like a vaccination. When you're vaccinated you receive a weakened version of the microorganism that threatens you. You then develop a resistance. Gradual exposure works the same way. Before you expose yourself to the full strength of a situation in which you lack self-confidence, you first experience a similar but far less daunting version. You then wait to develop a 'resistance'. Once you've done that, you have a 'booster' – a slightly stronger dose. Again you wait to develop a 'resistance'. And so it goes on until you're completely immunized against the full-strength situation. The rule is:

▶ *Never go jumping in at the deep end.*

Insight

I can't emphasize this too much. You won't rid yourself of your fears by confronting them head on at full speed. And certainly don't let anybody else 'help' you by 'proving' how groundless your fears are. All any of that will do is confirm to you how right you were in the first place. The word 'gradual' is paramount.

Let's again take a fear of heights. Let's suppose that whenever you have to go to a meeting in a tall building you're so nervous you just can't function properly. But the principles I'll describe can be applied to anything in which you lack self-confidence.

The first 'vaccination' could be to look at pictures in the safety of your own home. Get hold of some of those thrillers that feature the hero or heroine leaping about at the top of a skyscraper. Or maybe a documentary about climbing. Something that has plenty of those vertiginous shots looking down from a great height. The first time you watch you'll no doubt feel a bit dizzy and sick. This is where you use the relaxation techniques described above. Get your breathing under control and remember that you're safe and nothing can possibly happen to you. Then watch the scenes again. And again. And again. Until they have no effect at all.

The next stage would be to tackle a real-life situation. You might, for example, go to a tall building and look out of a first-floor window. If that doesn't bother you, progress to the second floor. If you feel anxious looking out of a second-floor window, stop there and do your relaxation exercises. Once you're comfortable, go down. Next day, return to the second floor. If you're no longer anxious, go up to the third floor. However, if you're still bothered, stay on the second floor and repeat your relaxation routine. And so it goes on. A key point is this:

▶ *Never progress to the next level of exposure until you're completely comfortable at the current level.*

Insight

Whenever you're desensitizing yourself through gradual exposure it helps enormously to have a laugh. Take some friends with you, having first primed them to kid around, tell jokes, tickle you and generally divert your conscious attention from your fears.

PRACTICAL EXERCISE

Draw up a 'gradual exposure' programme for one of your fears. Make sure each step is only a little harder than the previous one. Then go and do it.

How long does it take? As long as it needs to take. It could be a day, a week or a year. Don't set a timetable but do keep up the exposure regularly. Don't get disheartened if you get stuck at a certain level for a while. Be patient with yourself. You'll get there.

USING COGNITIVE THERAPY

By now you should be quite familiar with the principles of cognitive therapy. We've used them several times in this book so far and now we're going to use them again (but if you'd like to refresh your memory turn back to Chapter 1).

When you lack the confidence to do something – when you're afraid, in fact – there are two of those 'cognitive distortions' that you particularly need to work on. They are:

- ▶ *I feel like a failure so I must be a failure.*
- ▶ *I'm a label (weak/nervous/unco-ordinated or whatever).*

Let's say, for example, you have an idea for starting a business. You're convinced it's a good one. But your fears are holding you back. That's why you don't take your business plan to the bank.

Okay, let's get out another of those blank sheets of paper and divide it down the middle. On the left-hand side head it up 'Reasons for not going to the bank' (or whatever it may be in your particular case) and on the right head it up 'Cognitive distortions'.

Reasons for not going to the bank	Cognitive distortions
I've been a failure all my life and always will be so there's really no point in going to the bank.	If I don't go to the bank then, of course, it will be a self-fulfilling prophecy. This is just 'emotional reasoning'. It's only by going to the bank that I can make a success of this.
Yes, but there's no escaping that I'm a failure.	Failure at what? When I analyse it I've succeeded at quite a lot of things. It's true I haven't succeeded in business so far, but that's because I haven't been in business before. I've fallen into the trap of 'labelling' – giving myself a negative label that isn't deserved.

Now go ahead and fill in your own sheet according to your own fears.

Insight

Always keep in mind that when you're anxious about something and when you give yourself the label of 'not good at' something, you don't do it and you don't practise. So you just don't give yourself the chance to become good at it.

USING NLP

Neuro-Linguistic Programming (NLP) has various techniques for dealing with any nervousness, fears and phobias. The first of them is simply to change perspectives.

▶ *First position means visualizing something as seen through your own eyes.*

▶ *Second position means visualizing something through the eyes of any other person present.*

▶ *Third position means visualizing something through the eyes of an uninvolved outsider standing some distance away.*

PRACTICAL EXERCISE

Think of something that makes you anxious. Let's say you have to give a speech before a large audience and you're feeling so intimidated you don't think you can go through with it. I want you to visualize the situation from *multiple perspectives*, moving from *first* to *second* to *third* position, and from *association* to *dissociation*.

1 *Visualize the scene from* first position *(that is, through your own eyes). See the stage lights above you ... the audience out in front of you ... your notes in your hand ... Conjure it all up as vividly as you can. How do you feel? Probably tense.*

2 *Visualize the scene from* second position *(that is, through the eyes of someone in the audience). The scenario is the same but this time go through the whole thing again from this new perspective. Maybe another member of the audience is coughing. Maybe the seat is hard. Maybe it's hot. But the speaker looks fine and you can hear him okay (when that man isn't coughing). How do you, as a member of the audience, feel? Probably okay.*

3 *Visualize the scene from* third position *(that is, through the eyes of a detached observer). The scenario is still the same but this time you're neither giving the speech nor a member of the audience. In fact, you're, say, an usher, watching from a little distance away. You notice that some audience members are paying attention while others are fidgeting and looking around. How does it all strike you now? Probably far from the life-and-death situation that it seemed from the podium.*

When you imagine a scene from first position you're 'associated' and feel everything keenly, but if you switch to second or third position you become 'dissociated' and everything becomes less frightening. We're now going to take that principle and put it to work on a phobia.

The Fast Phobia Technique

This is a technique for dealing with a phobia caused by a specific incident. We're going to be revisiting whatever event it was that caused your phobia in the first place. So this won't work for a fear that developed in a different way. Let's say you had to give a speech at school and all the other children laughed at you. Ever since you've been terrified of public speaking. We're going to visualize this incident but to make sure you don't get upset all over again we're not just going to dissociate, we're going to *double-dissociate* – that is, we're going to go to the position of an outside observer, and then observe that observer.

PRACTICAL EXERCISE

1   *Imagine that you're in a cinema. In this cinema you're going to be in as many as three places at once – appearing in the film, watching it as a customer and working as the projectionist, all at the same time. (That's the wonderful thing about the imagination – you can do anything you like.)*

2   *Be a customer sitting in the cinema, watching a still black and white image of yourself on the screen the moment before you, as a child, had to get up and give that speech.*

3   *Now you're going to become the projectionist sitting in the projection booth. As the projectionist you can now see yourself in the cinema as well as the image on screen.*

4   *Still as the projectionist you run the black and white film of you, as a child, giving your speech. You see everything but it means almost nothing to you because you're just a projectionist, sitting in the safety of your projection booth. When you get to the end of the movie, where the person in the film (you) is 'safe' again, you stop the projector and freeze frame.*

5   *This is where things get really tricky. You have to leave the projection booth and step into the still picture on the screen. It now turns to full colour and as it does so the film runs backwards very quickly. In other words, the children laugh backwards and you talk backwards. So it should all look and sound quite funny and to underline how laughable it is you need to have a film score of comical music (the sort of thing*

you might hear at the circus). Hearing this music and the backwards voices and seeing the ridiculous movements, you now laugh.

6 *Repeat the backwards film sequence several more times, getting faster and faster each time.*

If, after completing the six steps, the idea of making a speech still scores a four or higher on your 'fearometer' (on a scale of one to ten) then repeat the procedure. If you rate it from zero to three then go out in the real world using the 'gradual exposure' technique described above.

KEEP CHALLENGING YOURSELF

How can you develop the confidence to deal with situations you haven't even thought of yet? Gradual exposure is all very well for a specific, known fear. But suppose you're an anxious sort of person generally. Supposing you're suddenly confronted with something new?

The answer is simple. The more ways you challenge yourself, the more confident you'll become in your ability to cope with all kinds of tricky situations. Even ones you've never encountered before and never practised.

If you've avoided challenging situations up till now, then your first step is to resolve to change your attitude. From now on, you've got to seek out challenges. If that sounds alarming, don't let it be. Because they don't have to be big ones. On the contrary, you should aim to proceed slowly and by little steps. There's no time limit. The aim is simply to keep moving in a positive direction.

Here are some of the ways in which you might challenge yourself:

▶ *giving a party*
▶ *training for and entering some kind of race*
▶ *riding a horse*
▶ *getting to the top of a mountain*
▶ *abseiling down a cliff*

- *learning to sail*
- *learning a new language*
- *making a trip abroad on your own*
- *helping other people with their problems.*

If you don't think this will work for you, reflect on the fact that a lot of very large companies spend considerable sums organizing challenges for their staff. It's partly about team-building but it's also about creating confidence. Those companies understand that activities like abseiling down cliffs or white-water rafting translate into better performance at work and, indeed, every sphere of life.

As time goes on, so you'll need to make the challenges that little bit harder. If you don't, you'll get stuck at a certain level. Rather, you should be aiming to progress all through your life.

Below we'll take a look at three different kinds of activities that can make a big difference to you.

Horse riding

I'm going to start with horse riding because it's one of the best ways to boost your confidence, develop your assertiveness and improve your interpersonal skills.

How?

Because when you sit on a horse you're obliged to take control of it. If you don't, the horse will take control of you, with potentially disastrous results. At the same time, you can't be aggressive towards the horse because that, too, could be dangerous. In other words, you have to learn to be assertive in order to get the horse to do what you want. That's an invaluable lesson.

When you sit on a horse you're also obliged to take control of yourself. A horse, after all, is a pretty frightening creature. How frightened you are depends on you and the horse. But here is a creature that weighs, maybe, half a ton, that has the strength of several men, that has a kick that can kill and a set of teeth with which it could rip the muscle right out of your shoulder. So you're right to be frightened. And yet, somehow, you've got to sit on it and entrust yourself to it. That takes a lot of self-control.

Believe it or not, many of the techniques you will learn when you ride a horse are exactly the same techniques that you need in your dealings with other people.

If you can master horse riding, then you'll go a long way in terms of self-confidence and, what's more, social skills. By 'master' I don't mean you have to be able to jump a fence – although that would be a wonderfully positive achievement. I simply mean that you should be capable of riding a horse alone – not following other horses – and getting it to do what you want.

Through riding you'll learn:

▶ *how to communicate*
▶ *how to give clear, unambiguous instructions*
▶ *how to maintain a firm, fair stance in the face of opposition*
▶ *how to control the emotions of fear and anger.*

As a bonus, you'll also discover:

▶ *how to relax*
▶ *the importance of body language.*

A horse acts as a sort of 'magnifying lens' when it comes to human emotions. An instructor will be able to tell at once if you're not relaxed – no matter how hard you may be trying to pretend you are – because your tension will be evident in everything the horse does. Horses, you see, are experts in body language. And that's something you may also need to improve when dealing with human beings.

Insight
Horses aren't like cars. Every one is different. If you don't get on with the horse you're given, ask for a different one. Coping with 'difficult' horses can come later. As a beginner,

start with a calm, well-disciplined animal. Sitting on a horse's back is only a small part of the process. Arrange to tack your horse up yourself at the beginning of each lesson. The more time you can spend hanging out with horses the better. For that reason, a week's trekking is ideal.

Climbing and abseiling

Human beings have marvellous imaginations. Extremely useful if you want to write a novel or paint a picture. But something of a liability in stressful situations. You're quite likely to imagine things far worse than the reality. So you need to get your imagination under control. You have to stop it running wild. Either shut down your imagination or use it, instead, to create an easier vision. It's all encapsulated in that old piece of climbing advice:

▶ *Don't look down.*

If you do, you start to imagine yourself falling and then you're in trouble. In other words, whenever you've got to tackle something that makes you nervous, try to find something non-threatening to focus on.

Climbing will teach you:

▶ *how to control fear*
▶ *how to formulate a plan and carry it out in a tense situation*
▶ *how to communicate clearly*
▶ *how to lead.*

You don't have to live near any mountains because many sports centres nowadays have climbing walls. However, as you progress, you should aim to tackle the real thing from time to time. You'll then experience climbing as a pair and take turns to lead.

Insight

Find a qualified instructor and explain your motives at the outset. If the instructor isn't sympathetic, find another one who is. As with all these kinds of things the secret is to

(Contd)

proceed slowly, one step at a time. Make sure the instructor understands that. The 'in at the deep end' approach will only reinforce your fears. Instead, go to a level at which you're challenging yourself just a little bit. Then stay at that level until you start to feel comfortable. When you do, it's time to move up to the next level. And so on.

Endurance sports

I'm lumping all the endurance sports together because, although they have their very different qualities, they're all concerned with the long haul. Whether it be running, swimming, cycling, all three together (triathlon) or whatever, they all teach you:

▶ *how to cope with projects in which the goal is a long way off*
▶ *not to be discouraged by short-term setbacks.*

Nowadays, everyone wants instant results but, in real life, that's seldom possible. Studying for a qualification, building up a company from scratch, investing in the stock market, establishing yourself in a career, living with somebody else – these are all examples of long-term commitments. And along the way there will be setbacks. It's the same with endurance sports. When you set out on that 26.2 mile marathon, or on a 10,000 metre swim, or on a triathlon, nothing is truer than this:

▶ *Every journey begins with a single step.*

Make that step, and then another and another. And keep going.

Insight
In your quest for greater and greater challenges, don't do anything dangerous. Always take proper instruction and proper

precautions. The challenge is in overcoming your own fears and in learning to trust both your own abilities and those of other people. You won't develop that trust if things go wrong.

So whether it's learning to ride a horse or abseiling down a cliff, make sure you get instruction from qualified professionals.

DON'T SABOTAGE YOURSELF

Quite often, when faced with a challenge, we unconsciously sabotage our own chances of success. But why would your unconscious do that to you? It could be because:

▶ *You just don't feel ready to take on the responsibility that goes with success.*
▶ *You identify yourself as a loser and, in a perverse sort of way, don't want to take on the identity of a winner.*
▶ *If you don't try too hard, you always have an excuse for failure.*

In that case, you need to start looking at things in a new way. Take pride in trying your best. Take pride in being able to say: 'I didn't get what I wanted but at least I gave it my best shot.'

The fact is, there's nothing wrong with failing. Everybody experiences failures. Even the most successful people. In fact, particularly the most successful people. Because those are the ones who keep trying.

▶ *Remember: You haven't failed until you've given up trying.*

Insight

On New Year's Day, review the progress you've made in every sphere during the preceding 12 months. Have you let things stand still in some areas? If so, make a resolution to challenge yourself a bit more.

10 THINGS TO REMEMBER

1   *Your imagination can create unnecessary fears.*

2   *Change the name of something intimidating and it can become easier to cope with.*

3   *Don't dwell on unrealistic, catastrophic outcomes; think instead of realistic outcomes.*

4   *Expose yourself gradually to stronger and stronger 'doses' of the things you're frightened of while using special breathing techniques to help you relax.*

5   *Never jump in at the deep end when trying to overcome your fears.*

6   *Switching perspectives can allow you to think about frightening situations without getting intimidated; the* Fast Phobia Technique *exploits this principle to help you overcome phobias.*

7   *Don't let the emotion of fear hijack your thinking and don't give yourself negative labels.*

8   *The more ways you challenge yourself the more confident you'll be in your ability to handle any kind of crisis.*

9   *Horse riding teaches you how to be assertive, climbing teaches you how to focus your mind away from fear, and endurance sports teach you not to give up.*

10 *We sometimes unconsciously sabotage ourselves.*

HOW CONFIDENT ARE YOU NOW?

▶ *Have you invented euphemisms for things that frighten you?*
▶ *Have you stopped imagining terrible outcomes?*
▶ *Have you used gradual exposure to reduce your fear?*
▶ *Have you learned to control your breathing in tense situations?*
▶ *Have you been able to eliminate cognitive distortions?*
▶ *Have you been able to reduce nervousness by switching perspectives?*
▶ *Have you reduced the impact of a phobia by using the Fast Phobia Technique?*
▶ *Have you challenged yourself in at least two ways this week?*
▶ *Have you taken up horse riding, climbing, abseiling or an endurance sport?*
▶ *Have you stopped sabotaging yourself?*

Score:

If you answered 'yes' to most questions, then you've obviously either overcome your fears or are well on the way to doing so. Go straight on to the next chapter.

If you answered 'yes' to between five and seven questions, then you can also go on to the next chapter but revisit this one from time to time and think about the issues it raises.

If you could answer 'yes' to only four questions or fewer, then you're obviously struggling with your anxieties. Keep working on the practical exercises in this chapter until you raise your score to five or higher, and only then read on.

9

The confidence chemicals

In this chapter you will learn:
- *the way to stimulate your confidence-boosting chemicals*
- *how you can develop the expectation of success week after week*
- *which activities are best for you.*

Running promotes good mental health, including increased confidence and self-esteem, positive mood, general well-being, and less anxiety and depression. Exercisers report being more alert, able to think more clearly and solve problems more efficiently.

Bob Glover, director of training clinics for the New York City Marathon

WORKOUT TIME

Exercise is good for confidence. And that's a scientific fact. Researchers have found it causes the levels of mood-boosting chemicals to shoot up. After a workout you'll feel more positive and better able to tackle the most intimidating problems.

But that's not the only way exercise can help you feel more confident. Exercise also:

- *provides endless opportunities to taste success as you attain one goal after another*
- *improves muscle tone and creates a healthy glow, so you feel more proud of your appearance*
- *builds self-confidence in physical situations*

- *builds self-confidence in confrontations*
- *creates the energy necessary for dealing with demanding tasks, whether mental or physical*
- *causes you to radiate energy to other people*
- *makes you feel more positive and clear-headed*
- *helps you handle stress more easily.*

Exercise also helps in other ways. As a further bonus you'll:

- *sleep better*
- *have a reduced risk of heart attack*
- *increase your levels of HDL or 'good' cholesterol*
- *lower your blood pressure*
- *increase your bone density*
- *boost your immune system*
- *enhance your sexual responsiveness*
- *increase your life expectancy*
- *feel happier.*

Exercise just isn't for me

Don't go thinking that because you're very unfit now (if you are) that an exercise programme isn't for you. On the contrary, the less fit you are the more rapidly you'll see an improvement. Just think about it. Someone who runs at the world record speed, for example, many never be able to run any faster. But someone who can hardly run at all can look forward to weeks, months and years of milestones achieved. It's all relative. You set goals that would represent progress for you. And you reward yourself when you achieve them.

And you will achieve them.

WARNING

The NHS warns that if you haven't been exercising regularly and have any of the following characteristics you should check with your doctor before beginning an exercise programme:

- *over 35 and a smoker*
- *over 40 and inactive*

- *diabetic*
- *at risk of heart disease*
- *high blood pressure*
- *high cholesterol*
- *experience chest pains while exercising*
- *difficulty breathing during mild exertion.*

GENERATING THOSE CONFIDENCE CHEMICALS

So why should exercise feel so good? When you think about it, it's not hard to understand how human beings evolved that way. Our ancestors had to be capable of vigorous activity if they were to eat. When their muscles screamed for respite, those whose bodies produced chemicals to ease the pain were the ones who ran down the prey and got the food. Logically, they were also the ones evolution selected. Well, that's a simplistic way of putting it but right in essence. Nowadays we only have to be capable of lifting a can off a shelf but our bodies remain unchanged. So if we want to enjoy those same chemicals, we have to exercise. Here are those confidence chemicals:

- *Noradrenaline/norepinephrine (NE): When generated by exercise, noradrenaline tends to make you feel confident, positive and expansive.*
- *Endorphins: The word means 'endogenous morphine', that's to say, morphine-like substances produced by the body. Endorphins combat pain, promote happiness and are one of the ingredients in the 'runner's high'.*
- *Phenylethylamine (PEA): This chemical is also found in chocolate as well as some fizzy drinks. Researchers at Rush University and the Center for Creative Development, Chicago, have demonstrated that PEA is a powerful antidepressant. Meanwhile, scientists at Nottingham Trent University in the UK have shown that PEA levels increase significantly following exercise.*
- *Serotonin: The link with exercise isn't so strong for this one but serotonin is a neurotransmitter for happiness and there's reason to think exercise elevates its level in the brain.*

In addition, exercise lowers the level of:

▶ *Cortisol: A stress hormone, cortisol is linked with low mood.*

There are also two further processes at work:

▶ *Thermogenics: Exercise increases the body's core temperature which in turn relaxes muscles which in turn induces a feeling of tranquillity.*
▶ *Right brain/Left brain: Repetitive physical activities such as jogging 'shut down' the left side of the brain (logical thought) freeing up the right brain (creative thought). It's a kind of meditation and it's why solutions to seemingly intractable problems often appear 'by magic' when exercising.*

HOW MUCH EXERCISE?

Remember, we're primarily looking at exercise as a way of boosting self-confidence, not physical fitness. So how much exercise does it take to increase those all-important positive-mood chemicals? The good news is, surprisingly little. Let's take a look:

▶ *Noradrenaline/norepinephrine (NE): This increases up to ten times following 8 minutes of vigorous exercise.*
▶ *Endorphins: The level of beta-endorphins, the chemicals the body releases to combat pain, increases five times after 12 minutes of vigorous exercise.*
▶ *Phenylethylamine (PEA): The researchers at Nottingham Trent University found that running at 70 per cent of maximum heart rate (MHR – see below) for 30 minutes increased the level of phenylacetic acid in the urine (which reflects phenylethylamine) by 77 per cent.*

So it would seem that around 10 minutes of vigorous exercise is already highly beneficial in terms of endorphins and NE but that PEA levels are slower to augment.

How vigorous is vigorous?
The word 'vigorous' may sound daunting, especially if you don't take any exercise at all at the moment. But, in reality, it doesn't take very long to achieve, even starting at zero.

You've probably got a pretty good idea already of what 'vigorous' feels like but let's pin it down a little more scientifically.

STEP 1 CALCULATE YOUR MAXIMUM HEART RATE
Your maximum heart rate (MHR) is the level at which your heart just can't beat any faster. It can be worked out in a fitness laboratory but there is an easier and less exhausting (although less precise) way. To calculate your MHR use the following formula:

▶ *220 − Your age*

For example, if you're 40 years old your MHR will be:

▶ *220 − 40 = 180.*

STEP 2 CALCULATE YOUR TRAINING HEART RATE
Experts argue about the percentage of MHR that provides the best training heart rate (THR). But most people are agreed that as a minimum, THR should be at least 60 per cent of MHR. Beyond 70 per cent of MHR, exercise would be classed as 'vigorous'. At 70 to 80 per cent you'd be in the zone where aerobic conditioning improves the most. Beyond 80 per cent you wouldn't want to go, unless you were seriously training to win races. So let's stick with the assumption that you're 40 years old and intending to exercise at the 70 per cent level. The calculation would look like this:

▶ *(220 − 40) × 70% = 180 × 70% = 126*

At that level you should be able to carry on a conversation − with a little bit of puffing.

STEP 3 DISCOVER YOUR RESTING HEART RATE

Your resting heart rate (RHR) is the level when you wake up in the morning and before you get out of bed. It's the measure of how well your exercise programme is going. The average RHR for men is 60–80 beats per minute while for women it's somewhat higher at 70–90 beats a minute.

If you're at 100 beats or more you're clearly not getting sufficient exercise. You should be aiming to get under 60. Athletes tend to be in the range 40–50. RHRs under 30 have been known.

It's not possible to say that your RHR is directly linked to self-confidence but there is an indirect link. If your RHR starts going down it's a good indication that those mood-enhancing chemicals are being produced during exercise.

Insight

In one way you're very lucky if you have a fairly high RHR right now, because you should be able to:

▶ *Reduce your RHR by one beat per minute per week during the first 10 weeks of an exercise programme (such as the one given below).*

In other words, you'll be able to see quick results and that's very good for motivation.

PROBLEM: HOW WILL I KNOW MY HEART RATE?

The easiest place to take your pulse is to one side of your Adam's apple (larynx). Just press gently with four fingers and you'll feel it. Another place is on your wrist. Turn your hand palm upwards and place four fingers of your other hand lengthwise with your little finger at the base of your thumb. You should feel the pulse either under your forefinger or middle finger. Count for 15 seconds and multiply by four.

However, it's not very easy taking your pulse accurately while you're exercising. A better idea is to buy a heart rate monitor with a watch-style display on your wrist. They're available quite cheaply in sports equipment shops.

How long and how often?
If you want exercise to make a significant difference to the way you feel it really comes down to this:

► *The minimum is 20 minutes of brisk exercise three times a week (and you'll need to allow 5 minutes at either end for warming up and cooling down).*

Five times a week would be better. Longer sessions, within reason, would be better still. Dr James Blumenthal carried out a study on people aged 50 or over at Duke University in 1999 and proved that exercise substantially improved their mood. In fact, all were suffering from depression but there's ample evidence that exercise works its magic on everybody. Dr Blumenthal also concluded that:

► *For each 50-minute increment of exercise, there was an accompanying 50 per cent reduction in relapse rate.*

So even a little is good but more is better (within reason).

THE EXERCISE HIGH

The so-called 'exercise high' (or runner's high) is somewhat controversial. Some people say it exists and others say it doesn't. Those who say it does describe it as a state of euphoria … an altered state of consciousness … a physical style of meditation. That, in turn, can lead to greater feelings of happiness and confidence.

It comes (if it comes at all) mostly with steady, repetitive exercise. In other words, you'd be far more likely to experience it in things like running, swimming, cycling and rowing than in stop – start sports such as tennis or basketball.

One marathon runner has written that: 'Anyone expecting a high or mystical experience during a run is headed for disappointment.' But many others insist that they do regularly enjoy such a state. The explanation probably lies at least partly in the nature of the exercise. Neither too little nor, on the other hand, too gruelling. It seems that those who push themselves very hard simply experience too much tedium, discomfort and pain to enjoy themselves. On the other hand, those who don't take things far enough never get to the point at which the runner's high starts to kick in.

But it's also a question of how you define words like 'high', 'euphoria' and 'mystical'. If you're expecting to come back from exercise a changed person, a sort of instant guru, then, of course, that isn't going to happen.

Here I'll declare myself on the side of the 'mystics'. For a bet I agreed to run a marathon. I had just over 9 months to prepare. A marathon is 26.2 miles and at that point, I swear, I couldn't run more than 26 seconds without getting out of breath. I was starting from zero. Now it's a principle of amateur preparation that you never run a marathon in training. It's just too debilitating. So when you line up for your first ever marathon you don't know for sure that you can do it. In my case, the furthest I'd run was 20 miles. The extra 6 miles were unknown territory. Well, I did do it and for those last few miles I was flying. I'd followed a well-established training routine and it worked perfectly. I'm not exaggerating when I say I could have carried on running without any problem. Without doubt I was experiencing the runner's high and it lasted the rest of the day. (Next morning was a different story.)

Insight

What does the runner's high feel like? Different people describe it differently. I'd say a certain immunity from pain, both physical and mental, coupled with a sense of detachment and a quiet sort of confidence.

I've carried on running, although I've never attempted a marathon again, and I can nowadays get a runner's high at much shorter distances. The key ingredients seem to be these:

- *The exercise should be at around 70 per cent of MHR – high enough to generate those happy chemicals, low enough to avoid real discomfort or pain.*
- *Don't think about the exercise; instead, let your mind wander over pleasant subjects such as your relationship or the beauty of the countryside.*
- *Stick with one type of exercise; it seems to help if the body is familiar with it.*
- *Exercise regularly – say, 5 days a week.*
- *Don't expect to feel euphoria early on – it'll probably take a few months before you have your first experience.*
- *You'll usually need to exercise for around 30 minutes before you start to experience an altered state of consciousness:*
  - *For the first 20 minutes, while your body cranks itself up, you'll more likely be wondering why you're doing it at all.*
  - *At 30 minutes you may start to feel a mild euphoria.*
  - *Between 45 minutes and an hour you may enter an altered state of consciousness.*

Insight

Once you've had the runner's high you'll find it comes more and more easily. You probably won't have the time or inclination to exercise for up to an hour regularly but you could aim to have, say, a one-hour session every weekend, coupled with two to four shorter sessions during the week. During that hour-long session you should get your runner's (or swimmer's or cyclist's or whatever's) high.

FIT FOR ANY CHALLENGE

Here are some simple tests for you to assess your fitness now. Try them again in a week, after you've got started on some exercise, and regularly thereafter.

1 *What's your resting heart rate (that is, your pulse when you wake up in the morning)?*
   a) *Under 50*
   b) *50–60*
   c) *60–70*
   d) *70–80*
   e) *80–90*
   f) *Over 90.*

2 *Can you touch the floor with your legs straight? (Warm up a little before trying this.)*
   a) *I can touch the floor with the palms of my hands.*
   b) *I can touch the floor with the tips of my fingers.*
   c) *I can touch my ankle bones.*
   d) *I can't get further than my calves.*

3 *How many sit-ups can you do in 1 minute? (Don't do this if you have a back problem. To do sit-ups, lie on your back on the carpet, knees bent, heels about 50 cm (18 inches) from your buttocks, feet flat on the floor shoulder-width apart and anchored under a heavy piece of furniture. Your hands should be on the sides of your head. When reclining you only need to touch your shoulders to the floor.)*
   a) *More than 50*
   b) *40–50*
   c) *30–40*
   d) *20–30*
   e) *10–20.*

4 *How long does it take you to walk half a mile? (Measure the distance along a flat stretch of road/pavement using your car.)*
   a) *Under 6 minutes*
   b) *6–7 minutes*
   c) *7–8 minutes*
   d) *8–9 minutes*
   e) *9–10 minutes*
   f) *Over 10 minutes.*

Your score

Question 1

	Men	Women		Men	Women
a)	23	25	d)	8	10
b)	18	20	e)	3	5
c)	13	15	f)	0	0

Question 2

	Men			Women		
	Under 30	30–50	Over 50	Under 30	30–50	Over 50
a)	15	20	25	13	18	23
b)	10	15	20	8	13	18
c)	8	13	18	6	11	16
d)	5	10	15	3	8	13

Question 3

	Men			Women		
	Under 30	30–50	Over 50	Under 30	30–50	Over 50
a)	20	25	–	25	–	–
b)	15	20	25	20	25	–
c)	10	15	20	15	20	25
d)	5	10	15	10	15	20
e)	2	5	10	5	10	15

Question 4

	Men			Women		
	Under 30	30–50	Over 50	Under 30	30–50	Over 50
a)	20	25	–	25	–	–
b)	15	20	25	20	25	–
c)	10	15	20	15	20	25
d)	5	10	15	10	15	20
e)	1	5	10	5	10	15
f)	0	1	5	1	5	10

What your score means

If you scored 75–100 you're already extremely fit and are no doubt already enjoying the self-confidence that goes with it; if you scored 50–75 you're not in bad shape but if you do a little more you'll gain benefits in terms of health as well as self-esteem; if you scored under 50 then, in one way, you're very lucky because you're going to improve rapidly once you start exercising regularly – you'll notice a difference in mood very quickly.

SETTING YOUR GOALS

You can use the little test above to set some goals. Establishing appropriate targets is one of the keys to success. It's very difficult to, say, make a lot of money, but achieving exercise goals is something that's not only 100 per cent within your personal control, it's also very easy. I guarantee you'll regularly experience and even become very used to the feeling of success if you'll only follow my advice.

For example, if it takes you 11 minutes to walk the half mile, set yourself a target of 10 minutes within 2 weeks. If you can do ten sit-ups now, aim to make it 12 at the end of a fortnight. And so on. Keep on raising the bar just a little bit. Do the same with whatever activity or activities you select. If you can just swim a width of the pool, set yourself the challenge of swimming a length. If you can't swim at all, then enrol in a course of lessons. And give yourself a reward for enrolling. That's already an achievement.

There's one unbreakable rule:

▶ *Don't compare yourself with other people, only with your own previous best.*

Insight

Remember, you're 'competing' with yourself, not with anybody else. To 'beat' yourself is good enough and, when you do, take pride in your achievement. That's what it's all about. Making progress and feeling good about it.

WHAT TYPE OF EXERCISE?

The best exercise is something you enjoy and will be happy to do several times a week. It's no good relying on, say, a ski trip once a year or a game of tennis once a month. So when you're choosing, bear in mind practical considerations such as cost, distance from your home and the availability of friends (if it's something you can't do on your own). But, of course, you don't have to do just one thing all the time. It's a good idea to find two or more activities you can enjoy. That way you'll combine their benefits and always have things to do whatever the weather conditions. It could be swimming when it's hot, jogging when it's cold and self-defence classes when it's raining.

Self-defence classes
I'm kicking off with self-defence classes because, although they might not necessarily be the best form of exercise, they introduce an important psychological element. They can improve your self-confidence in a very direct way. If you feel yourself physically intimidated by other people then this could be the solution for you.

There's plenty of evidence to show that people who appear nervous or who look vulnerable are more likely to be the victims of aggression than people who radiate physical self-assurance. Self-defence classes are the way to gain that assurance.

Nowadays all kinds of martial arts are available, from judo to kick-boxing, and great sports and hobbies they can be. However, I'd suggest you opt for a really practical course. Martial arts often involve stylized movements and specific conventions which criminals are unlikely to follow. So look for a course that teaches things like:

- ▶ *distraction techniques*
- ▶ *locks*
- ▶ *kicks*

- ▶ *how to respond if held by the wrists, lapels, hair or neck*
- ▶ *how to respond to a punch or kick.*

To find details of courses near you enquire at your local police station or sports centre or put 'self-defence course' into your Internet search engine. Don't go thinking these courses are only for fit young people. No matter what your age, shape, size or level of fitness, there are techniques you can learn that are appropriate to you. Get a book or a video by all means but, in the first instance, you can only learn by being shown the moves by a qualified instructor. After that you need to practise regularly so that the moves become automatic.

Here's some general advice from self-defence experts:

- ▶ *Avoid hazardous situations.*
- ▶ *Be aware of what's going on around you (don't, for example, listen to music on headphones while walking alone at night).*
- ▶ *If you are in an area that makes you feel uneasy, always be thinking ahead to what might happen and how you'd respond.*
- ▶ *Carry an alarm and have it ready.*
- ▶ *Carry a mobile phone and have it ready.*
- ▶ *Keep to well-used, well-lit streets.*
- ▶ *Don't hitch-hike.*
- ▶ *Make sure your home is protected by security locks.*
- ▶ *Fit a door-chain and some kind of viewing system; don't let strangers in.*

Insight

Physical response is always a last resort. If possible, diffusing the situation or getting away are always preferable. But knowing you have the ability to defend yourself creates confidence and confidence reduces the likelihood of being a target in the first place. Take whatever tests are available and get a certificate to remind you how good you are. For best results, combine your self-defence classes with a more vigorous form of exercise.

Tai chi
Some people say tai chi (or tai chi chuan) is meditation in motion.
But you could also call it self-confidence in synchronization.
Because it's all to do with flowing from one specific position to
the next in a way that increases physical awareness and leads to
enormous physical presence. When a tai chi master calmly enters a
room you know he or she is there.

It also:

▶ *increases flexibility and agility*
▶ *increases strength and stamina*
▶ *improves balance*
▶ *reduces stress and lowers blood pressure.*

The movements derive from martial arts but have become
stylized, so you don't have to worry about getting hurt.
Nevertheless, there is a self-defence school of tai chi, using the
principles of yielding and blending, which can further enhance
physical self-confidence. Once you've mastered the basics you
can move on to that if you want. Or you can simply make a daily
routine of the solo form.

Tai chi lessons are widely available. To find a class near you
try putting 'tai chi classes' and the name of your town into
your Internet search engine. Or contact one of the national
organizations:

▶ *UK: www.ntcca.co.uk*
▶ *USA: http.nqa.org*

Insight
Give yourself a reward each time you master a movement.

Jogging
Jogging is a lot of fun. The steady, rhythmical movement seems to
generate more mood-enhancing chemicals per minute than many

other activities. Just think about it for a moment. Here's an exercise that:

▶ *doesn't require any special equipment*
▶ *doesn't have to cost anything*
▶ *doesn't require any special training*
▶ *provides plenty of fresh air and sunshine out of doors*
▶ *can be done indoors on a machine when the weather is bad*
▶ *can be done alone or with friends*
▶ *can be done anywhere*
▶ *enhances creative thinking and permits 'meditation'*
▶ *makes progress very easy to measure.*

For all those reasons, jogging is one of the most useful forms of exercise. And even if you take up some other activity, jogging is always a good thing to build into your weekly routine.

Insight

One of the problems is running slowly enough. Yes, slowly. Beginners tend to associate the word running with 'going fast'. Wrong. Don't rush. You're aiming for a pace you can sustain over a long period. That means going a lot slower than your sprinting pace. In fact, to begin with you should try to run no quicker than the pace of a brisk walk. It's not as easy as you might think to go that slowly. If you can hardly speak you're going too fast.

Here's a little programme to help you build up from zero to a reasonable level of confidence-building fitness in just 10 weeks. At the end of it you can just continue at the Week 10 level for 3–5 days or, if you really get inspired, you might like to run further.

YOUR 10-WEEK JOGGING PROGRAMME
Exercise for 20 minutes in accordance with the following programme plus 5 minutes' warming up and 5 minutes' cooling down, making a total of 30 minutes in all. Exercise

at least three times a week and build up to five times. Don't run too fast – at all times you should be able to carry on a conversation.

- ▶ *Week 1 Alternate 1 minute of running with 2 minutes of walking*
- ▶ *Week 2 Alternate 2 minutes of running with 2 minutes of walking*
- ▶ *Week 3 Alternate 3 minutes of running with 2 minutes of walking*
- ▶ *Week 4 Alternate 5 minutes of running with 2 minutes of walking*
- ▶ *Week 5 Alternate 6 minutes of running with 1.5 minutes of walking*
- ▶ *Week 6 Alternate 8 minutes of running with 1.5 minutes of walking*
- ▶ *Week 7 Run 10 minutes, walk 1.5 minutes, run 10 minutes.*
- ▶ *Week 8 Run 12 minutes, walk 1 minute, run 8 minutes*
- ▶ *Week 9 Run 15 minutes, walk 1 minute, run 5 minutes*
- ▶ *Week 10 Run 20 minutes.*

Insight

It's always good for confidence to be able to measure success. Set yourself goals (such as jogging 100 metres without stopping) and reward yourself when you achieve them. Wearing a heart rate monitor (available in sports shops) will allow you to track the improvement in your recovery rate.

Swimming

Swimming is a really good aerobic exercise and, in addition, presents some easy ways to challenge yourself. For example, can you dive in from the side? From the diving board? Can you swim underwater? Touch the bottom? These are all examples of the tests you can set for yourself and, by succeeding, boost your self-esteem. If, in summer, you can swim in the sea, a lake or a river, why not set yourself the goal of swimming somewhere particular, such as the next bay or the far side?

Swimming is:

- *an excellent aerobic exercise*
- *a good upper body exercise*
- *easy on the joints*
- *an easy activity in which to monitor progress*
- *the most enjoyable exercise in hot weather.*

But it's:

- *poor exercise for the lower body*
- *boring if you're doing lots of laps in a swimming pool.*

Insight

Set yourself challenges (such as swimming a certain distance or diving in from the side of the pool) and reward yourself for achieving them.

Cycling

The biggest advantage of a bicycle is that you can use it in a practical way, such as pedalling to work, and don't have to make a special time for it. In a hectic schedule that can be very much in its favour. Given the right sort of conditions – quiet lanes, beautiful landscape, pleasant weather – cycling can also be marvellous recreation. If you don't live in an area where cycling would be enjoyable, then there's always the indoor cycling machine – you certainly won't run the risk of being knocked over by a car.

Cycling:

- *is one of the best aerobic conditioners that exists*
- *is easy on the joints*
- *will give you wonderful-looking legs*
- *is a practical means of transport.*

But it:

- *can be dangerous (so always wear a helmet).*

Gym

If you join a gym, you'll have access to all kinds of exercise equipment. There's almost certain to be a static bicycle, treadmill, rowing machine, weight-training machines, free weights, possibly a swimming pool and almost certainly classes in things like aerobic dance and yoga. Most important of all from the point of view of self-confidence, working out with weights and resistance machines is the most precise and effective way of sculpting your body. No other activity comes close. If you want to tighten that stomach or banish those flabby upper arms, then this is the way to do it.

Membership of a gym:

▶ *doesn't require you to have any special equipment of your own*
▶ *can be used whatever the weather*
▶ *can be visited alone or with friends*
▶ *can exercise a wide range of muscles as well as the heart/lung system*
▶ *gives access to a professional on hand to advise and motivate you*
▶ *makes progress very easy to measure*
▶ *is trendy.*

But:

▶ *you will require training before you can use the equipment safely*
▶ *if the gym is a long way from home you may not always feel like going*

▶ *gyms are expensive*
▶ *the exercises can seem boring.*

Insight

Set yourself realistic challenges, such as the number of repetitions you can manage. Keep an exercise diary so you can take pleasure in your progress. And once a month have a good look at yourself in a full-length mirror so you can admire the improvements in your contours.

Dancing

To a lot of people dancing sounds like a good deal more fun than, say, weight training. But is it really a serious exercise option? Well, it certainly can be. The right sort of dancing has all the benefits of jogging plus a few more of its own. The only difference is that it's somewhat harder to measure progress. Look out for aerobic classes or more exotic hybrids such as 5Rhythms, a synthesis of indigenous dance, Eastern philosophy and modern psychology developed by Gabrielle Roth in the 1960s.

Dancing is:

▶ *a fun way to get aerobic exercise.*

But it's:

▶ *hard to measure progress and, therefore, to feel a sense of achievement.*

Insight

If you feel nervous about attending a dance class, start off by buying a DVD and learn at home. Then join a class for absolute beginners (although you won't actually be a beginner).

KEEPING MOTIVATED

Now you know all the benefits of exercise you should be pulling on your exercise gear right now. But, unfortunately, life isn't like that.

We seldom do the things that are good for us and even if we start out with the best of intentions it's all too easy to backslide. So here are a few tips on keeping motivated:

- *Try to take your exercise regularly at a certain time every day and on your days 'off' just go for a leisurely stroll; then, when the time comes round, your body will soon start demanding that you do something active with it.*
- *If your favourite exercise is out of doors, try to have an indoor back-up you can turn to in bad weather.*
- *Exercise together with friends and jolly one another along (unless, of course, you prefer to be alone).*
- *Don't strain; take it easy and build up gradually.*
- *Keep an exercise diary and enter your distances, times, heart rates, scores or whatever; look at it from time to time and take pride in your progress.*
- *Give yourself rewards whenever you achieve a particular goal; if it's a cup you covet, then award yourself a cup – or it could be new clothes, a meal out, a massage or whatever you fancy (and can afford).*
- *Hang up a poster of your ideal body; remember, that's how you're going to look.*
- *Keep thinking of the benefits – improved appearance, greater fitness, an aura of positive energy, better health (lower resting heart rate and blood pressure) and 2–10 extra years of life.*
- *Keep a diary. Does it show you're more self-confident, fitter and happier than you used to be? If you are, then for goodness sake don't stop.*

PRACTICAL EXERCISE

Choose a challenge by which you feel intimidated. It might be, for example, phoning for a job. Do your favourite activity until you begin to feel 'charged up'. Then go and do the thing you've been dreading. You'll find it much easier than you thought.

10 THINGS TO REMEMBER

1 *Exercise can make you feel more confident because it releases various mood-enhancing chemicals including noradrenaline/ norepinephrine, endorphins and phenylethylamine; it also lowers cortisol, the stress hormone.*

2 *Exercise will increase your fitness level, improve your self-image and make you more resilient.*

3 *By setting realistic exercise goals you can regularly enjoy a sense of achievement.*

4 *The minimum amount of exercise for creating a significant improvement in your physical and mental states is 20 minutes three times a week.*

5 *You should exercise at around 70 per cent of your Maximum Heart Rate (MHR).*

6 *When you exercise enough you can enter of a state of euphoria known as the 'runner's high' – but you can experience it in many activities.*

7 *It's important to discover activities you can enjoy regularly in all weathers – jogging, cycling, swimming and working out at the gym are all good examples.*

8 *Self-defence training can help you feel more self-assured.*

9 *Doing some brisk exercise before a challenging task can make you feel less anxious.*

10 *If you're not used to exercise, consult a doctor before starting an exercise programme.*

HOW CONFIDENT ARE YOU NOW?

▶ *Are you taking 20 minutes or more of brisk exercise at least three times a week?*
▶ *Are you taking 20 minutes or more of brisk exercise at least five times a week?*
▶ *Have you experienced the exercise high?*
▶ *Over the course of this week have you been able to improve your score in two of the four fitness tests in this chapter?*
▶ *Over the course of this week have you been able to improve your score in all four fitness tests in this chapter?*
▶ *Have you succeeded in reaching any of your personal exercise goals?*
▶ *Have you improved your body self-image?*
▶ *Have you taken up a new physical activity?*
▶ *Have you started an exercise diary?*
▶ *Before a challenging event, have you used exercise as a way of combating nerves?*

Score:

If you answered 'yes' to most questions, then you're obviously producing plenty of 'confidence chemicals'. Go straight on to the next chapter.

If you answered 'yes' to between five and seven questions, then you can also go on to the next chapter but revisit this one from time to time, think about the issues it raises, and try to increase your score.

If you could answer 'yes' to only four questions or fewer, then you're probably not producing enough 'confidence chemicals'. And yet you're probably one of the people who could benefit the most rapidly from an exercise programme. Do give it a go.

10

The confidence to lead

In this chapter you will learn:
- *how you can be an effective leader*
- *why reward is more effective than criticism*
- *how to create reputations for people to live up to.*

> *If your actions inspire others to dream more, learn more, do more and become more, you are a leader.*
>
> John Quincy Adams (1767–1848), sixth President of the USA

How can you possibly be in charge of other people? How can you be a leader? How can you give guidance and instructions to your children, other people's children, friends or relatives? To fellow members of a sports team, adults undergoing training, or colleagues at work? How can you cope with the rows, the shouting, the conflict, the assaults on your authority and all the rest? Maybe you've tried it and concluded: 'I'm no good as a leader. I'm hopeless. I'm not cut out for this.'

Well, in fact, it doesn't have to be like that.

Conflict isn't an essential part of the job. Your task as a leader is to help other people perform their best. And people perform at their best not when they're attacked and criticized but when they're praised and supported. So there's really no need to be apprehensive about it. On the contrary, it can be a very fulfilling and enjoyable position to be in. And you can do it.

But, even so, you have to be tough. Don't you? You have to be ruthless. Resilient. So full of self-confidence as to be able to face down any challenge to your authority. Well, actually, no. The confidence you need most of all is confidence in your team. I'm now going to show you how you can be an effective leader, even though you yourself may doubt it. These are the vital principles:

- *reward not criticism*
- *appreciation*
- *people live up to their reputations*
- *empowerment*
- *set clear goals and methods.*

REWARD NOT CRITICISM

There are two different styles when it comes to getting other people to do what you want:

- *You can reward positive behaviour.*
- *You can punish negative behaviour.*

Some leaders are all one thing, some are the other and most use a mixture. I'm going to suggest to you that you should lean pretty heavily towards rewards and be very sparing with punishments.

Why? Because:

- *it's much easier to be confident about handing out rewards*
- *rewards are more effective than punishments.*

Let me tell you about my husky. I got her, age five, from a man who was emigrating. He always used to keep her on a lead and I did the same until she got to know me. Then one day I let her off. It was fine for a minute or two but very soon she got the scent of something and disappeared into the woods. I called. Nothing. I called a lot more. Nothing. I went on calling. Finally she turned up. What did I do? If you're a dog owner yourself you'll know the answer. I gave her a dog biscuit.

You see, if I'd smacked her she'd have thought I was punishing her for coming back. Instead, I needed to reward her when she came back. I persisted like that every day and it hasn't stopped her running off but she comes back pretty quickly now. Which, for a husky, is good going.

Okay, people aren't dogs and can't be subjected to dog training methods. But the story illustrates a point that's relevant. Suppose your 11-year-old son was to come to you and confess that while he'd been larking around he'd accidentally smashed a window. What would you do? Punish him? You see, he already knows he's done something wrong. So what would be the point? In a way, you'd be punishing him for good behaviour – for owning up to his mistake. And you'd actually make it less likely that he'd confess to his mistakes in future.

So I suggest you should reward him for owning up and, as to the broken window, let him help install the new one so that he learns (a) how to fix a window and (b) to take responsibility for putting right his mistakes. Then reward him for that, too.

Another illustration. Suppose you're in charge of a complaints department. One of your staff takes a call. She begins well enough but the customer is angry and soon your junior is getting angry back. That's no good. What should you do? Tell her off for losing her temper with a customer? Following the ear-bashing she's just received that might make her resentful and demoralized. Instead, you could try something like this: 'I was really impressed by the way you handled that call. He was a very difficult customer and you managed to keep calm during most of it. The way you were to begin with is exactly how you need to be. Keep on like that. If you can show that you can keep calm even under provocation I'll recommend you for a bonus.'

PRACTICAL EXERCISE
Whatever spheres you're involved in this week as some sort of leader:

▶ *watch out for people making mistakes*
▶ *devise a way of tackling the errors by rewarding positive behaviour rather than by criticizing negative behaviour.*

At the end of the week, review your performance to see if the reward system has improved it.

NLP and motivation direction

Neuro-Linguistic Programming (NLP) has its own variation on this theme of reward and criticism. It's known as 'motivation direction'. We're all motivated *away from* things that are negative and unpleasant, and *towards* things that are rewarding and enjoyable but, according to NLP, we're all much more responsive to one than the other.

So if you want to encourage somebody you need to know their motivation direction. Generally speaking:

▶ *You'll recognize 'towards' people because they're fired up by goals and plans for the future and tend to be ambitious, energetic and optimistic. In that case you motivate them using words such as achieve, target, drive, reach, top and summit.*

▶ *You'll recognize 'away from' people because they tend to be more aware of possible problems and are therefore more cautious. In that case you motivate them using words such as avoid, overcome, prevent, bunker and trap.*

APPRECIATION

What is it that we're living for? Applause! Applause!

Lyrics from the musical *Applause*

Not many of us are literally living for the applause of an audience in a theatre. But everyone likes to feel appreciated. It's warm. It's inspiring. It's energizing.

To be a good leader you need to show appreciation.

Learn from sports stars

Have you ever heard top tennis players interviewed after winning matches? Then, almost certainly you'll have heard them say something like this: 'The crowd was great. They really gave me a lift.'

If you've never experienced it for yourself you might have been mystified. After all, if you know how to hit a tennis ball you know how to hit a tennis ball. What's all this about the crowd?

Well, I have experienced it. I was running my first marathon. Most of the route was along busy shopping streets that had been closed to traffic. But some sections were out in the countryside and they were so tough I often felt like giving up. Yet in the city I was flying. At first I couldn't understand what was going on. Then I realized it was entirely to do with the spectators. Where they lined the city streets two or three deep, all cheering and holding out hands for a high five, I was somehow energized by them. Where there were only a few cows to watch I felt flat and drained. Which just goes to show what sensitive creatures we all are. We can't perform at our best unless other people show their appreciation in some way.

So the moral is, cheer on your staff, your colleagues and your family. It's not even necessary to identify any particular thing that's been well done. Just cheer them anyway.

PRACTICAL EXERCISE

1 *As you go around today show your appreciation for everyone you come into contact with. Here are some of the things you might say:*
   ▷ *Nobody could have done that as well as you, Gerald.*
   ▷ *Susan, I want you to know how much I enjoy your company.*
   ▷ *That was a tremendous achievement, Wendy, and we're all proud of you.*
Notice that I've made a point of inserting people's names. That's very important if your appreciation is to sound personal and genuine. In fact, the more specifically you express your appreciation the better. Don't let it sound like a formula.

2   *If you are in charge of a group of people (and that includes a
    family), start every day or session with some appropriate little
    ritual that's inspiring. Sports teams often do this. They know
    the value of it. For example, if you're the head of a sales team
    you might start the day like this:*
    YOU: We're the best sales team in the industry. What are we?
    TEAM ALL TOGETHER: The best sales team in the industry.
    YOU: I couldn't hear you.
    *TEAM ALL TOGETHER (shouting): The best sales team in
    the industry.*
    YOU: Okay! Go get orders.

Now you work out your own ritual for your own particular
circumstances. You can certainly make it more elaborate than I've
done or more subtle. On a sports occasion you might include, say,
banging a drum or a gong, singing a song or chanting. Within a
family, on the other hand, it could just be giving everyone a hug
before they leave the house. Remember, the whole idea is to raise
morale, increase confidence and, in the case of a group of people,
create a team spirit that will carry everyone along. Never use the
occasion to criticize anyone. That will ruin the effect.

PEOPLE LIVE UP TO THEIR REPUTATIONS

We all like to gain something every day but we're even more
concerned about losing something we already have. Think about
it for a moment. What would be worse? If you were to fail to win
£1,000 (US $1,580 approx.) in a lottery today? Or if someone stole
the £1,000 (US $1,580 approx.) you won in a lottery last week?

It's the same with reputation. We're all far less concerned about
gaining a good reputation than we are about losing a good
reputation we already have. So it's excellent psychology to create
a reputation for someone that is, in truth, a little elevated. That
person will then try their hardest to live up to it.

Think of things you can say to bolster the reputations of people around you. Work out something suitable for:

- *someone you're in charge of*
- *your children*
- *your partner*
- *someone who is providing you with goods or services.*

But don't create a reputation that the person has no chance of ever living up to. That would either cause unfair and even dangerous pressure or, alternatively, run the risk of being ridiculed. Just set the bar a little higher than the person's current level.

Here are some suggestions to get you started:

- *To someone you're in charge of: I wouldn't want other people to know I'd said this because it might affect their motivation but, between you and me, you're the best in this company.*
- *To a child: You behave with a maturity beyond your years and I want you to know how proud I am of you.*
- *To a partner: I want you to know how much I enjoy you being so romantic with me.*

Insight

An easy way to increase people's reputations is to give them more elevated titles. For example, instead of 'Salesman, Northern Region' try 'Sales Manager Northern Region' (even if there aren't any other salesmen). If you're dealing with something where titles aren't appropriate you can still give 'quasi-titles'. For example, you might call that recalcitrant teenager of the household 'Technology Expert'.

EMPOWERMENT

Empowerment is vital to performance. Most people achieve their best results when:

▶ *they have some degree of control over what they're doing – in other words, they need to be given the independence to make decisions within certain parameters*

▶ *they can see that what they're doing makes a tangible difference.*

Let's look at these principles in action.

Let's say you've asked someone to write a report which is going to be presented at a board meeting. When you receive it you notice some things that are wrong. Do you (a) correct it yourself and send it on to the board (b) call the author in and tear him off a strip (c) call the author in, praise the things in the report that are good and ask him to bring the unsatisfactory elements up to the same high standard?

Solution (a) might be an option if the matter is urgent but the author isn't going to learn anything as a result. What's more you're disempowering that person. Solution (b) will damage the author's self-esteem without anything positive coming out of it. Solution (c) is the path to follow. Why? Because, the opportunity to correct the matters you've drawn attention to is empowering – and educational, too. Moreover, although the author has made some mistakes, you've actually raised the bar that he's going to set for himself in the future. He now wants to live up to the reputation you've just given him.

Insight

If you think the person is ready, say that you're no longer going to check their work which means they have to take full responsibility for it.

In that way, the person can see that what they do makes a direct difference.

PRACTICAL EXERCISE

This week, in every sphere, give people a little more control and a little more responsibility than you ever have before. See what happens.

SET CLEAR GOALS AND METHODS

When someone underperforms it's all too easy to criticize and to overlook a simple explanation. It could be that they've just never been properly shown:

▶ *what's expected of them*
▶ *how to do it.*

This kind of underperformance happens a lot when someone is new to something. And it happens when someone who has been very good in the past is elevated to the next level and then 'thrown in at the deep end'. Of course, some people do learn to swim that way but many others sink.

Remember that people tend to go about things in the way they're first shown, until somebody shows them something better. So make sure initial training is thorough and sound.

Jill was beginning a new job. Her boss delegated Mary, a colleague who had been at the company about a year, to 'show Jill the ropes'. Unfortunately, Mary had some sloppy habits which Jill inevitably copied. The result? Jill underperformed and was given a warning. But it was the boss who should have taken responsibility. It was his poor training methods that were at fault.

The principle applies in every walk of life, not just in business.

Let's take a completely different example. Say you have a 14-year-old and you decide it's now about time he helped with the washing-up. He moans, slouches off to do it, makes a mess, breaks a glass ... You know, or can imagine, the scenario. You end up feeling demoralized and resolve that, in future, you'll do it yourself. You lose confidence in your ability to get other people to do things. Why, you ask, am I so ineffectual?

Well, what was your mistake? Not being more assertive? Not being more persistent? No, your mistake was for 14 years (well, in practical terms, let's say 10 years) training your son to believe he didn't have any contribution to make to the running of the home. Yes, training. Every day he didn't have to do anything was a day he learned that nothing was expected of him. Naturally, being asked to wash up came as a terrible shock.

What you were trying to do when you asked him to wash up was not 'training' but 'retraining'. And that's a whole lot harder. 'Training', whether it be a child or a business executive, has to begin at the right moment, before bad habits have crept in.

Remember, you can't confidently lead people who haven't been properly trained.

PRACTICAL EXERCISE
Wherever people are underperforming, analyse the situation and ask yourself: 'Have they been properly trained?'

Insight

A quick way to discover people's characters, especially their aptitudes and weak spots, is to play games with them. In the case of young children these can be simple games like asking them to stand up and say something about themselves. You quickly get to see which children are the confident ones, which the nervous ones and so on. In the management sphere, try sports such as climbing and sailing – you'll quickly see who's good at organizing. And shared challenges are a good way of creating bonds.

USING SUGGESTION AND SELF-HYPNOSIS

If you have any doubts about your ability to lead use the suggestion technique described in Chapter 2. Before you go to sleep at night plant an idea like this in your unconscious:

▶ *I am an effective leader. I inspire and encourage others to perform to the maximum of their abilities.*

Alternatively, you could use self-hypnosis. Refer back to Chapter 2 for the complete method.

PRACTICAL EXERCISE

1 *Complete the 'external' phase of the process of self-hypnosis stating the aim of the self-hypnosis as follows: 'I am entering into a state of self-hypnosis so that I can hand over to my unconscious mind the task of making me more a confident leader.'*

2 *Having completed the 'external' phase, close your eyes and move on to the 'internal' phase, visualizing a scene in which you are behaving as a confident leader. See, hear and feel just as if it was all actually happening. Select examples of each 'representational system' exactly as described in order to deepen the trance.*

3 *Come out of trance.*

4 *Repeat the process from time to time until you feel you have become fully confident as a leader.*

MORE APPLICATIONS FOR NLP

Neuro-Linguistic Programming (NLP) has quite a lot to say about leadership. First of all, let's take a look at some more of the 'presuppositions' that we first met in Chapter 1.

YOU CANNOT *NOT* COMMUNICATE
THE MEANING OF YOUR COMMUNICATION IS THE RESPONSE YOU GET
These two presuppositions are a big part of what you, as a leader, need to know about communication. It's very important to realize that you're communicating all the time, whether you intend to or not. Even silence is a kind of communication. As to *what* you're communicating, the second presupposition puts the responsibility for clarity firmly on you. If someone else doesn't react in the way you expected or carries out an instruction in the wrong way, then you have to accept that your communication was faulty and that you need to find a better way of expressing your meaning.

UNDERLYING EVERY BEHAVIOUR IS A POSITIVE INTENTION
PEOPLE ARE ALWAYS MAKING THE BEST CHOICES AVAILABLE TO THEM
PEOPLE WORK PERFECTLY
These three presuppositions should have a significant effect on your
management style. What they're all saying in their different ways
is that the people you're leading will do the best they can with the
cards you deal them. If someone doesn't behave as you wish, try to
understand what positive intention lies at the root of the situation
and why the 'right' choice didn't seem to be available.

PEOPLE ALREADY HAVE ALL THE RESOURCES THEY NEED
This doesn't mean that the people you're leading already know
how to use a spreadsheet, check a contract, design a machine tool
or whatever it might be, But it does mean they have within them
the capability – the mental structures, the reasoning powers, the
emotions, the experiences and so on – that will allow them to
learn. It's your job to help them.

**THE MOST FLEXIBLE PEOPLE HAVE THE GREATEST CHANCE
OF GETTING WHAT THEY WANT**
Look around in nature. The creatures that are the most adaptable
are the most numerous and successful. If, like a panda, you insist
on eating a special kind of bamboo and nothing else, then you're in
danger of extinction. As a leader, be willing to change tactics.

IF WHAT YOU ARE DOING ISN'T WORKING, DO SOMETHING ELSE
THERE'S NO SUCH THING AS FAILURE, ONLY FEEDBACK
We met these two presuppositions in Chapter 1 – turn back if
you've forgotten about them.

Modelling
If you want to know how to lead other people with confidence
then it wouldn't be a bad idea to watch an expert. NLP has its
own special way of going about this, called 'modelling'.

Broadly speaking there are two stages to the modelling process, implicit and explicit:

Implicit modelling means unconsciously *absorbing* what someone else does, without asking questions and without applying verbal descriptions.

Explicit modelling means consciously deducing which of the expert's actions you've now absorbed are important and which are irrelevant.

Modelling is the way infants acquire knowledge and skills. They observe – the implicit phase. Then they try things out for themselves. What works they keep, what doesn't work they reject – the explicit phase.

Why not ask questions during the implicit modelling phase? Because even experts don't necessarily know how they do what they do. It's not in their conscious minds but in the unconscious. What's more, asking questions can actually *change* things. Let's suppose I ask you to imagine a dog in the park. Now I ask you some questions. Does the dog have a collar? What colour is it? Is it playing with a ball? What colour is the ball? Is the dog wagging its tail? Is it sniffing the ground? In all probability, each question will change the image you first created in your mind.

How best can you uncover the information contained in someone else's unconscious mind and transfer it to your unconscious mind, so you can do the same things? NLP sees conventional learning as divided into four main stages:

▶ *Unconscious incompetence. At this stage you know nothing.*
▶ *Conscious incompetence. You've now begun to practise the skill. You're not very good at it but at least improvement is rapid because you're starting from a low level.*
▶ *Conscious competence. By this stage you've acquired a good level of skill but further improvement takes enormous time and effort and everything still requires concentration.*

► *Unconscious competence. You've now arrived at the stage at which you can perform the activity automatically at a high level without having to think about what you're doing.*

A faster way of learning would be to skip the conscious stages and accomplish the whole process unconsciously – from unconscious to unconscious. But is it possible? Almost certainly. Neurophysiologists at the University of Parma, Italy, have discovered that macaque monkeys have 'mirror neurons' that fire not only when the monkeys carry out a particular action but also when they see another monkey, or person, perform that action. In other words, seeing an action carried out creates the same 'experience' in that part of the mind *as actually doing it.* If they're proven to exist in humans (and not all scientists have accepted that) then they provide an explanation of implicit modelling.

PRACTICAL EXERCISE
1 *Find your model. Ideally, this is the world's greatest expert in confident leadership, but at least make sure you are observing someone who is genuinely worth it.*
2 *Prepare for each modelling session by using self-hypnosis to get yourself into a heightened state of awareness (see Chapter 2). When required to state the purpose you say something like: 'I am entering into a state of self-hypnosis so that I can hand over to my unconscious mind the task of absorbing the techniques used by my model.'*
3 *Observe your model in action. Do* not *make any attempt to describe what's going on, either by writing it down, or describing it out loud, or even by thinking it in words. Nor should you ask any questions. Simply try to absorb.*
4 *As soon as you feel able, try copying your model. Continue observing and copying until you can achieve the same results.*
5 *Try leaving things out and see what impact that has on your results (explicit phase). Retain what works, jettison the rest.*

Insight

Clearly, the explicit phase can be laborious and time-consuming. There could be hundreds of things to check. You may well conclude that, for your purposes, it's enough to be able to get the results you want, even if some of the things you're doing are irrelevant. On the other hand, if you want to be a world-beater in confident leadership, that's the kind of attention to detail that's essential.

NEVER KEEP RIVALS DOWN

One of the greatest challenges to leadership is a rival who wants your position – and can do it. So how should you, as a confident person, respond? Be obstructive, right?

Wrong.

Let's just analyse that fear of able people 'below' you. Everyone is employed to do a job. Your job is to manage, not to perform other people's tasks for them. If you can encourage people to do those jobs better than you could have done them then that's not a failure on your part. That's a success. By being obstructive, on the other hand, you're only demonstrating incompetence. Look upon yourself as the manager of a sports team (which maybe you are). Your job is not to get on the field and score. Your job is to help your team score. If you do that, your position is secure.

So never try to hold good people down. Encourage them. Build them up. Help them. If it turns out that one of them is suited to move up to a higher level, to leapfrog you, then that's great. It means you've done a fine job.

10 THINGS TO REMEMBER

1 *Conflict isn't an essential part of leadership.*

2 *Leadership means helping other people to perform at their best.*

3 *Reward is more effective than criticism – and it calls for less self-confidence.*

4 *Always show appreciation for things well done.*

5 *Create little rituals to raise morale.*

6 *People live up to their reputations – so give them reputations to live up to.*

7 *Give people some independence to make decisions.*

8 *People need to know that what they do makes a tangible difference.*

9 *Underperformance is most likely the result of undertraining.*

10 *Modelling confident leaders is a good way to learn leadership skills.*

HOW CONFIDENT ARE YOU NOW?

▶ *Have you shown your appreciation to at least three people with whom you are in contact?*
▶ *Have you introduced any inspiring rituals at home or at work?*
▶ *Have you given slightly elevated reputations to at least two people?*
▶ *Have you trusted someone with a little more power?*
▶ *Have you made sure people know what's expected of them and how to do it?*
▶ *Have you used suggestion and/or self-hypnosis to improve confidence in your leadership?*
▶ *Have you absorbed the NLP presuppositions?*
▶ *Have you modelled someone who is a confident and inspiring leader?*
▶ *Have you helped someone 'below' you to be more successful?*
▶ *Have you any evidence that you're now a more successful leader?*

Score:

If you answered 'yes' to most questions, then you're obviously either a confident and inspiring leader or well on your way to becoming one. Go straight on to the next chapter.

If you answered 'yes' to between five and seven questions, then you can also go on to the next chapter but revisit this one from time to time and think about the issues it raises.

If you could answer 'yes' to only four questions or fewer, then you obviously find it very hard to be in charge of other people. Keep working on the practical exercises in this chapter until you raise your score to five or higher, and only then read on.

11

··

Developing confidence
with the opposite sex

In this chapter you will learn:
- *how to be confident with the opposite sex*
- *how to work with the opposite sex*
- *the one quality that can resolve gender conflicts.*

> *Without the awareness that we are supposed to be different,*
> *men and women are at odds with each other.*
>
> John Gray, *Men Are From Mars, Women Are From Venus*

Men are always complaining that women are a mystery. And
women are always complaining that men are a mystery. And, of
course, men and women are different. But before I deal with those
differences I first of all want to deal with the ways men and women
are the same.

Here's the thing that both men and women equally want:

▶ *To be valued as a person.*

It means that dealing with the opposite sex is much easier and
far less frightening than you thought. Whatever else you do,
always treat members of the opposite sex as valued people first.
Everything else, beautiful, handsome or whatever it may be,
comes second.

And, indeed, when you think of the big picture there can be more differences between two men or between two women than between a man and a woman. We all, irrespective of gender, want to be loved, to feel fulfilled, to be happy and so on. So let's not exaggerate. We're all from the same planet.

By comparison with some of the issues that can cause a divide between one person and another, gender issues are quite small stuff. More a matter of approach than substance. Here are some of them:

▶ *Women tend to favour empathy over action; men tend to favour action over empathy.*
▶ *Women see all the grey; men like to simplify things into clear black and white.*
▶ *Women tend to be conciliatory; men tend to be confrontational.*
▶ *Women tend to get irritated by people who are too emphatic; men tend to get irritated by people who appear indecisive.*
▶ *Women like to discuss problems from every angle; men prefer to make a decision and then forget about the problem.*

I stress that these are generalizations and they certainly don't always apply. But it's as well to keep them in mind.

In this chapter I'm first of all going to take a look at gender issues in the workplace. Then I'll move on to those initial romantic encounters and, finally, to issues to do with confidence within relationships.

PRACTICAL EXERCISE
If you're not very used to being with members of the opposite sex, then make a point of it now. Don't treat them only as potential partners, either going mad over them or, at the opposite extreme, ignoring them because you don't fancy them. Treat them all as people who are valued for a variety of different reasons.

Here are some ideas to help you:

- *Have your hair done in a mixed sex salon.*
- *Don't group together with your own sex at parties – move across to the other side of the room sometimes.*
- *If you have a close relative of the opposite sex, discuss gender issues.*
- *Read novels and self-help books aimed at the opposite sex.*
- *Watch films and TV programmes aimed at the opposite sex.*
- *Don't make judgements about the attitudes of the opposite sex, just accept them as different but valid.*

MEN AND WOMEN AT WORK

Two weeks earlier Chloe had passed her final exams and been promoted to head of auditing. Now she faced her first big dilemma. John, one of the trainees, had returned from audit without having made any of the necessary stock checks. It was her job, as head of auditing, to sort the matter out. Meanwhile, her boss, the senior partner, had got wind of John's error and summoned both Chloe and John to a meeting. Chloe wasn't looking forward to it at all. The sexual politics were potentially explosive. She was caught in the middle, in charge of one man, but subordinate to the other.

This is the kind of situation that frequently crops up nowadays. It embodies the two biggest confidence issues in the workplace today:

- *being a woman in charge of men*
- *being a man taking orders from a woman.*

Let's look at the subordinate male first of all. A lot of men find it very difficult to relate to women other than in certain clearly defined roles. Here they are:

- *the mother figure*
- *the schoolmistress figure*

- *the partner figure*
- *the daughter figure.*

The mother and schoolmistress figures have their distinctions but when it comes to giving orders they merge into one. The defining characteristic is that they both curtailed the young male's freedom. As soon as a woman boss issues instructions to a man she risks becoming, in his eyes, the omnipotent but hugely resented mother/schoolmistress figure trying to restrict his independence. All the bitterness he feels over the things he was forbidden in childhood now wells up.

But that's not all. Adult men believe themselves to be 'protectors' of women and therefore 'superior'. So when the positions are reversed, and a woman is put in charge, many men find it extremely difficult to cope. The situation becomes even more fraught if the man finds his female boss attractive because his position of 'inferiority' is then intolerable.

Now let's look at the superior female. Although she's the boss she quite possibly feels threatened. She, too, has childhood issues and, what's more, she knows she still lives in a male-dominated world. She may either respond by giving in to confident males, even though she thinks they're wrong, or, more usually, by rejecting all ideas from men and refusing to discuss the issues.

So how can you, as a woman, confidently manage men? Here are some guidelines (and many of them equally apply to managing female staff):

- *Set goals and give as much freedom as possible to make decisions but within clearly defined limits.*
- *Avoid admonitions of the sort used for children ('I'm really surprised at you', 'You've let me down', and so on).*
- *Make use of the male's instinct to be a 'protector' by assigning 'protective' roles. (For example, you could say: 'I'm going to get a lot of stick over this from the powers that be; I want you to write a report that answers all possible criticisms.')*

- *Don't become defensive if a male subordinate tries to press his views – consider the merits of the case not the gender.*
- *Be clear – men understand directness but aren't so good on subtlety.*
- *Plant a suggestion into your unconscious, along the following lines, as described in Chapter 2:*
  I'm a highly capable executive, promoted on ability, and equally capable of dealing with men and women.

And how can you, as a man, maintain your self-confidence when you're subordinate to a woman? Again, here are some guidelines:

- *What's being a woman got to do with it? You'll do much better if you forget all that stuff about men being naturally 'superior'.*
- *See your boss first of all as a person, not a woman.*
- *Don't assign preconditioned roles ('Who does she think she is, my mother?').*
- *Bear in mind that women are presidents, prime ministers and chief executives of major corporations – working for a woman doesn't make you 'inferior'.*
- *Plant a suggestion into your unconscious, along the following lines, as described in Chapter 2:*
  I'm extremely good at my job and working for a woman is a positive opportunity to enlarge my perspective even further.

CONFIDENCE IN SEDUCTION

Your mouth is dry. Your heart is thumping. The blood is pounding in your temples. You feel sick and dizzy. But you're not ill. No, you're in love. Or, at least, infatuated. You've just seen the most marvellous person across ... what? A crowded room, perhaps? Well, not just a person, more a god, or a goddess. And you know beyond any doubt you have to be with that exceptional being. That creature like no other on the planet. Your whole happiness and future depend entirely on it. But there's just one insurmountable hurdle:

You can't speak.

The projection problem

I'm sure the next person you fall in love with will be wonderful. I'm equally sure there won't be any gods or goddesses involved. And if you do 'fall in love at first sight', well, it just can't really be love. If you don't know what someone is like, you're falling in love with your own fantasies. It's what psychologists call 'projection'. You project onto somebody the way you'd like them to be. It's not how they really are. And it's because the fantasy you've created in your own mind is so exalted that you can't speak.

One of the most famous examples of projection was the relationship between D.H. Lawrence, the novelist, and Frieda Weekley, who became the model and inspiration for so many of his female characters. Lawrence was instantly infatuated, calling Frieda 'the most wonderful woman in all England' and 'the woman of a lifetime'. And she equally projected onto him her fantasies of the great novelist. Obviously, neither of them was lacking in self-confidence because Frieda ran away with Lawrence, leaving a home, a husband and three young children, just 8 weeks after first meeting him. But you can see how, for anyone lacking confidence, such projections would be utterly daunting.

And here's the second problem that for Lawrence and Frieda was far more important. Disappointment is bound to follow when you put someone on the proverbial pedestal. Before long they were battering one another.

OVERCOMING PROJECTION

When it comes to projection, your fantasies have an ally in a chemical called phenylethylamine (PEA). When you see that 'special person' PEA starts whooping around inside you and produces that lovely 'walking on air' feeling. Now, I wouldn't want to take that away from anybody. In fact, I would thoroughly recommend you always to maintain a happy level of PEA. But PEA can coexist with realism. And a little more realism would do wonders for your self-confidence.

So take out yet another sheet of paper, divide it vertically in two, and head up the columns 'My feelings about this person' and 'Are these feelings valid?'. Then fill it in. You might write something like this:

My feelings about this person	Are these feelings valid?
He's the most handsome man I've ever seen.	Ever? Come on! He's good-looking but there are plenty of others just as good. And, anyway, looks are not the most important thing.
He looks kind.	Looks kind? What sort of evidence is that?
I sense that we're made for each other.	I don't even know if he shares any of the same interests as me, likes the same music or has the same political outlook.

Now you write out your own 'balance sheet'. It may not completely eliminate the awe you feel about approaching this person but it should at least get the PEA down to manageable levels.

The template trap
We all tend to carry within us a sort of template of the ideal partner. That's why, when one relationship breaks down, we tend to seek out another partner identical to the previous one. So, naturally, that relationship also breaks down. And the next one. Eventually, your confidence is destroyed. You think like this:

▶ *I just can't make a success of any relationship. I've been out with six different people in the past year and every time it's ended in failure. I'm no good. I'll never find happiness with anybody.*

Well, you will if you'll just break that template. The truth is, you haven't been going out with various 'different' people. They've all been slight variations on a single theme. So it's not true to say you can't make a success of 'any' relationship. It's just that particular type of relationship. You need to open up your horizons to include people who truly are different.

This business of templates is also why we try to remodel our partners. You've probably had experience of that. Someone is attracted to you but once you start going out together he or she then starts to criticize you. The reason is this. You fitted some aspects of the template but not all of them. The other person then starts trying to cut pieces off here and add bits on there to make a perfect fit.

So how can you overcome the template trap? The answer is very simple. Go out with people you're not instantly attracted to. That's right. With men or women who don't immediately make your head spin. One benefit is that you'll probably find your conversational skills much improved. But the biggest bonus is that you'll put your rigid template to the test. And if you do, I think you'll end up throwing it away.

USING COGNITIVE THERAPY

When you lack confidence in romantic situations it's so often due to 'cognitive distortions' – ways of thinking about yourself that don't match with reality. (If you don't recall the details, turn back to Chapter 1.) Here are some of the thoughts that can destroy your confidence:

▶ *She/He's better than me.*
▶ *I know she/he's not going to like me.*
▶ *I feel like a failure so I must be a failure.*
▶ *I'm a label (stupid/boring/unattractive or whatever).*

And here's one that women are probably more susceptible to than men:

▶ *It's obviously my fault (again).*

Let's deal with them one by one.

SHE/HE'S BETTER THAN ME

This can be an example of what the psychotherapists call the 'mental filter'. You focus on one negative and that then colours your whole outlook. Here's how it works in the romantic context. You see someone you're attracted to but you notice, say, that he or she drives an expensive sports car. You, on the other hand, drive an old banger. You then think like this (I'll assume that you're a man and she's a woman but the same kind of negative thinking could just as easily apply the other way around or in same sex relationships):

> ► *She is vastly superior to me. She obviously has a lot of money and must be very stylish and know important people. I'm just a nobody. She wouldn't want to go out with me.*

The error in this kind of thinking is to believe that because someone is 'superior' in one thing (in this case, money) that they're superior in everything. This then leads to the feeling that you have nothing at all to offer. You're a 'nobody'. Let's do one of those divided sheets of paper and weigh up the arguments. On the left-hand side we'll head it up 'Reasons why she's better than me' and on the right 'Errors in my thinking'.

Reasons why she's better than me	Errors in my thinking
She has more money.	Money doesn't make anyone 'better'. In fact, being wealthy can lead to character faults such as a lack of empathy. I may not have money but I score highly in other ways.

She must be far more dynamic than I am to have made so much money.	How do I know she made it? Maybe her parents gave it to her. If she did make it, I admire that but I've been dynamic in other ways.
She must be cleverer than me.	You don't have to be clever to make money. Lots of very clever people have very little money.

If you've seen someone you're attracted to but lack the confidence to approach, try to gain perspective by reasoning things through in this way.

I KNOW SHE/HE'S NOT GOING TO LIKE ME
This is the error of jumping to conclusions. And the sad thing is that when you think like this it probably becomes a self-fulfilling prophecy. You feel nervous. You don't push your warmth ahead of you. So you come across as cold and disdainful. And, naturally, people don't take to you.

You can also make the same kind of mistake when you're in a relationship. The other person doesn't return your call right away and you conclude: 'He's avoiding me.' Or he can't make a particular date and you think: 'He's having an affair with someone else.' When you do get to speak on the phone or meet up you act strangely as a result – you're anxious or angry or aloof, or something like that. And the relationship suffers.

A good way of checking the validity of your prophecies is to keep a note of them. All this week, whenever you find yourself 'jumping to conclusions', write them down in your diary. Later, review them and see how many of them turned out to be true. You'll almost certainly find you've made yourself anxious and damaged your self-confidence without any reason.

I FEEL LIKE A FAILURE SO I MUST BE A FAILURE
This is 'emotional reasoning'. Because you feel a certain way you assume you are a certain way. And it becomes another of those circular problems. Let's say you see someone you're attracted to. You'd like to start a conversation but, as you approach, you're suddenly overwhelmed by nerves. The person seems unattainable. Then you begin to think like this: 'I feel so insignificant. This is ridiculous. I'm just going to be laughed at. I'm a failure in this and in everything I do.'

You've just allowed an understandable feeling of hesitancy in one situation destroy your self-image. Because of that, you feel even more nervous. You no longer have the resolution to act and you're stuck in a circle from which there seems to be no escape.

But there is one. The way out is to realize that your negative emotions are unwarranted. You can argue with yourself inside your head. But, better still, take a sheet of card and write on it the reasons your negative emotions aren't justified.

It might look something like this:

- ▶ *I passed my exams.*
- ▶ *I have a good job and the prospect of promotion.*
- ▶ *I recently finished the 10,000 metre charity run.*
- ▶ *I'm good at drawing.*

Now you fill in a card for yourself and keep it with you in your handbag or wallet as a reminder. Next time you're overwhelmed by negative emotions carry out a 'reality check' by reading the card.

I'M A LABEL (STUPID/BORING/UNATTRACTIVE OR WHATEVER)
Having labels is a great way of simplifying life but a terrible way to live. Labels are black and white. They miss out all the grey, which is where the truth really lies. Moreover, when you use labels you come to believe them. Let's say you give

yourself the tag of 'unattractive to men'. Then this is what
happens:

- ▶ *You don't pay attention to your clothes.*
- ▶ *You don't pay attention to hair or make-up.*
- ▶ *You don't take care of your body.*
- ▶ *You don't make any attempt to meet men.*
- ▶ *You don't signal interest to any of the men you happen to*
  come into contact with.

The label becomes a self-fulfilling prophecy. Never apply negative
labels to yourself. If you have been doing that, you need to counter
their effect in your unconscious by replacing them with positive
suggestions, as described below.

IT'S OBVIOUSLY MY FAULT (AGAIN)

Men have a knack of getting women to think they're the cause of
any problem that happens to occur. And women have a knack of
believing it. (Of course, it can happen the other way around but
this is by far the most common scenario.)

You possibly know the kind of thing. He fails an exam and says it's
your fault because you asked him to do a few chores around the
house. He gets lost and says it's your fault for not spotting the sign.
And there are other kinds of things. Dinner one night isn't quite
right and he says you're a lousy cook. Or you spill something and
he says you're clumsy. And so on.

That's already bad. But the worst thing is that you come to
believe it all yourself. Your confidence is so shot to ribbons
that, ultimately, you almost can't do anything.

And here's the paradox. This man will actually fall out of love with
you precisely because you're no longer the woman he fell in love with.

How can you deal with it? The first step is to stop believing you're at
fault. So here we go again. Yes, divide that sheet of paper. This time, on

the left-hand side, head it up 'Things he says are my fault'. And on the right put 'Why it's not my fault'. You might fill it in something like this:

Things he says are my fault	Why it's not my fault
He says I'm clumsy because I spilt the soup on the carpet.	Everybody drops things and spills things sometimes. In fact, he spilt oil in the garage last week – but I didn't say anything about it.
He says it's my fault his boss ticked him off for wearing a creased suit because I didn't iron it properly.	It's not my job to iron his suit. He should take responsibility for his own appearance. He's just as capable of ironing as I am – or he could take it to the cleaners.
He says it's my fault we don't have enough money because I spend too much on clothes.	He spends far more on golf and fishing than I spend on clothes.

I'll have a lot more to say about people who destroy your confidence in Chapter 12.

USING SUGGESTION, VISUALIZATION AND SELF-HYPNOSIS IN SEDUCTION

These techniques were all described in Chapter 2. Using suggestion you might increase your self-confidence by planting the following idea in your unconscious:

▶ *I'm an attractive and interesting person with a great deal to offer and I feel confident in romantic situations.*

You might also visualize yourself being successful and, for maximum effect, you should do that under self-hypnosis. Turn back to Chapter 2 to refresh your memory. In Step 3 state the purpose of self-hypnosis along the following lines: 'I am entering into a state of self-hypnosis so that I can hand over to my unconscious mind the task of making me confident when I'm wanting a date.' Don't forget the key word *unconscious*. During the 'internal' phase of the self-hypnosis you might then imagine yourself behaving confidently with your potential date and getting the response you want.

THE ART OF THE CHAT-UP

If only you knew a sure-fire way to chat someone up then you could feel a lot more confident about trying. Right? Well, I can't guarantee success but I can certainly improve your chances.

But let's first of all take a look at the mechanism. Men may think they initiate the chat-up but, in fact, research shows that it's normally women. Most men won't approach a woman in a setting such as a bar without some encouragement. In fact, quite a lot of encouragement. The best way for a woman to give that encouragement is simply to smile broadly and make eye contact. In one experiment, a woman who made frequent eye contact while smiling was approached by 60 per cent of her male targets. How frequent? Ladies, it's important to be persistent. On average it took *nine* bouts of signalling. And that was for the most successful tactic! Men are just not as daring as they like to think.

Okay, guys, so you've received the signal. Now you probably think that if you can only come up with the right 'chat-up line' you can't miss. Wrong! So often, relationships are formed *despite* men's chat-up lines, not because of them. In other words, most chat-up lines simply confirm women's fears that men are not serious.

Chat-up lines can be funny to read or hear in a film but in real life they're just that – lines. Everybody will recognize them as the superficial ear candy they are. At best they might make someone laugh. And that's good because everyone likes a good sense of humour (GSOH). But, on balance, something less facetious would probably give a better impression.

So here are some chat-up lines to smile about – *but never use*:

▶ *Do you believe in helping the homeless? (Yes.) Then take me home with you.*
▶ *If I said you had a beautiful body would you hold it against me?*
▶ *Do you know the difference between sex and conversation? (No.) Then let's go upstairs and talk.*
▶ *Do you have any raisins? (No.) Then how about a date?*

Instead of chat-up lines, engage in some normal conversation. Research shows that simply opening with 'hello' is as good as anything. From that point on, here's a ten-point plan that will give you the best chance of success:

1 *Quickly identify how the other person likes to be viewed.*
    (In other words, if you detect that your potential date likes to be thought of as, say, caring, or unique, or dynamic, or funny, then respond in a way that shows you have recognized and appreciate that quality. You'll get a clue by asking what their career is and what their favourite activities are.)
2 *Show that you like the other person.*
3 *Show that you have similar values.*
4 *Keep your face animated and make long eye contact.*
5 *Laugh at their jokes.*
6 *Match and mirror but keep it subtle (see Chapter 5).*
7 *Disagree for a time but then switch back to agreement.*
    (This comes from an experiment in which researchers compared the effects of agreeing all the time, disagreeing all the time and, thirdly, initially disagreeing with everything then, later, agreeing with everything. The third technique was the most successful.)
8 *Demonstrate in some way that you're very choosy.*
    (No one likes to think they're being chatted up by someone desperate or who is not considered desirable by others.)
9 *Try to have something happen that creates a modicum of fear.*
    (Research shows that fear increases arousal and makes other people seem more attractive, which explains the

popularity of fairground rides. Even walking over a high, narrow footbridge was shown to have such an effect.)

10 *Try to make acceptable physical contact, such as touching a hand or arm.*

(Physical contact generates a chemical called oxytocin which creates a bond and a desire for further touching.)

Insight

Here's a final piece of advice. If you're not having much success at the bar or disco early on, stay right till the end. Research shows chatting-up then has a much higher success rate.

WHAT MEN WANT

What men want is a lot simpler than what women want. It's sex. As a woman you won't have much problem attracting a man as long as he thinks there's a good chance of sleeping with you. In one famous study on an American college campus, an attractive woman approached various men and asked one of three questions:

▶ *Would you go out on a date tonight?*
▶ *Would you go back to my apartment with me?*
▶ *Would you have sex with me?*

Fifty per cent of the men agreed to a date, 69 per cent were willing to go back to the apartment and 75 per cent accepted the offer of sex. In other words, the greater the likelihood of sex, the more men were interested. (For how women responded in the same experiment, see below.)

So if you're interested in sex, you only have to make that apparent, but without seeming to take the initiative (a turn-off for men who like to believe they're in charge). But supposing you're not? At least, not for some time yet. In fact, you'd be well advised not to be open for sex on a first date if it's a long-term relationship you're interested in. Men still behave in accordance with the principle of a 'bad' woman for fun and a 'good' woman for marriage.

Here, according to research, are some of the other things that attract men:

- *feminized versions of their own faces*
- *a waist-to-hip ratio of 0.7*
- *a woman who is younger (on average in the USA, women are younger by 2–3 years for a first marriage, 5 years for a second marriage, and 8 years for a third marriage)*
- *a woman with the same 'market value' as themselves*
- *a good body of normal weight with a medium bust*
- *long hair*
- *a high voice*
- *a woman slightly less intelligent than themselves*
- *ovulation*
- *the scent of copulins (fatty acids found in vaginal secretions).*

WHAT WOMEN WANT

The evidence is that women enjoy sex just as much as men but they're far more discriminating. As part of the same study quoted above, women on an American college campus were approached by an attractive man and posed one of the same three questions:

- *Would you go out on a date tonight?*
- *Would you go back to my apartment with me?*
- *Would you have sex with me?*

Fifty per cent of the women – the same proportion as men – accepted a date but only six per cent agreed to go to the man's apartment and not a single woman agreed to sex. That's a huge if not surprising difference. So there certainly isn't any point in a man being overtly sexual in a chat-up. Quite the reverse. You'll usually have more success by taking things slowly.

Here, according to research, are some of the things that attract women:

- *masculinized versions of their own faces*
- *a V-shaped but not overly-muscular torso*
- *a man who is financially successful with a strong work ethic (the less physically attractive a man the more money he needs)*
- *a man with the same 'market value' as themselves*
- *height – the man must be taller and, ideally, over six feet (1.83 m)*
- *high testosterone (as evidenced by a deep voice, a square jaw and a strong handshake) for a short-term relationship, but a man with a more feminine side for a long-term relationship*
- *a man who is well-dressed*
- *a man who is polite, helpful and caring*
- *a good sense of humour (women seem to believe GSOH implies other desirable qualities such as intelligence, sensitivity, height, adaptability, masculinity and happiness)*
- *a man whose smell indicates that the segment of his DNA known as the major histocompatibility complex (MHC) is sufficiently different from her own (yes, women really can tell that, although they don't know that's what they're doing when they think he smells 'nice').*

Priming

Everyone understands that, say, wearing expensive jewellery will make others believe you're financially successful (even though you might have borrowed it). Less well understood is the way things in the environment, over which you have little or no control, can also influence another person's view of you. Let's say you've been attracted to someone while out-and-about somewhere. You've done some chatting-up. Now you're both hungry. And there's only one restaurant. Here's the strange thing. If that restaurant is glamorous and romantic then you're more likely than otherwise to view one another as glamorous and romantic. But if it's a scruffy, plate-crashing café, then you'll come across to one another as unsophisticated.

This impact of subtle – and sometimes not so subtle – stimuli is known as 'priming' which we first met in Chapter 5. So you need to think about this very carefully at the beginning of a relationship.

PRACTICAL EXERCISE
Take a look at the lists of things men and women want and work out how you could prime a date to make it more likely you'll be viewed favourably.

GENDER ROLES

Men and women have different 'pre-programmed' insecurities. A man's stem from the fact that evolution has assigned him the role of pursuing women (and sex). As a result, he constantly battles with the fear of rejection. A woman's insecurities come from the fear she might not be pursued.

Now, modern culture has exacerbated those male anxieties. Here's the thing modern men fear most of all:

▶ *Women can get along without us.*

Well, yes, women no longer need men to go out hunting because food nowadays comes from the supermarket. Nor do they even need men any longer to go out to work because there are plenty of job possibilities for women. It might be nice to have a man around for protection but, compared with the prehistoric environment, the world is pretty safe. And, anyway, there are things called police officers.

So men are no longer required to be 'manly'. In which case, why should women bother with them?

Well, that's how the thinking allegedly goes.

But, in fact, men, you can relax. Thousands of years of evolution have gone into creating the traditional gender roles and they can't be undone in a few decades. The world may have changed but the male and female mindsets haven't. Indeed, they can't.

Yes, there are some women getting along very happily without men and who wouldn't have it any other way. But, in practice, it's a non-issue. The vast majority of women are attracted to men. The vast majority of men are attracted to women. And the vast majority of both sexes are happiest when they fall approximately into the traditional roles. So that's that.

But one question still remains.

WHO OPENS THE DOOR?

At one time it was a simple matter. Men opened doors for women, gave up their seats on trains and even raised their hats. Nowadays life is very different.

Here's an interesting little scenario. You're driving along in town and, just ahead of you, a car is tentatively nudging its way out of a parking bay. You're not in a hurry so you stop and wave the driver on. What happens next?

Well, that depends on the sexes of the people involved. If a woman is in the parking bay and a man is doing the waving then, almost certainly, she'll gratefully pull out. But if it's a man in the parking bay and another man doing the waving the situation becomes much more complicated. Chances are the man in the parking bay won't pull out but, instead, will wave the other driver to come on by.

What's going on here? In a word, status. The driver doing the waving on is granting the other person the opportunity to pull out. Being, as it were, magnanimous. Lordly. Giving permission gives status. The person accepting the permission is, for the moment, cast in the role of the underling. The subject who depends on another's favour.

Women tend to accept that role more readily than men. Hence the two different reactions.

Of course, there are other things going on as well. Manners. Practical issues. Time considerations. But the principle holds good. Men were traditionally cast in the role of 'protectors' which, inevitably, also made them 'superior'.

Many women now object to that. And that's the whole problem. If all women objected, life would be simple. Men would simply stop doing it. But there are other women who feel the opposite. That men should open doors and that failing to do so reveals a considerable lack of style.

So how do you know what kind of woman you're dealing with? Sometimes it will be fairly obvious. But, if it's not, why not ask? You could say something like this:

> ▶ *I'm the kind of guy who likes to open doors for women. Does that bother you?*

You can then go on to discuss it.

Now let's look at the subject from the woman's point of view. There are really three possible positions:

> ▶ *Men should open doors for women; it's the polite thing to do.*
> ▶ *I would feel insulted if a man made a point of opening doors for me.*
> ▶ *I don't care either way.*

Let's say you're attracted to a man. But you're independent and proud of your equality while he is plainly the type who opens doors. How can you handle that? Well, once again, why not just discuss it? Nicely. Because it may not have any undertones of superiority and inferiority. Some men just think it's the elegant thing to do. So just say something like this:

> ▶ *I appreciate you opening doors for me. It's stylish. But I also have my own personal style and I'd sincerely prefer it if we open doors on the basis of whoever is there first.*

Of course, doors are not the only issue. But you get the idea. The same approach goes for all the other gender issues. Don't allow ignorance to damage your confidence. Talk about them. Don't argue about them. And then you can do the right thing.

DEVELOPING CONFIDENCE THROUGH CONVERSATION

Steve's partner Jill was in the habit of phoning him at work at least once a day. The things she said were not urgent. They could have kept until he got home and, in fact, he wouldn't have minded if he didn't hear them at all. So Steve got more and more irritated. He even wondered if the point of the calls was to check up on him. And, anyway, didn't she realize he had important work to get on with? Did she think his job was so insignificant that he had time for small talk? One day he barked: 'Will you stop bothering me at work.'

Naturally, Jill was upset. She assumed Steve liked to hear from her and she couldn't understand his attitude. Thinking that he didn't care about her she lost confidence in herself.

The anecdote illustrates an important distinction between the way men and women use talking.

▶ *For women, talking is a way of establishing and maintaining connection.*
▶ *For men, talking is a way of conveying information.*

As far as Steve was concerned, the information Jill had to impart wasn't important so there was no point in phoning.

Well, that's a generalization but it's fairly true to say that women value conversation far more than men do. Silence is a negative. And, even, in certain circumstances, a punishment. Many women therefore prefer to say anything rather than nothing.

An extreme example of the male outlook is given in Kent Nerburn's *Neither Wolf Nor Dog*. Nerburn is a passenger in a car with two

Native Americans, Dan and Grover, the driver. Grover picks up another hitch-hiking Native American. Mile after mile nothing at all is said and after a time Nerburn records: 'The silence was disconcerting me.'

So he decides to break it. 'Going up to the grave site?' he asks the hitch-hiker.

It turns out to be completely the wrong thing to do and the newcomer immediately freezes and asks to be let out again.

'White man's disease!' Dan snaps, and goes on to explain: 'We're not like white people who have to fill up every damn second of silence with a bunch of talk.'

Nerburn was writing about the difference between Native Americans and white Americans. But they were also men and the event can also be seen as an illustration of the way many men are. Nerburn, reacting more like a woman, believes they should talk to establish connection. The three other men don't feel any such need. Their sense of connection comes about in another way.

The moral of all this is simple:

▶ *If you're a woman, don't let silence destroy your self-confidence – it doesn't necessarily indicate a lack of interest by a man.*
▶ *If you're a man, you'll be much more successful with women if you learn to use language for connection.*

DISCUSSING EXTERNAL PROBLEMS

Men and women use language in different ways. In fact, you could almost say there's feminine English and masculine English. They sound more or less the same but the meanings vary.

Probably the clearest distinction is in the way men and women use language to talk about problems. Men like to solve problems and, if they can't be solved, to forget about them. Women come to terms with problems by talking about them, without necessarily trying to solve them. I'm certainly not saying that women never solve problems because, of course, they do. But in terms of the purpose of talking about them it holds pretty good.

Here's a fairly common scenario. A woman comes home and tells her partner that she's having problems at work that are making her unhappy. Her partner immediately leaps into problem-solving mode.

'So leave and get another job,' he says.

But she doesn't want another job. She wants to be able to talk through the things that are bothering her and to hear some empathetic words of support. Here's how the situation then deteriorates:

1 *He becomes irritated because she won't follow the 'obvious' course of action.*
2 *She becomes upset that she's not hearing the words of support she wants.*
3 *He feels he's being criticized for not having come up with an acceptable solution, becoming either increasingly defensive or increasingly aggressive – or both.*
4 *She becomes conciliatory to try to placate him.*
5 *The issue is now no longer one of problems at work but power within the relationship – sensing 'weakness' he now takes advantage of her conciliatory overtures to announce he's not going to discuss the situation any more, or even to speak to her again.*
6 *End of conversation.*
7 *Both partners lose confidence.*

So how should you handle these kinds of issues?

If you're a man: When your partner tells you about a problem don't immediately try to come up with a solution. (Of course, this doesn't apply to a problem such as the house burning down.) Just listen, try to understand what she's feeling and offer sympathetic words. That's probably everything she's hoping for. However, if you sense that a solution is subsequently needed, try approaching it like this:

▶ *What would you like to have happen?*

If you're a woman: Understand that finding solutions is a man's natural response to problems. And it can be very useful at times. But if you're not looking for a solution say something like this:

▶ *Do you mind if I just talk this through with you? It makes me feel better.*

If he continues to offer solutions which are unwelcome, say something like this:

▶ *I appreciate you trying to solve my problem. However, at the moment what I'm looking for is emotional support to cope with the situation as it is.*

DISCUSSING RELATIONSHIP PROBLEMS

John Gottman is the head of the Gottman Institute, more popularly known as the 'Love Lab'. He's been studying relationships since the 1970s. By analysing an hour-long conversation between partners he's been able to predict with 95 per cent accuracy whether or not a couple would still be together 15 years later. In fact, he's been pretty accurate on the basis of watching just a 3-minute conversation. Intriguingly, Gottman discovered that 69 per cent of couples never resolve their conflicts, no matter how many discussions they have. But that in itself does not predict marital failure. Far more important is *how* couples discuss their differences.

What, then, are the clues?

1 *How the conversation opens (normally the woman's role). If it's soft and conciliatory that's a good sign but if it's immediately harsh that's a bad sign.*

2   *How personal any criticisms are. In other words, it's reasonable to say 'I'm upset because you never help me in the kitchen.' (Best of all would be to use the three steps to assertiveness described in Chapter 7.) But saying, 'You're a lazy, selfish, self-centred person' would be a bad sign.*

3   *The reaction of the partner on the receiving end. If that person remains calm and open to considering the points made, that's good. But anger, defensiveness and stonewalling (mostly a male tactic) are all bad signs.*

4   *How amiable the couple remain. Using devices to keep the emotional temperature down is a good sign (telling a joke, recalling something nice in the past, making a cup of coffee). Letting the conflict escalate is a bad sign.*

5   *The nasty/nice ratio. In other words, being nasty to one another infrequently, and nice frequently, is a good sign. The reverse is a bad sign. Worst of all is contempt.*

6   *Damage limitation. Rushing to soothe and heal any wounds is a good sign. Leaving wounds to fester, and brooding over wounds, are bad signs.*

Of course, we have to be careful to distinguish cause and effect. Successful couples display the good signs because they already feel affection, love and respect for one another. If your relationship is in serious trouble, robotically switching to 'best practice' is not necessarily going to save it. But it certainly *will help* to avoid the negatives Gottman has identified and to adopt the positives.

Insight

It seems that once an argument escalates and their heart rate goes above 100, people are no longer capable of being rational and reasonable. The technical term for this is 'flooding'. Some people are more easily flooded than others, and men are generally more easily flooded than women. This is why it's important to keep the emotional temperature down.

PRACTICAL EXERCISE

Next time a difficult issue comes up between you, STOP. Open this book, refer to the six points above and endeavour to conduct your discussion in accordance with 'best practice'.

FREEDOM CRY

It was the day before St Valentine's Day and Peter and Sarah were shopping together.

'I've got some things I need to do,' said Sarah. 'You go off and buy me a romantic CD for tomorrow and we'll meet up later for a coffee.'

Sarah wanted to get rid of Peter for a while so she could buy him a present. And she was looking forward to it. She considered her words completely harmless. But, to her astonishment, Peter was furious and the whole occasion was a disaster. Sarah lost confidence. She began to feel she couldn't say anything without risking Peter's anger.

What's going on here? In fact, something easily explained. Justified, no, but simple, yes:

> ▶ *Most men can't stand anything that strikes them as a restriction on their freedom.*

Peter already had been planning to buy something but now it would look as if he was only getting a present because he'd been asked, not because he wanted to. What's more, Sarah seemed not only to be ordering him to buy her something but even instructing him what to get. To demonstrate his independence he decided not to buy her anything at all and St Valentine's Day was a failure.

Why are men like this? It goes back to those mother/schoolmistress figures I dealt with at the beginning of the chapter. As soon as a woman gives a man an instruction ('nags') she becomes transformed from his lover into his mother/schoolmistress. His jailer. Men feel that independence is an absolutely vital aspect of being male. Anything that reduces it is interpreted as an attack with subjugation as its aim. Worse, by taking on the role of mother/schoolmistress, the woman makes herself 'superior' and the man 'inferior'. And no man can relate to his lover with confidence from a position of 'inferiority'. Refusing the request, or ignoring it, seems to be the only option.

What's the real solution?

If you're a woman: Try to express your desires in a way that gives the man some freedom to make a decision. Sarah could easily have said something like this. 'I need time to do one or two things. Where would you like to meet up?' And left it at that. In that way she makes her position known but gives him some room to make a decision.

On a more general point, men like to feel they're doing things of their own free will. If a woman asks a man to do something now he instinctively puts off doing it. Otherwise he feels he's been ordered around and has given in. By doing the job later he retains his self-respect. For more on the technique of 'seeding' ideas rather than giving orders see Chapter 7.

If you're a man: Take a sheet of card and write on it all the things your partner does for you. Humbling, isn't it! Then add this thought: 'Asking me to do something doesn't make me inferior.' Keep that card with you and refer to it from time to time.

Insight

Work on everything in this book to do with self-confidence. The more self-confident you are, the easier you'll find it to accede to reasonable requests without losing self-respect.

CONFIDENCE IN BED

The first time you have sex with someone is very, very unlikely to be the 'best'. Of course, there are those who find novelty so exciting that the thrill of it overrides everything else. But they are rare. Nor are the second or third times likely to be the most mind-blowing. Or the tenth. What I'm getting at is this. Unless you're both extremely experienced, extremely uninhibited and extremely well-matched, it's going to take a while.

So don't let initial 'poor performance' damage your confidence. It will automatically get better as you come to know more about one another.

Most people feel guilty about at least some of their sexual practices and desires. So it's extremely unlikely that any relatively new partner is going to say: 'I'd like you to do this to me', or 'I'd like to do that to you'. Not, anyway, if it's something that's 'daring' – that's beyond what's believed to be 'normal'.

So how can you find the confidence to progress? One way is to use the technique of swapping intimacies described in Chapter 4. You reveal something about your desires that go just a little bit further than anything you've done so far. If your partner responds and moves even further ahead, then you can both explore until you sense resistance has been reached. But if your partner freezes, then you know you have to back off.

Men are, generally speaking, far more interested in experimenting than women are. So, if you're a woman, you can feel quite confident about proposing most things. However, even men have their limits and some reach theirs sooner than others. One danger area is the sharing of fantasies. Be cautious about that.

If you're a man, you'll almost certainly find your partner is less enthusiastic about experimentation than you are. The attitude is likely to be: 'I'm enjoying things as they are so why bother to try something else?'

The extreme manifestation of a lack of confidence is, of course, impotence in a man and failure to orgasm in a woman. It's very important never to entertain doubts about your sexual performance.

As described in Chapter 2 you might plant an unconscious suggestion such as this:

▶ *I love my genitals. They are wonderful. They make me very happy and they make my partner very happy, too.*

For even greater impact you could use visualization, especially under self-hypnosis.

PRACTICAL EXERCISE
Follow the procedure for self-hypnosis as described in Chapter 2. When you get to Step 3 state the purpose of self-hypnosis along the following lines: 'I am entering into a state of self-hypnosis so that I can hand over to my unconscious mind the task of making me confident about ...' You would then add the thing that makes you feel insecure, such as 'being seen naked by my partner' or whatever it might be. Don't forget the key word *unconscious*. During the 'internal' phase of the self-hypnosis you would then imagine yourself undressing and your partner's eyes lighting up with admiration and desire.

Insight

Sex is a big subject. You might like to take a look at *Teach Yourself: Have Great Sex* or *Teach Yourself: Get Intimate with Tantric Sex*.

THE SOLUTION TO ALL GENDER PROBLEMS

I've already written about the importance of acceptance and now I'm going to emphasize it some more.

Acceptance is the solution to gender problems. And in this context, one of the most important things to accept is that men and women are different. In lots of ways. You can't 'cherry pick' the differences. You can't, as a man, be delighted that women have, say, breasts but then complain about their desire for connection.

You have to take the whole package. You have to accept it.

Listen to Richard's story:

'We had a pretty good relationship but it had its tensions. Mostly on my side. She'd say something I took exception to and I'd explode. Silly little things usually. But I took them as attacks on me. I see now that I was lacking in confidence. Then one day I had a kind of revelation. I realized that she loved me. I mean, I already knew it in one sense. But I hadn't really embraced it until that moment. I saw that the things she said, which sometimes so enraged me, weren't meant as attacks on me at all. She didn't even realize the significance to me of what she was saying. So how could I be angry? They were just the result of the fact that she was a woman. And I decided to accept that. I decided to accept her love in the terms that she expressed it. And now all that insecurity is gone. All that tension is gone. And it feels wonderful.'

Each night, before going to sleep, plant this suggestion in your unconscious:

▶ *I love my partner and my partner loves me. Therefore, I accept the things my partner says and does as tokens of my partner's love.*

10 THINGS TO REMEMBER

1 *Value members of the opposite sex as people first and as men or women second; you're much less likely to be overawed.*

2 *Get 'inside the heads' of the opposite sex by reading their books, watching their films and spending as much time as possible with them in a non-sexual context.*

3 *Being a woman in charge of men is liable to exacerbate male insecurities – men instinctively feel that they're 'protectors' of women and find it hard to accept a subordinate role.*

4 *Don't 'project' superhuman qualities onto potential partners and don't work with a fixed template of how a partner should be.*

5 *Avoid chat-up lines; instead try to identify the way the other person likes to be seen and show that you've recognized and appreciate that quality.*

6 *Use cognitive therapy, suggestion, visualization and self-hypnosis to boost your confidence with the opposite sex in daily life, in romance and in bed.*

7 *Discuss differences without making personal attacks or getting angry – when you feel the emotional temperature rising too far, STOP.*

8 *Men like to solve problems and, if they can't be solved, to forget about them; women often use language to come to terms with problems.*

9 *Independence is very important to men – but they're also very insecure about it; the more confidence you have as a man the more secure you'll feel about acceding to reasonable requests.*

10 *Acceptance is the key to many gender conflicts.*

HOW CONFIDENT ARE YOU NOW?

- *Are you enjoying the company of the opposite sex in non-romantic situations?*
- *Have you been getting inside the heads of the opposite sex by reading books by female/male authors and watching films by female/male directors?*
- *At work, are you able to consider suggestions by the opposite sex on the merits of the case rather than on gender?*
- *Are you able to view potential partners realistically, without projecting your fantasies onto them?*
- *Have you tried going out with people who don't match your 'template' for the ideal partner?*
- *Have you stopped putting yourself down?*
- *Have you practised identifying the way other people like to be viewed?*
- *Have you successfully chatted anyone up using the ten-point plan?*
- *Have you discussed a relationship problem without making personal attacks, stonewalling or getting angry?*
- *Have you accepted that members of the opposite sex are different?*

Score:

If you answered 'yes' to most questions, then you're obviously fairly confident dealing with members of the opposite sex. Go straight on to the next chapter. If you answered 'yes' to between five and seven questions, then you can also go on to the next chapter but revisit this one from time to time and think about the issues it raises. If you could answer 'yes' to only four questions or fewer, then you obviously find it very hard to behave as you'd like with the opposite sex. Keep working on the practical exercises in this chapter until you raise your score to five or higher, and only then read on.

For where and how to meet potential romantic partners see Taking it further.

People who put you down

In this chapter you will learn:
- *how to stop other people undermining your self-confidence*
- *how to disarm critics*
- *how you can live happily without the approval of others.*

> *Do what you feel in your heart to be right – for you'll be criticized anyway. You'll be damned if you do, and damned if you don't.*
>
> Eleanor Roosevelt (1884–1962)

Why are you lacking in confidence? So far we've been looking at internal explanations, that's to say, the way you look at life. Now we're going to do something different. We're going to look outside. We're going to look at the attitudes of other people towards you. You see, it could well be that other people, either deliberately or unconsciously, have undermined you and made you lose faith in yourself. And it could still be going on right now. If that's the case you must put a stop to it as soon as possible.

It could be any of the following and more:

- *a boss who wants to aggrandize himself or herself at your expense*
- *an instructor who always seems to be picking on you*
- *a customer or client complaining about a product or service*
- *a friend who is jealous*

- *parents who are/were too demanding*
- *a partner needing an ego boost.*

DEALING WITH CRITICISM

Most of us find it hard to deal with criticism. We feel hurt. We lose self-esteem. We dwell on the 'attack'. We build it up. And up. And up. We may get angry and bitter. Depending on personality, we may plot revenge of some sort or we may enter a period of demoralization.

I want you to stop handling criticism in that kind of way. I want you to look at the whole subject in a new light. What I'm going to say next is easy to write and hard to do. But I want you to understand that, when you're criticized, it's you who makes yourself upset. Not the other person. Not the criticism.

Sounds crazy? Let me explain. Someone criticizes you – let's say at work – and then you have all, or at least some, of the following thoughts: 'I knew I wasn't cut out for this. I'll never be any good at it. I'll probably get the sack now. I just don't know if I'll ever be any good at anything. What's going to become of me? I should have settled for an easier job. It's hopeless. I'm a loser. Still, it wasn't right to say that. Who does he think he is? He thinks he's Mr Bloody Perfect. He's arrogant.'

Do you recognize any of that? I'm sure you do.

If you think back to Chapter 1 where we looked at cognitive therapy you should be able to identify several 'cognitive distortions'. See if you can pick out the all-or-nothing thinking, generalization, exaggeration, jumping to negative conclusions, 'should' statements and labelling.

Now let's see if there's another way. In general terms, a criticism will either be right or wrong. So let's think about this.

- *If it's right, then you can accept the criticism and take action to correct your mistake.*

It's really not a big deal. Everyone makes mistakes every day. There's no need to think less of yourself or paint a doomsday scenario. In fact, correcting mistakes is a good learning experience so, afterwards, you'll actually be better than before.

▶ *If it's wrong, then you can reject the criticism and explain why.*

In which case, you have absolutely no reason whatsoever to lose self-esteem. On the contrary! The other person was wrong and you were right.

So what does all this mean? It means there's no logical reason for criticism to dent your belief in yourself. Think about it for a moment. Let it sink in. Once you understand that you'll be far more resilient in the face of negative comment and your self-confidence will increase.

Let's dwell on this a little longer because it's a key point. Your worth as a human being does not go down because someone criticizes you. You're the same person. The same valuable human being that you were before the criticism was made. There's a lot more to you than that. If the criticism is right, just be sure to learn from it and then you'll emerge 'better' than before. If the criticism is wrong, then there's no need for your self-confidence to be dented at all.

Ah yes, you say. But the other person may still think I'm wrong, even if I'm not. And, even worse, the very fact that they voiced the criticism must mean they don't like me. Okay, I understand those points. So let's now take a look at a way you can deal with the people who are making the criticisms.

DISARMING YOUR CRITICS

How exactly do you go about either accepting criticism or rejecting it? When people consider themselves 'under attack' there are, broadly, three kinds of response. They 'fight back', they 'flee' or they try to 'disarm' their opponents. I'm now going to try to convince you that the third option is usually the best.

- ▶ *'Fighting back' is something you should almost never do. It only raises the emotional temperature and leads to an escalation. Remember the principle of both science and Eastern philosophy: Every force creates an equal and opposite force. You may both start saying things you don't mean with the result that the situation just gets more and more wounding.*
- ▶ *'Fleeing' is an option only in extreme cases. The problem with fleeing is that it leaves the situation unresolved.*
- ▶ *'Disarmament' is the best response because it keeps everything calm and allows for a constructive resolution.*

Let's see then, how the 'disarmament' process works.

STEP 1 ASK FOR CLARIFICATION OF THE CRITICISM
There are three reasons for that:

- ▶ *Firstly, you make sure you fully understand the other person's point of view.*
- ▶ *Secondly, you show that you're engaging positively, which should reduce any feelings of irritation or anger on the other person's part.*
- ▶ *Thirdly – and this is very important – you force the other person to re-examine their position and, if it's unbalanced or unfounded, to modify it.*

STEP 2 FIND SOMETHING TO AGREE WITH
Do this even if you consider the other person to be wrong. At first this may seem hard to swallow. But there's a very good reason for this tactic. It continues the 'disarmament' process and keeps everything calm so you can move on to Step 3.

STEP 3 RESOLVE THE SITUATION THROUGH AMICABLE DISCUSSION
I'm now going to give you some examples of this process in various different situations. Each little scenario is designed to be the basis for role-playing. That's to say, you enlist the help of a friend and act out the scenes, improvising your own dialogue as you go. Be as realistic as possible. If you remember, in Chapter 2 I suggested this kind of

'trial run' as a way of reducing anxiety. It also, of course, allows you to practise handling different situations. Initially, cast yourself in the role of the person being criticized. But, later, switch roles and become the person doing the criticism. This will increase your insight.

If you don't have someone you feel sufficiently comfortable to role-play with, then I suggest you write down your own imaginary dialogues. At the very least, visualize the exchanges, as explained in Chapter 2, and keep replaying them in your head.

YOUR BOSS

You have your job. Your boss has his. Which is, in part, to oversee what you do. So it's almost inevitable that, on occasion, you'll receive criticism. In this scenario you've made some small errors to which your boss has completely overreacted.

PRACTICAL EXERCISE

BOSS (played by your friend): Can't you ever do anything right?

YOU (playing yourself): I think I usually do things correctly. What exactly are you referring to?

BOSS: This report you've written is full of spelling mistakes for a start.

YOU: I apologize for that. How many exactly?

BOSS: There's one right on the first page. And another on page three.

YOU: I'll put those right. However, I don't think that amounts to never doing anything right. What else?

BOSS: Well, I don't agree with your final conclusion.

YOU: I was confident in my analysis. However, I'd be pleased to hear where you think I've got it wrong.

By responding in this kind of way you achieve several things:

▶ *You compel your boss to be more balanced.*
▶ *You make it clear, in a non-confrontational way, that you won't accept unwarranted criticism.*
▶ *You show that you're willing to correct errors where genuine and learn from the experience.*
▶ *You demonstrate that you're an employee who can work together with other people and handle criticism.*

The result is that you come out of the situation a winner because you've used the incident in a positive way.

Now you create your own role-play, using the scenario above as a model, and continue it for a couple of minutes.

YOUR CLIENT

In this scenario we meet the complaining client. The client feels she has a genuine grievance but, in reality, it's all due to a misunderstanding on her part. In your life you may or may not have clients to deal with but the broad principles apply in all kinds of situations.

PRACTICAL EXERCISE
CLIENT (played by your friend): Why can't you do your job properly? I'm not paying for this kind of thing.

YOU (playing yourself): What exactly is the problem?

CLIENT: You've just made a complete mess of everything. You're completely useless.

YOU: I do sometimes make mistakes like everybody else. But I'll do my best to put it right. Tell me what I've got wrong.

CLIENT: It's all very well saying that now. It's a pity you didn't care enough before.

YOU: What gives you the impression that I don't care?

CLIENT: Look at this for a start. Is this what you call a proper job?

YOU: I can understand why you would think I didn't care if I had done a bad job. Let me explain why I think I've done the right thing and you then tell me what you think.

That's just a brief outline. Adapt it to your own circumstances and carry it on for a minute or two.

Insight

The principles are clear. First of all try to clarify the problem and then try to find something to agree with as a way of 'disarming' your critic and making him or her a little more amenable to reason.

YOUR INSTRUCTOR

Let's say you're on some kind of course, together with other people, and that you seem to be getting more than your fair share of criticism. This sometimes happens. The instructor picks on someone as a 'fall guy' to entertain the others. If you don't defend yourself there's no end to it. In this scenario we'll assume you're completely in the right. You're now going to try to disarm your critic without causing any bad feeling.

PRACTICAL EXERCISE
INSTRUCTOR (played by your friend): Here comes Ms Hopeless. Last again!

YOU (playing yourself): I really don't understand why you're calling me Ms Hopeless. That suggests I have no ability to improve whereas I think I have learnt a lot on this course. What exactly are you referring to?

INSTRUCTOR: Well, that's fairly obvious.

YOU: Not to me. I need to know more precisely so I can have the chance to correct my mistakes and improve.

INSTRUCTOR: You were very slow completing the test.

YOU: It's true that I was slow. I do like to double-check things. My feeling is that reliability comes first and that speed will follow with practice. How did I compare with the others in terms of accuracy?

INSTRUCTOR: Well, let's see. Hmm! Actually, you have one of the highest marks. But that's no good without speed.

YOU: I take your point about speed. Accuracy without speed is less than optimum performance. On the other hand, it seems to me that speed without accuracy is of no value at all.

INSTRUCTOR: Okay, I shouldn't have said 'hopeless'. But you do need to work on speeding up.

YOU: I'll do that. Under your marking system who scores highest overall? The people who were wrong but fast? Or the people who were slow but right?

Insight

Once again the same principles are at work. Find out the exact nature of the criticism, then find something in the criticism that you can agree with. Only then can you move on to the 'negotiation' phase.

YOUR PARENTS

Coping with parental criticism is extremely difficult when you're young but even middle-aged people can find it hard to deal with domineering parents. Recently a man of 60 consulted me because his father has just committed suicide at the age of 93 and this man was distraught because there was so much 'unfinished business'. I'll call him 'H'.

'All my life I was never good enough for him,' H told me. 'And now I'm never going to have the chance to have it out with him.'

In reality, even if his father had lived to be 120, H would never have raised the subject. And that's a pity because if he had, and if he'd done it in the right way at the appropriate time, his relationship with his father might have been a lot better.

Most critical parents are only acting from what they think are the best of motives. They see criticism as a form of motivation. But, usually, it has the opposite effect. In this scenario, you play yourself and a friend plays the father or mother who undermines your confidence. You're now going to tackle your parent.

PRACTICAL EXERCISE
YOU (playing yourself): I got a promotion today.

PARENT (played by your friend): Well, it's about time.

YOU: Why do you say that?

PARENT: Because you've been in the same job about three years.

YOU: It's true that some people are promoted more quickly but others don't get promoted at all, so I think congratulations are in order.

PARENT: You always set your sights so low. At your age I was managing 100 people.

YOU: How do you know what I've set my sights on? It's true that my ambitions are different to yours. However, I'm not you, so they're bound to be different. Nevertheless, I can admire your achievements. Can't you find it in you to admire me for anything?

PARENT: Such as what?

YOU: For having won a promotion despite the fact that you've undermined my self-confidence all my life.

PARENT: I'd show confidence in you if you achieved something.

YOU: In my opinion it's the other way around. Self-confidence comes first and achievement follows. Don't you think that's right?

PARENT: Well, maybe.

YOU: In fact, I've had to overcome terrible feelings of inadequacy and self-doubt to get where I am. I feel proud of that.

Once again, adapt the scenario to your own case.

Insight

Dealing with critical parents is always complicated because we always want them to feel proud of us. That old desire to say, 'Look Mum – no hands' never goes away. So it's very important to understand that the approval of other people – including those close to you – has nothing to do with your worth as a person.

YOUR PARTNER

It's an unfortunate fact that two people who start out loving one another can end up destroying one another. If your partner is always putting you down, criticizing you, and generally finding fault with everything you do then that's a situation that needs to be tackled immediately.

Why does it happen? There are several possible reasons:

▶ *Competition: Some people are so highly competitive they have to compete with everyone they're in contact with. In order to raise themselves up they put everyone else down. And that includes you.*
▶ *Projection: Your partner may have fallen in love with an ideal image that was 'projected' onto you, rather than with the reality. They then set about trying to change you into the 'projection' by making criticisms.*

- ▶ *Association: That's to say, your partner may feel everything you do is somehow a reflection on him or her by association. If you do something differently to the way they would have done it they don't like it.*
- ▶ *Control: Your partner may feel inferior. Threatened. Insecure. He or she therefore tries to take control of you. In this case, the aim is quite specifically to destroy your self-confidence so that you become almost a slave, always doing what your partner tells you.*

Unfortunately, these kinds of attitudes are very common in relationships and ultimately self-defeating. Which is why so many couples separate and divorce.

In the following scenario we'll imagine your partner has voiced yet another criticism. Adapt it to your own situation and continue it for a couple of minutes. The three-step formula described in Chapter 7 is a little disguised here but you should still be able to recognize it.

Insight

If you're in a relationship in which you're constantly being criticized you need to tackle the situation as soon as possible. Don't allow it to continue because it can only end badly.

PRACTICAL EXERCISE

YOUR PARTNER (played by your friend): You're absolutely hopeless. I thought I told you the proper way to do this.

YOU (playing yourself): I understand that you're frustrated. However, that doesn't entitle you to call me 'absolutely hopeless'. Do you realize how frequently you criticize me?

YOUR PARTNER: When the boot fits.

YOU: Constructive criticism is one thing. However, what you said was simply insulting. Do you know why you're constantly finding fault with me?

YOUR PARTNER: Because you're always doing things wrong.

YOU: Always? I don't think I get things wrong any more than anybody else. Do you really think your criticisms are fair or valid?

YOUR PARTNER: Well I certainly don't make that mistake.

YOU: Even if your criticisms are correct, do you think it's always appropriate to voice them? Why do you feel you have to do that?

YOUR PARTNER: If I don't point them out, how will you ever improve?

YOU: Have you ever considered that by lowering my self-esteem you're actually diminishing the person you fell in love with?

By answering in this way you're compelling your partner to consider the real motivations behind the criticisms, as well as the consequences. If you can move on to have a dialogue like this with your partner you can both be winners in the end.

Insight

If your partner continues to undermine you then you'll have to consider the 'fleeing' option. That's to say, separating. The whole point of a relationship is to have a better life together than you would have had otherwise. If, on the contrary, the relationship is a source of unhappiness and demoralizing, then there's no point in continuing it.

(If you turn back to Chapter 11, about developing confidence with the opposite sex, you'll also find there a technique for maintaining your self-confidence, even in the face of constant criticism from a partner.)

LIVING WITHOUT APPROVAL

We all seek love and approval in our lives. And there's nothing wrong with that. On the contrary. But there's one thing you must understand. Living without love and living without approval doesn't diminish your worth as a human being. I want to be quite clear about this. I'm not suggesting you should deliberately learn to live without love or approval. Love is a wonderful thing. But what I am saying is that if it so happens you live alone, if it so happens you have no close relatives, if you have no close friends, if you have no one to approve of your achievements and even if there are people who disapprove of you, you can nevertheless still have confidence in yourself.

What counts is what you feel about yourself.

You see, the problem with relying on other people's approval is that you become like a rudderless boat, completely at the mercy of the wind and the waves. When people compliment you, your spirits soar up to the crests. Very nice. But when people criticize you, your spirits go into the troughs. That's not good. And it's all the worse if the criticism comes from someone very close to you. Then you're literally like the pricked balloon. One minute you're on a high. The next minute you're a little shrivelled-up remnant of what you had been.

I'm not suggesting you should cut yourself off from other people or close your mind to criticisms they might make. Those criticisms could turn out to be very useful. What I am aiming to do is get you to see that a criticism about one thing, or even about several things, doesn't amount to a criticism of everything that you are. A key phrase here is:

▶ *Know your worth.*

Insight

Don't rely on the love and approval of other people for your sense of self-worth. Instead, learn to love and approve of yourself. Then you have something you can always rely on.

PRACTICAL EXERCISE
If you live alone and are unhappy about it, or if you live with a partner and fear a life alone, the following exercises should help.

1 *Draw up a list of all the advantages of being alone. In fact,
   there are quite a lot. Here are some suggestions to get you
   started:*
   ▷ *I can do anything I want whenever I want.*
   ▷ *My enjoyment of the things I like won't be marred by a
      partner who doesn't enjoy them.*
   ▷ *I can experiment with different things without feeling
      constrained by a partner's expectations.*
   ▷ *I can change my appearance and my beliefs as I wish.*
   ▷ *I will become stronger and more resourceful.*
   Reflect on those and then add some more of your own.
2 *Divide a sheet of paper into two columns. On the left-hand
   side set down all the things you consider to be the advantages
   of living with someone else. Then on the right-hand side see if
   you can find any counter-arguments. For example, you might
   begin like this:*

Advantages	Disadvantages
We can enjoy doing things together.	There's no reason I can't enjoy the same things on my own. In fact, I might enjoy them more because I won't have to make concessions to another person who doesn't like the same things.
There will be someone else to help take decisions.	I can learn to take decisions on my own; that will make me a more self-confident person.

3 *Try doing more things alone. It may be you've always told
   yourself 'I'm not going to do that on my own.' Well, give
   it a go and see what happens. You may well enjoy yourself
   far more than you thought. Why not go to the beach alone?
   Why not go to a social event alone? Why not make yourself
   a special meal alone? In this way you can learn to enjoy
   the thing for itself rather than for your reflection in another
   person's eyes.*

10 THINGS TO REMEMBER

1 *Other people may try to undermine your self-confidence for various reasons.*

2 *There's no logical reason criticism should reduce your feelings of self-confidence or self-worth.*

3 *If a criticism is right you can learn from it and become a 'better' person.*

4 *If a criticism is wrong then just ignore it.*

5 *Don't 'fight back' against a critic or 'flee' but, instead, try 'disarmament'.*

6 *To 'disarm' a critic first clarify the problem, then find something to agree with and, finally, negotiate in an amicable way.*

7 *You can practise 'disarmament' by role-playing with a friend.*

8 *Living without love and approval doesn't diminish your worth as a human being.*

9 *When you rely on love and approval your spirits constantly rise and fall; when you love and approve of yourself you can always maintain a positive outlook.*

10 *Discover the enjoyment of doing things alone.*

HOW CONFIDENT ARE YOU NOW?

▶ *Have you stopped upsetting yourself when someone criticizes you?*
▶ *Have you been able to recognize that a criticism was correct and made the appropriate changes?*
▶ *Have you been able to reject an invalid criticism, explaining why clearly and calmly?*
▶ *When last criticized, did you ask for clarification?*
▶ *When last criticized, did you find something to agree with?*
▶ *When last criticized, did you resolve the situation through amicable discussion?*
▶ *Do you feel that 'disarming' a critic is preferable to either 'fighting back' or 'fleeing'?*
▶ *Are you now able to hear criticism from those close to you without losing your sense of self-worth?*
▶ *Have you forced yourself to go alone to something you'd normally only go to with someone else?*
▶ *Do you love and approve of yourself?*

Score:

If you answered 'yes' to most questions, then you're obviously able to handle criticism fairly easily, a very important skill. Turn to the final chapter and start your one-month confidence plan. If you answered 'yes' to between five and seven questions, you don't allow criticism to unravel your life but it hurts all the same, especially when it's from someone close. You can also go on to the next chapter but revisit this one from time to time and think about the issues it raises. If you could answer 'yes' to only four questions or fewer, then you obviously find it very hard to handle criticism. It hurts and it makes you question so much about yourself that you find it difficult to function normally for a time. Keep working on the practical exercises in this chapter until you raise your score to five or higher, and only then read on.

13

Your one-month confidence plan

In this chapter you will learn:
• **how to put everything together.**

Reading this book is only the start. You now have to put
everything into practice. Here is a one-month plan to do just
that. If you complete it I guarantee you'll be a far more confident
person. And don't stop just because the month has come to an end.
You need to keep on following the same principles and practices so
you continue to grow in poise and assurance.

Before you start decide on your motto (Chapter 2).

EVERY DAY

Do:

▶ Begin with a 'pep' talk for yourself, incorporating your motto,
  then, as the day progresses, have 'pep' sessions with everyone
  else you're responsible for, using rituals as appropriate
  (see Chapter 10).
▶ Push your warmth ahead of you (see Chapter 3).
▶ Give a greeting kiss to as many people as possible. Answer
  questions about how you are by saying 'wonderful' or
  'marvellous' (see Chapter 3).
▶ Start a conversation with a stranger or someone to whom
  you've previously spoken only a few words (see Chapter 4).
▶ Speak to as many members of the opposite sex as possible
  (see Chapter 11).

- Tell a joke (see Chapter 4).
- Accept the love that's on offer to you (see Chapters 3 and 11).
- Pay attention to what your partner says (if you have one) and try harder to understand what he or she really wants.
- Make a point of finding out about something and incorporating your new knowledge into your conversation.
- Challenge yourself in some new way. It doesn't have to be something very big or elaborate (we'll be leaving that for the weekends). But every day should be a different kind of thing. For example, one day could be a social challenge such as telling a joke, another day could be a mental challenge such as starting to learn a new language and on yet another day you could set yourself a physical challenge such as diving into a swimming pool. Don't make the challenge too difficult. It's enough that you go slightly further than you ever have before. Remember, every long journey begins with one step.
- Sow those seeds by the handful. As we saw in Chapter 7, it's not a good idea to give yourself just one single chance of success. When you invest all of your emotions in one hope then failure becomes overwhelmingly destructive. Instead, give yourself a lot of chances and hope for one positive outcome. From job hunting to Internet dating to making a sales pitch or whatever else it may be, multiply the possibilities for success.
- Set aside some time for meditation (see Chapter 6). Even a few minutes is better than nothing but half an hour would be a more worthwhile target. As part of your meditation technique you'll have to get to grips with your breathing – vitally important for controlling anxiety.
- Review the progress you've made at the end of every day. In bed can be a good place. Don't give yourself a hard time. Just run through the day's events before going to sleep and take note of the things you did well and the things you didn't do so well. Give yourself a pat on the back for the good things. Reflect on the progress you've made. As for the rest, try to analyse how you could do better next time. Be constructive, not critical. Everybody makes mistakes every day. The important thing is to learn

from them. In that way, even your errors become something positive.

▶ Make suggestions to your unconscious, as you're drifting off to sleep, and visualize yourself being confident in tomorrow's situations (see Chapter 2).

Don't:

▶ Do one thing that you 'should' do; revel in not doing it.
▶ Indulge in Schadenfreude; instead, offer friendly support.
▶ Be judgmental about other people.
▶ Let other people make you feel things are your fault when they're not – talk back using the three-step technique.

EVERY OTHER DAY

▶ Select one of the ten 'cognitive distortions' discussed in Chapter 1 and work on it. That means you'll devote some time every other day to eliminating that particular confidence-destroying thought pattern. As a reminder, here are the ten distortions:
  ▷ They're better than me.
  ▷ I'm not first so therefore I'm a loser.
  ▷ The things I do have faults so I'm obviously no good.
  ▷ I'm always making an idiot of myself.
  ▷ I know they're not going to like me.
  ▷ I feel like a failure so I must be a failure.
  ▷ I'm a label (stupid/boring/unattractive or whatever).
  ▷ I feel guilty that I'm not doing the things I should.
  ▷ It's obviously my fault (again).
  ▷ They're only saying that to be nice.
▶ Get physical. As we saw in Chapter 9, physical exercise causes your body to produce chemicals that make you feel expansive, happy and confident. Set aside 30 minutes for exercise every other day – that's 5 minutes to warm up, 20 minutes for the exercise and another 5 minutes to cool down again. If you're already exercising at that level, then move up to five sessions a week.

EVERY WEEK

▶ Spend some time alone. Maybe you already have too much time alone. But if you're one of those people who's constantly surrounded by family, friends, colleagues and acquaintances, make space to do something on your own every week. It's important to understand that you have the ability to be self-sufficient and that you can enjoy yourself alone.

▶ While you're alone, practise body language in front of a mirror and then use it for real (see Chapter 5).

▶ You can also use the time to invent euphemisms for all the things that challenge your self-confidence (see Chapter 8).

▶ Use self-hypnosis to improve your confidence and make other changes to your behaviour (Chapter 2).

▶ Role-play with a sympathetic friend (see Chapter 2).

▶ Study a subject that's new to you. Ideally, you should attend evening classes.

▶ Make a point of watching a film or TV programme that's aimed at the opposite sex, and read a book written by a member of the opposite sex for members of the opposite sex (see Chapter 11).

▶ If you're in charge of others in any way (we almost all are sometimes) show appreciation for the good things they do.

EVERY WEEKEND

▶ Take advantage of your weekends to tackle challenges that are too time-consuming for weekdays. Horse riding and climbing are good ones, but anything of which you're a little fearful will be beneficial (see Chapter 8).

▶ Spend time trying on new clothes and experimenting with new looks.

▶ Rearrange your home to make more of a statement about who you are. Use your creativity to decorate it with your own artworks – paintings, sculptures, wall hangings, photographs, 'found objects' or whatever it may be (see Chapter 6).

▶ Try something completely at random (see Chapter 6).

▶ Have at least one really long exercise session (see Chapter 9).

DURING THE MONTH

▶ At least once, throw some kind of party and include people who don't know one another. Be a good host or hostess by making introductions and ensuring that everyone mixes and has a good time (see Chapter 4).

▶ Spend time reviewing the work of charities that interest you and then commit yourself to donating £2 (US $3.1 approx.) regularly every month (or more if you can afford it). Reflect on the good that you're doing and enjoy it.

▶ Spend time thinking about your job and reviewing other possibilities. If you conclude that you're a square peg in a round hole, apply for a square hole – something that more closely reflects your interests and personality (see Chapter 6).

▶ If you have a relationship problem, make a point of discussing it without either of you stonewalling or getting angry or defensive (Chapter 11).

Taking it further

Making friends

Where can you get to meet people and make friends? The modern solution is the Internet. Don't go thinking of it as something artificial. It's no more artificial than, say, going to a party. It's new, that's all.

It's also an excellent medium for anyone lacking self-confidence because nobody has to see you or hear your voice. At least, not to begin with.

SOCIAL NETWORKING SITES

http://badoo.com Multilingual London-based site with 69 million registered users worldwide. Here you can share photos and videos and accounts of your life.

www.bebo.com A general social networking site based in California.

www.blogger.com Get in touch through blogs and chats.

www.care2.com With about 14 million members this website aims to connect people who want to make the world a better place, with a view to joint action.

www.dontstayin.com If you want to know where all the best parties are taking place this is where you'll find out.

www.facebook.com Originally restricted to students of Harvard College, Facebook has expanded to become the largest social networking site worldwide. As a user you can join networks organized by city, region, school or workplace, which gives you a good chance of making contact with other people.

www.faceparty.com Young, brash and geared to organized social events.

www.friendsreunited.co.uk Why not try contacting old school or university friends, or people you were in the armed forces with, or even those where you used to work?

www.jaiku.com Social networking site founded in 2006 and based in Helsinki.

www.lifeknot.com Lifeknot focuses on interests, activities and hobbies, allowing you to make contact with others who share your enthusiasms.

www.linkedin.com LinkedIn is essentially a business networking site, with over 75 million members worldwide. Everyone lists their contacts (known as connections) making it possible to make new contacts via people you already know.

http://multiply.com Originally a social networking site to link people who share the same interests, the focus now is on online buying and selling.

www.myspace.com The emphasis is on music and video.

INTERNET DATING

There are now literally thousands of Internet dating sites and many, many couples have met through them. But a word of warning: It's easy to lie on the Internet. Never reveal your personal contact details until you are very sure of the respondent. And make that first date in a secure environment.

Here are a few sites to get you started:

▶ *www.dateline.co.uk*
▶ *www.datingdirect.com*
▶ *www.datingforparents.com Specializing in single parents.*

- *www.fitness-singles.com* For singletons interested in keep-fit and sports.
- *www.guardian.co.uk/soulmates*
- *www.meetic.co.uk*
- *www.plentyofdatingsites.co.uk* A useful directory.

HOLIDAYS FOR SINGLETONS

www.friendshiptravel.com Tel: 0871 200 2035. Wide range of summer and winter holidays all over the planet.

www.globetrotters.co.uk Share travel information and team up with like-minded travellers.

www.solosholidays.co.uk Tel: 0844 815 0005. Holidays and short breaks in the UK and elsewhere. Holds 'Newcomers Events' in various parts of the UK for those who'd like to know more before committing themselves.

www.solitairhols.co.uk Tel: 0845 123 5515. Wide range of holidays in Europe, the Middle East, North Africa and Thailand, ranging from the adventurous to the sedentary.

www.travelone.co.uk Tel: 08445 766 866 brochures/0207 392 8988 reservations. Holidays in southern Europe, North Africa, Kenya, Mexico and Cuba.

www.travel-quest.co.uk/tqsingles.htm Online travel directory including a special section for singles.

www.wayn.com Stands for, Where Are You Now? Allows you to meet up with people all over the world.

MORE BOOKS ABOUT CONFIDENCE

Anthony, R. *The Ultimate Secrets of Total Self-Confidence* (GP Putnam's & Sons, 1994).

Back, K. and Back, K. *Assertiveness at Work: A Practical Guide to Handling Awkward Situations* (McGraw-Hill Professional, 2006).

Bishop, S. *Develop Your Assertiveness* (Kogan Page, 2006).

Bourne, E. J. *The Anxiety and Phobia Workbook* (New Harbinger Publications, 2005).

Burns, D. D. *Feeling Good: The New Mood Therapy* (Avon Books, 2000).

Butler, G. *Overcoming Social Anxiety: A Self-Help Guide using Cognitive Therapy Techniques* (Robinson Publishing, 1999).

Carnegie, D. *How to Develop Self-Confidence and Influence People by Public Speaking*, new edn (Vermilion Press, 1998).

Carnegie, D. *How to Win Friends and Influence People*, (Dale, new edn Vermilion Press, 2007).

Dryden, W. and Constantinos, D. *Assertiveness Step by Step* (Sheldon Press, 2004).

Edelmann , R.J. *Coping with Blushing* (Sheldon Press, 2004).

Fennell, M. *Overcoming Low Self-Esteem: Self-Help Using Cognitive Behavioural Therapy Techniques* (Robinson Publishing, 1999).

Forsyth, J. and Eifert , G. *The Mindfulness and Acceptance Workbook for Anxiety: A Guide to Breaking Free from Anxiety, Phobia and Worry Using Acceptance and Commitment Therapy* (New Harbinger Publications, 2008).

Frohart, P. *The Book of Fabulous Questions: Great Conversation Starters About Love, Sex and Other Personal Stuff* (BRG Publishing, 1998).

Gawain, S. *Creative Visualization* (New World Library, 2002).

Gray, J. *Men are from Mars, Women are from Venus: The Classic Guide to Understanding the Opposite Sex* (Harper Paperback, 2006).

Jeffers, S. *Little Book of Confidence* (Rider & Co, 1999).

Keirsey, D. *Please Understand Me* (Premethus Nemesis Book Company, 1998).

Leigh, A. *The Charisma Effect – How to Make a Powerful and Lasting Impression* (Prentice Hall, 2008).

Lowndes, L. *How to Talk to Anyone – 92 Little Tricks for Big Success in Relationships* (Thorsons, 2008).

Markway, B.G. and Pollard, A. *Dying of Embarrassment: Help for Social Anxiety and Social Phobia* (New Harbinger Publications, 1992).

Markway, B.G. and Markway G.P *Painfully Shy: How to Overcome Social Anxiety and Reclaim Your Life* (Thomas Dunne Books, 2003).

McKenna, P. *Instant Confidence*, with CD (Bantam Press, 2006).

O'Connor, J. and Seymour, J. *Introducing NLP Neuro-Linguistic Programming* (Thorsons, 2003).

Peale, N.V. *The Power of Positive Thinking*, (available *with The Positive Principle Today and Enthusiasm Makes The Difference*) (Wing Books, 1994).

Reneau, Z. Peurifoy, *Anxiety, Phobias and Panic: A Step-by-Step Programme for Regaining Control of Your Life* (Piatkus Books, 2006).

Wills, P. *Visualization for Beginners* (Hodder Arnold, 1999).

Wilson, R. *Cognitive Behavioural Therapy for Dummies* (John Wiley and Sons, 2005).

Young, J.E. *Reinventing Your Life: How to Break Free from Negative Life Patterns* (Penguin Putnam, 1991).

Yeung, R. *Confidence – The Art of Getting What ever You Want* (Prentice Hall Life, 2008).

WEBSITES ABOUT CONFIDENCE

www.anlp.org Website of the Association for Neuro-Linguistic Programming, with information and details of practitioners and courses.

www.babcp.com Information on cognitive behavioural therapy (CBT) from the leading UK organization.

www.johngrinder.com Website of John Grinder, co-founder of Neuro-Linguistic Programming (NLP).

www.mind.org.uk Long-established organization for all forms of mental and psychological problems. Includes explanation of cognitive therapy. List of counsellors throughout the UK.

www.nhsdirect.nhs.uk Follow links or use Search for a clear and authoritative explanation of cognitive therapy (also see www.nhs.uk).

www.personality-power-for-everyday-living.com Includes details of the Myers-Briggs personality indicator (which you can take for a fee).

www.rcpsych.ac.uk Information on cognitive therapy and more from the Royal College of Psychiatrists.

www.relatebetter.com Follow links to relationship section which, for a fee, includes a useful diagnostic questionnaire.

www.relate.org.uk Authoritative relationship advice for couples and singles; you can also receive a Reveal report into your relationship for a small fee.

www.richardbandler.com Website of Richard Bandler, co-founder of Neuro-Linguistic Programming.

www.wikihow.com A wide-ranging user-edited site including a section on how to be yourself.

The author
I'm always delighted to hear from readers. If you'd like to get in touch with me please visit my website: www.pauljenner.eu

Index

Notes

Notes

Notes